The Legend Of
HONEYWELL

From the days of inventor Albert Butz and the damper–flapper, to commercial airlines and Space Shuttles, Honeywell has been providing controls for 110 years. W.R. Sweatt, a forefather of Honeywell, is pictured on the left. The Sweatt and Kerstater Clock Thermostat, introduced around 1908, the Honeywell Round, introduced in 1953, and the TDC 3000, introduced in 1983, are just a few of the innovative products that helped Honeywell become the multibillion dollar company that controls the controls industry.

The Legend Of
HONEYWELL

Jeffrey L. Rodengen

Published by Write Stuff Syndicate, Inc.

For Judy,
who taught me to tie my shoes.

Also by Jeff Rodengen:

The Legend of Chris-Craft
Iron Fist: *The Lives of Carl Kiekhaefer*
Evinrude-Johnson and The Legend of OMC
Serving the Silent Service: *The Legend of Electric Boat*
The Legend of Dr Pepper/7UP
The Legend of Ingersoll-Rand
The Legend of Briggs & Stratton

WRITE STUFF SYNDICATE

Write Stuff Syndicate, Inc.

1323 S.E. 17th Street, Suite 421
Ft. Lauderdale, FL 33312
(800) 900-Book/(800) 900-2665
(305) 462-6657

Library of Congress Catalog Card Number: 94-61806

ISBN 0-945903-25-1

Completely produced in the United States of America

10 9 8 7 6 5 4 3 2 1

TABLE OF  CONTENTS

CONTROLLING OUR WORLD

Perhaps the single most easily recognized control instrument in the world is the Honeywell thermostat. You know the one: round, gold, sleek. The T–86 "Round" is probably the most common thermostat in the world, and rivals Coca–Cola and McDonald's for name recognition.

As depicted with some artistic license on the jacket of this book, the Honeywell Round is a fitting icon for the vast global company which was founded in Minneapolis, Minnesota over one hundred years ago. This odd little device is also recognized around the globe, and has made the word "Honeywell" synonymous with it. One might easily hear, "Turn up the Honeywell" in Mandarin Chinese, Russian, Swedish, or in the hundreds of other languages spoken throughout the world where the thermostat is used.

In continuous production since 1953, the Round has achieved an unusual status, a result not only to its well–known ability as a temperature regulating device. It has become an icon not only of a large global corporation, but of the modern home and modern living. Today, Honeywell is an organization with thousands of products and services. An individual thermostat can scarcely represent the organization in all of its diversity, yet considering what it accomplishes, the thermostat is an ideal symbol for Honeywell's history and vital force, for the thermostat represents control in a most literal sense.

The idea of control, plays a central role in human history, stretching back into the past as far as the most basic desire to survive and thrive. Civilization itself can be seen as the end result of a complex process of building more and more sophisticated tools for the purpose of control. In fact, we've gotten so good at controlling our world, that we have developed forms of control that are automatic.

Webster's Dictionary describes automatic as "free from human organs of observation, effort, and decision." The attraction lies primarily in creating freedom for people, freedom from the uncertainties of manual control. Automation gives us freedom to do other kinds of work and play, and lets the control of our world take care of itself.

More than this freedom, automation can lend precision to the process of control which isn't otherwise possible. For example, can you detect a one degree change in temperature in your living room? Probably not, but your thermostat can. It detects a change long before you do, and automatically compensates by starting up or shutting down your source of heat or cooling. This precision has other advantages, such as increasing the efficiency of your heating and cooling systems by eliminating human error from the process, minimizing waste, and providing energy savings. For over 110 years Honeywell has played a central role in making use of automatic control, and in manufacturing, promoting, and distributing automatic controls like — but not limited to — the thermostat.

In the 1950s, Honeywell — then still called "The Minneapolis–Honeywell Regulator Company" — adopted the slogan "First in Control." This slight change reflected a new emphasis on the capacity to control, rather than on the actual products themselves. The change reflected the company's commitment not only to its product line, but also to what its product line could provide. By 1990, Honeywell had further refined this commitment to read, "Helping you control your world."

While the T–86 Round has been manufactured continuously for over 40 years, the company has designed, manufactured, and marketed such diverse controls as automatic pilots and tank periscopes for the U.S. Army during World War II, computers and cameras in the 1960s, and components for the Space Shuttle in the 1980s and 90s. Honeywell even manufactured flour sifters during the Great Depression, when the firm took on piecework for the Pillsbury company to help maintain its skilled work force.

Honeywell from its earliest days has helped define the modern advertising campaign through its aggressive marketing and sales. Yet, though the company recognized the value of automatic controls, public demand for them was by no means automatic. As early as the 1890s, the company that would become Honeywell advertised thermostatic regulators directly to homeowners and furnace manufacturers on a massive national level, creating demand for its products and educating both the public and the home heating industry as to the benefits of automatic control. In a very real sense, Honeywell was responsible for the development of and the demand for constantly improved conditions of environmental and process control. A good example is Honeywell's very first product, the "damper flapper," which was fitted for a specific coal furnace of modest renown. Honeywell created demand for its product directly with homeowners, who in turn pressured furnace manufacturers to provide heating plants that could accommodate the new controls.

Aggressive marketing techniques are not enough to create a company of Honeywell's stature – the product must have integrity. From the earliest days, Honeywell has committed to a program of significant research and development. The company is proud of what one of its early and famous presidents, H.W. Sweatt, called "a spirit of restlessness" to constantly strive to realize creative inspiration. A significant — often disproportionate — portion of the company's profits has been consistently invested in research and development. The investment has contributed to the growth of what was once a small Midwestern thermostat company, into a multinational corporation with the reputation as, "the company that controls the controls market."

In the first half of the 20th Century, Honeywell salesmen were known as complete heating–system experts, able to identify and resolve just about any problem with a furnace system. So while they were selling and installing thermostats, they were often performing double duty as repairmen and maintenance men. This gave them a reputation of being completely accessible to their customers; they became a real asset with their constant "reports back to the company" about the performance of their products, and possible improvements in their design, manufacture, and installation. This level of service has been a trademark of Honeywell, and one which flourishes in no small part because of the "Honeywellers" — the roughly 55,000 people in over 90 countries worldwide who are employed by Honeywell, Inc.

Today, the company conducts about one third of its business internationally, so it is little wonder that Honeywell employees speak 80 languages and represent 50 cultures. In the spectacular boom and bust atmosphere that has been characteristic of the American business landscape since the middle of the last century, it is rare indeed for a company to have survived for over one hundred years. Honeywell has not only survived and thrived, it has done so while remaining engaged almost exclusively in its original market — a market it nearly invented and surely defined: controls.

So Honeywell's story is a biography of American industry from its inception. It is the chronicle of many generations engaged in the business of devising and building controls for all sorts of processes, systems, and environments. The product may have a thousand different names or uses, but if it's a Honeywell, it probably has something to do with control.

ACKNOWLEDGEMENTS

A great many individuals and institutions assisted in the research, preparation and publication of *The Legend of Honeywell*. The development of historical time-lines and a large portion of the principal archival research was accomplished by my valued and resourceful research assistant, Hans Eisenbeis. His thoughtful and careful investigations into the early years of Honeywell history have made it possible to publish much new and fascinating information on the origins and evolution of this unique organization.

The research, however, much less the book itself, would have been impossible without the dedicated assistance of Honeywell executives, employees and retirees. Principal among these is Frederick L. Klein, director of corporate identification and design, whose courteous and affable guidance made it possible to locate and identify both prominent records and individuals crucial to the Honeywell legacy. Instrumental to our research team was the remarkable dedication of J. Michael Stapp, communications and audio visual specialist, whose own broad understanding of Honeywell's roots and whose knowledge of company archival assets helped us to understand the maze of rooms and buildings where archives are stored. Also assisting whenever help was needed was Sally McNeil, senior administrative assistant; Ron Dow, manager of corporate photographic services; Lynda Nordeen, manager of corporate public relations; Mark A. Greene, curator of manuscript acquisitions at the Minnesota Historical Society; Robert Jansen, head librarian at the Minneapolis Star-Tribune; and Nena Jones of NASA Media Services, among many others.

A very special thanks is due to Karen Bachman, vice president of communications at Honeywell, for her skillful leadership and valuable advice during the course of the project. Her intimate knowledge of the human resources instrumental to the continued success of the company was of invaluable assistance in selecting the scores of individual interviews conducted during the lengthy research.

The interest and courtesy of the many interview subjects for the book was most gratifying, and I would like to thank Michael R. Bonsignore, chairman of the board and chief executive officer; D. Larry Moore, president and chief operating officer; John R. Dewane, president—Space and Aviation Control; Brian M. McGourty, president—Home and Building Control; Edward T. Hurd, senior vice president; Giananntonio Ferrari, president—Honeywell Europe; Ray Alvarez, vice president and group executive—Sensing and Control; Dana B. Badgerow, vice president and general manager—Skinner Valve; Jim Binger, Herb Bissell, Clyde Blinn, Phyllis Cooper, Mary Jo Feickert, Mannie Jackson, Roger Jensen, Geri M. Joseph, Steve Keating, Stan Nelson, Elaine Porter, Nicole Renault, Dean Randall, James J. Renier, Ed Spencer, Charlie Sweatt and Warde Wheaton, among others.

Finally, a very special thanks to the dedicated staff at Write Stuff Syndicate, Inc., especially my Executive Assistant and Office Manager Bonnie Bratton, Executive Editor Karen Nitkin, Creative Director Kyle Newton, Project Analyst Karine N. Rodengen, Logistics Specialist Joe Kenny, and Graphic Illustrator and cover artist David "Spuds" Rubinson.

HONEYWELL

Designed by Albert Butz between 1883-1885, the "damper-flapper" wasn't so much a gadget as a system of gadgets designed to automatically regulate a hand-fired coal furnace. The thermostat had been in existence for some time, but never used in such a system. The bi-metal strip opened and closed a circuit which ran a motor, and the motor opened and closed the damper on the furnace, providing more or less ventilation to the fire. When the fire heated up sufficiently, the bi-metal strip would activate the circuit again, and the damper would close.

CHAPTER ONE

STAYING WARM

"We hear a lot of talk these days about 'the good old days,' but I wonder just what what was so good about them. In fact, I am getting just a bit bilious over that nonsense."

— C.W. Nessell

Until the Industrial Revolution, the single greatest advance in the control of fire had been the chimney. For thousands of years, the control that humankind had over fire was quite limited. It was all people could do to keep fire from spreading, once kindled. Fire was a naturally occurring resource of a kind that resisted control, and as a result represented certain dangers. While indispensable as a source of heat for cooking and warmth, fire remained a mysterious entity for thousands of years, one that could be only partially understood and harnessed. Fire is not typically thought of as a tool—but it is perhaps the most important tool of all.

Man's first encounters with fire must surely have occurred with volcanic lava. Throughout most of history, fire was kindled using wood or charcoal for fuel. Wood was ideal because it was so readily available. Charcoal, the charred, partially burned remains of wood formerly set afire, was also a common fuel.[1] It was not until shortages of wood and charcoal threatened Europeans in the late 17th Century that coal was used as a fuel.[2] Until recently, petroleum wasn't considered useful. In fact, crude oil was frequently cursed as late as 1850 for its propensity to flood salt mines and render them a complete loss.[3]

The earliest form of controls for fire were the tools developed to produce it. The fire drill, for example, consisted of a bow and string used to turn a dowel in a wooden socket. Friction and perseverance brought a small smoldering flame. The flint and steel method was an equally time–consuming and tricky affair, involving the rain of sparks into a small pile of extremely dry tinder. These methods were exacting and hardly sure–

fire. As a consequence, once started, fire was hoarded and protected. A fire was kept burning as long as possible, and was even moved from one location to another by carrying embers in dirt wrapped in skins.

By the Industrial Revolution, making fire had become a common notion. The earliest forms of the match were often given poetic names which reflected their importance. The "Phosphoric Candle" and the "Pocket Luminary" were among the earliest forms, usually awkward affairs consisting of components that were often-dangerous. For example, the "Instantaneous Light Box" involved a wooden splint tipped with potassium chlorite. This splint was then dipped in a vial of sulphuric acid, causing the fire to ignite by chemical reaction. Needless to say, a vial of sulphuric acid carried around in a gentleman's vest pocket was inconvenient—as well as deadly poisonous—and these early matches were positively hazardous.[4]

The first friction match was developed in 1827 and was given the evocative title "Jones Lucifer." The Jones Lucifer consisted of a wooden splint topped with antimony sulphide. It was drawn through a piece of abrasive paper, causing friction which ignited the match.[5]

The advantages of heat and light obtained by fire are counterbalanced by the obnoxious presence of smoke. Quite early in the experience of fire, people became concerned with the separation of fire and smoke, no doubt when fire was first brought into the shelters fashioned for protection from the elements. The simplest solution was to make a hole in the roof, and to create a funnel into which the smoke could enter as it billowed out to the open air. The Indian tepee is an example of a simple solution applied for centuries to the problem of smoke.

The Romans employed a portable brazier to heat their homes and public places, a sort of tray mounted on legs in which charcoal was burned. They used aromatic or perfumed wood, in order to make the smoke more agreeable.[6] During the heating season, the Romans would use a separate set of furniture, which would presumably become smoky and soiled, and was probably less decorous than the furniture they brought out from storage in warm weather.[7] The term "barnburner," sometimes used to describe a raucous social gathering, probably has its origins in ancient methods of home heating: It was common in Roman times to judge the size and success of a party by the amount of smoke billowing from the windows and roof of a citizen's home.[8]

The Chimney: Where There's Fire There's Smoke

The chimney, which first came into general use in the 15th Century, was the first device to effectively separate heat and smoke.[9] The draft created by the fire served the dual purpose of introducing more oxygen to the fire, causing it to burn hotter and faster, while drawing the smoke away from the lungs of inhabitants. With the invention of the chimney came the fireplace and hearth, which replaced the ancient fire ring. The chimney was a tremendous advance, but far from perfect as a solution to the problem of home heating.

Unfortunately, the draft of the chimney caused about 80 per cent of the fire's heat to be lost with the smoke. And without a means to control the introduction of oxygen to the fire, a strong draft could accelerate the fire, burning fuel too quickly.

Furthermore the quality of the heat generated was poor, because it was so uni–directional. Sitting in front of the open fireplace, one's face and front might become toasty and warm, while the draft caused by the fireplace actually chilled one's posterior. The fireplace, though,

A 19th century *Füllregulierenöfen.* This ceramic oven was one of the earliest coal-burning heaters.

was the best available technology until the Industrial Revolution. As the casting of iron became possible, the complexion of fire control and home heating changed completely .

Iron proved to be an ideal material to contain fire for a number of reasons. It transferred heat extremely effectively, while remaining mostly unscathed by fire. Iron was particularly suited to an improvement on the chimney and fireplace principle. The effect of chimneys in wasting 80 percent of the heat of a fire could be countered by increasing the transfer of heat from the fireplace itself to the air in the room. Ceramic tiles, glass, and iron were all incorporated into early stoves in order to increase efficiency.

The stove and oven existed in various forms long before the casting of iron, however. The Chinese had a brick oven they used to heat a room and cook, the fuel being reduced to embers in the course of a day. By night, the oven cooled enough to sleep on.[10] Europeans used brick ovens for baking and cooking for centuries, and a variety of kilns, oasts (a kiln to dry herbs or leaves), and other fire boxes were used for special purposes such as pottery and brick firing. But the stove as a universal heating and cooking unit did not emerge until the 18th Century.

Hot Iron

The use of iron was common in the earliest stoves, which were used in Germany.[11] A cast iron floor or base provided the surface on which a wood or charcoal fire was built. This base was elevated on four legs in the style of the Roman braziers, and enclosed by ceramic tiles, forming a kind of ceramic closet in which the fire burned. These early stoves often stood over twelve feet tall. The first stove in North America was the Ben Franklin stove,[12] which was more a cast iron fireplace than anything else. It provided better heat transfer than ceramic tiles, bricks, or stones, and was more or less inserted into an existing fireplace. In this way, it extended into the room from the hearth, while still channeling smoke up the existing chimney. Before long, perhaps influenced by German designs, the Ben Franklin stove was fitted with four legs and a door, to better control the flow of oxygen to the fire. These innova-

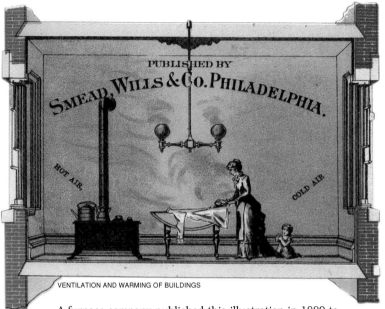

VENTILATION AND WARMING OF BUILDINGS

A furnace company published this illustration in 1889 to depict common heating problems encountered by 19th Century householders.

tions were further refined in the Box stove, which was introduced around 1800.[13]

Before long, manufacturers realized they could maximize the transfer of heat by increasing the surface area of their cast iron wares in artistic ways.

"The early stoves were not very efficient because they lacked heating surface, so the stove designers increased the heating surface by using unique and ornamental designs. To enhance their beauty—if a cast-iron stove could ever be a thing of beauty—the surface casings were decorated with flowers, fruits, garlands of leaves and vines, and pure baroque."[14]

The cast iron stove was originally designed to be used with wood and charcoal as fuels. But shortages of these resources led to the increased use of coal, which became nearly universal once the Industrial Revolution got under way.

The qualities and abundance of coal, along with its relative proximity to urban industrial centers, marked it as the fuel that fired the revolution. Wood and charcoal were both inefficient and unavailable in the quantities needed for massive industrial expansion. As industry grew, the use of coal as a fuel for firing stoves, furnaces, and ovens grew apace.

The old-fashioned baseburner is a well-remembered centerpiece of the days when coal was the fuel of choice. The baseburner was a corpulent fixture with nickel-plated footrests, ornate trappings, and mica windows through which could be seen the ruddy glow of burning coal.

"The family gathered about it every evening while the wind howled around the corners of the eaves, and the snow and sleet beat against the window panes. The ruddy glow of the fire through the mica windows bathed the room in a soft and mellow light while we ate popcorn and apples. I thought we gathered there every night because we loved to be together, but a suspicion lurks in my mind that the real reason was that it was the only room in the house warm enough to sit in."[15]

Coal was not the only fuel in use, just the most common. Since coal wasn't mined in the American West until later, stoves were developed there which burned hay, corn cobs, and even "buffalo chips." In the Pacific Northwest, stoves that burned sawdust were often used.[16]

However, coal remained the standard fuel well into the 20th Century, because it was so readily available to an increasingly urban, industrialized society. But there were a number of troubling aspects to this wonder fuel, which eventually contributed to the demise of fixtures like the baseburner. Most homes built in cold weather latitudes had a cellar or basement. This fact encouraged stove and furnace salesmen to urge homeowners to dispense with stove heating, and install central heating. This was an attractive idea to the homeowner because of the somewhat dirty nature of a hand-fired heating plant. Coal is a filthy fuel, and its ashes can make an unpleasant mess. Smoke and fire soiled the "sittin' room" with annoying regularity, so it seemed like a good idea to move the whole mess down to the cellar.

Moving To The Cellar

Central heating simply requires a heating plant and a means of distributing heat to the rest of the home. It had already been the subject of experimentation with steam by 1769, the same year James Watt perfected the steam engine. For coal-fired furnaces, the idea was simply to provide ventilation from the combustion chamber to the other rooms of the house. Moving the stove from the living room to the basement also changed heating terminology, which today defines the stove as primarily a heat source for cooking located in the kitchen, and the furnace as primarily a heat source located in the cellar. Before central heating, this distinction did not exist.

The first central heating system using a coal furnace was probably the "Cockle stove," a system used to heat a cotton factory in England after 1792. Really just a stove adapted to heat a large public building, it was the first gravity hot-air furnace.

VENTILATION AND WARMING OF BUILDINGS

THE AIR-WARMER AS MANUFACTURED IN 1867.

A wide variety of iron furnaces provide evidence of many approaches to the coal-burning heating plant. Most furnaces in the late 19th Century were warm air units, though steam and hot water were developed as early as the 1870s.

"The Cockle stove was made of cast iron and constructed with thick and heavy walls – top, bottom, and sides, or in other words a cast–iron case to enclose the fire. This case was called the cockle, and in turn it was enclosed in a brick casing with a minimum of 3 or 4 inches between the inside surface of the casing and the cockle or heat exchanger, to provide air circulation. Openings at the bottom of the brick enclosure allowed cold air to enter. The heated air was conveyed in pipes and flues to the rooms to be heated, from the top of the enclosure."[17]

The advantages of moving the heating plant to the cellar or basement were immediately known to the home-owner, who was probably happy to have the dirt and dust out of sight. The larger advantage must have been the more

A large brick and iron furnace from 1889. This was an institutional coal furnace designed to heat a school classroom or church sanctuary. Cool air entered the brick casing at the floor, came into contact with the iron jacket of the furnace, and proceeded through a venting system.

complete heating of the home, with flues and ducts directed into every room, instead of heating only the room containing the stove.

Socially, the introduction of the basement furnace may have had the interesting effect of decentralizing the family. Since there was no longer an impetus to gather in the single, well–heated parlor, and since every room in the house was theoretically as comfortable as the next, the family members were able to retire to separate rooms. Certainly the decor of the home was enhanced, since the chances of soiling fine fabrics and bric–a–brac were reduced by moving the coal fire to the basement.[18] "Central heating systems were often sold to the reluctant homemaker on the strength of 'we will take the dirt from the fire in your living room and put it down in the basement where it belongs.' She was not told that she would chase down the stairs several times a day to throw coal on the fire."[19] This was precisely the moment when a clever gadget was invented which would usher in an age of automatic control, and which would forever be associated with the birth of Honeywell.

A Clever Invention

Albert Butz is the man who happened upon the idea of automatic control, especially as it applies to the thermostatic control of heating plants. By 1885, the most common heating

VENTILATION AND WARMING OF BUILDINGS

COLD AIR OPENINGS.

systems consisted of a coal-burning furnace in the cellar which provided heat for either a steam or gravity air system. The typical homeowner needed to journey to the basement several times a day in cold weather, take up the coal shovel, and stoke the hand–fired furnace. Any adjustments in the system, in terms of flues and vents, dampers and intakes, had to be made at the furnace itself. Albert Butz approached this aggravation as a challenge, and developed an idea to regulate the coal furnace. His invention was nicknamed "the damper flapper," which describes exactly what the system accomplished.

Albert Butz is a somewhat mysterious figure in the history of Honeywell. While his invention is the foundation of the company, he is not normally identified as its founder. For reasons that are not entirely clear, Butz's association with the company that would become Honeywell was a loose, if not cold relationship. Butz was primarily an inventor, and company lore suggests that he was unable or unwilling to market the devices he contrived. Although the historical record is somewhat incomplete, there is no shortage of popular mythology regarding Butz and his landmark contributions to Honeywell's history.

Albert M. Butz was born in Switzerland in 1849, and at age eight he emigrated (probably with his family) in what is commonly called the "first wave" of mass immigrations from central and eastern Europe to the United States. At age sixteen, he enlisted in the Union Army during the Civil War, serving in Wisconsin's 47th Infantry for the last six months of the conflict. Apparently his company did not see combat, and his service was uneventful.[20] Nothing is known of the years between Butz's 1865 enlistment and 1881, when he first appears as a resident of Saint Paul, Minnesota. He was apparently a man of eclectic talents, listed variously in city directories as a florist, a bookseller, and a gardener.[21]

By 1884, Butz had become involved with the invention of fire–related devices. He and a partner, R.J. Mendenhall, formed a company with the unlikely name of The Butz and Mendenhall Hand Grenade Fire Extinguisher Company.[22] The partners developed a fire–extinguishing system that consisted of glass spheres filled with water which were hung from the ceiling in wicker baskets. If the room was set ablaze, the baskets would in theory burn up, and the glass spheres would fall to the floor, break, and extinguish the fire. Though the effectiveness of such a system was dubious, it contained the useful notion of feedback, upon which automatic control is based. Feedback is the simple principle that a part of the output of a process can return to the origin as input and effect successive output. The hand

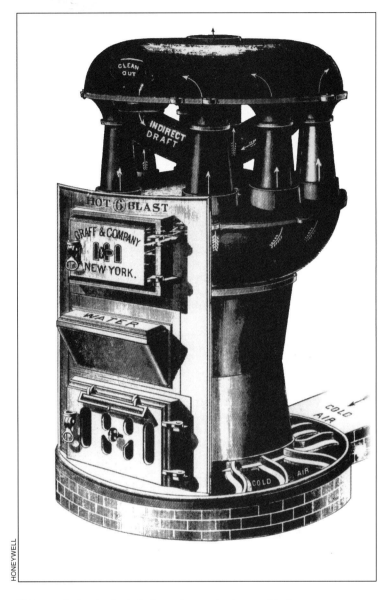

HONEYWELL

This gravity heater included a water carrier to provide for humidifying the notoriously dry air. Constructed of cast iron, a furnace like this could weigh more than a half-ton (1,200 pounds).

grenade system seemed to have been a one–shot deal. There is no evidence that Butz and Mendenhall advertised, sold, or even manufactured their product, beyond an assumed prototype or model.

Around this time, Butz also experimented with a system that would become the cornerstone of Honeywell—the thermostatic heat regulator.

It is a common misconception that Butz or Honeywell invented the thermostat. Thermostats had been in existence for over a century by the time Butz adapted one for use in his system. In fact the term "thermostat" was used as early as 1831 by a Scottish chemist. It described any instrument constructed to exploit the principle of the variable expansion of metals. Different metals have different rates of expansion depending upon the temperature. It is fairly easy to compare the rates of two different metals, simply attaching them to one another, applying heat and watching the results. If a strip of copper and silver are attached to each other, they will bend in one direction or the other as heat is applied or removed. The early thermostat was simply a bi–metal strip which could be used to indicate variations in temperature.[23] This gadget was for the most part ignored through the 18th Century, viewed more as a curiosity than as a useful tool. By the end of the 18th Century, however, the bi–metal strip had been used to compensate a "chronometer" for variations in temperature. By the middle of the 19th Century, a Frenchman had developed what he called a "thermoscope," most likely an ancestor to the modern thermostat.[24]

By the mid–1800s, thermostats and bi–metal strips were used with increasing frequency to monitor and signal variations in temperature. The thermostat could be connected to a DC circuit, and when temperatures reached a high or low threshold, the circuit would close and a bell or light would alert people to the condition. This system was useful in cases where a janitor needed to be awakened to shovel more coal or close down the damper.

In 1879, Julien Bradford was issued a patent for "Electric Heat and Vapor Governors for Spinning and Weaving Rooms." Bradford's invention was probably the first application of a thermostat to the automatic control of heat. His device provided for a DC circuit running through the thermostat, which acted as a switch to a gear train which performed work. More than simply signalling a need for manual control as earlier thermostats had done, Bradford's thermostat acted as part of an automatic system.

Albert Butz was aware of Bradford's patent, and cited many of the same principles in his own patent application six years later. In fact, Butz purchased Bradford's patent after forming a business to manufacture his own device. Other systems also resembled the Butz invention, and may have influenced or inspired it. For example, the J.A. Larkin Company of Westfield, Massachusetts advertised an "Automatic Damper Regulator and Horse Feeder" in 1885. The advertisement copy was unadorned.

"This little machine will open the drafts of your Stove or Furnace any time in the morning, and your house will be warm when you get up. It never oversleeps. It is reliable, durable, and economical...It will feed your horse at any time in the morning, and

will be found very convenient for those wishing to get an early start with a team, such as Milkmen, Grocers, Marketmen, and others." [25]

Though the idea of automatically operating the dampers on a stove or furnace was growing, no one had thought to apply the thermostat to the task, until Butz created his "damper flapper."

In 1885, the same year Larkin's advertisement appeared, Butz applied for his first patent on a device that automatically, *thermostatically* controlled the dampers on a coal–fired stove, and the patent was granted in 1886. Honeywell commonly cites 1885 as the date of its e s t a b - lishment, and by 1895, its advertising claimed that the company had been in business for 10 years.

The damper flapper was a system composed of three basic parts. The thermostat acted as a bi–metal trigger, placed in the living space of a home. Adjustments could be made to two points on either side of the bi–metal strip to conform to the desired temperature. The thermostat would complete an electric circuit which began with a battery pack, and terminated with a solenoid in a windup motor. The solenoid engaged and disengaged the clockwork mechanism

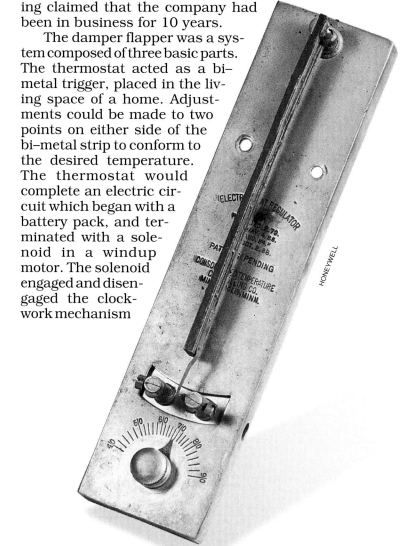

This thermostat was manufactured around 1894 after Consolidated Temperature Controlling Company became Electric Heat Regulator Company. Though Albert Butz did not invent this or any thermostat, he probably devised one much like it for his damper-flapper system, which became the founding product of Honeywell. He had inexplicably left the company by 1888.

of the windup motor, serving as a lynch–pin. The whole mechanism worked on half turns. For example, if the thermostat was set at 70 degrees, the circuit would close when the temperature fell to 69 degrees. The solenoid would disengage the flywheel, and the windup motor would make a one–half turn with its bell lever. The lever would pull a chain running through a series of pulleys to the hinged damper door of the furnace, opening it, and introducing more oxygen. The fire would burn hotter and faster, causing an increase in the temperature of the living space. When the room had warmed to 71 degrees, the thermostat would again close the circuit, and this time, the motor would turn another 180 degrees, closing the damper door and cooling the fire. This was the Butz system, and it constituted one of the first automatic controls based purely on reliable feedback.

Someone still had to shovel coal into the furnace, so to many it may have seemed unnecessary to have automatic control from the living areas, when one had to make periodic trips to the cellar anyway.

And yet, advantages to automatic control quickly became obvious, once the system could be made to operate smoothly. In the first place, the Butz heat regulator was a more precise method of controlling the heating plant because it could measure relatively small variations in temperature. There are few individuals who can actually feel a one degree change in temperature, but the Butz system responded immediately to even a single degree of variation.

This precision saved coal by avoiding over-stoking and over–ventilation of the heating system, usually caused by members of the household over-compensating for their slow–reacting senses.

An additional benefit was the labor it saved, because the damper–flapper system allowed the homeowner to shovel all the coal in one visit in the morning, with no additional coal needed for twenty-four hours, even in bitter weather. The damper flapper made control of the home heating plant as simple as deciding what temperature would be comfortable.

Albert Butz probably conceived his damper flapper in 1884 or 1885, and it is generally believed that R.J. Mendenhall urged Butz to patent, manufacture, and sell it. He may have introduced Butz to Amasa Paul, Rufus Sanford, and T. Dwight Mervin, the patent attorneys in Minneapolis who prepared Butz's application. Mendenhall also most likely introduced Butz to a group of investors known as Hay & Company, Investors and Business Brokers. They, in turn, provided Butz with the funds he needed to incorporate the Butz Thermoelectric Regulator Company, on April 23, 1886. Two weeks later, on May 4, 1886, Butz's patent was granted. The world was about to buy an Electric Heat Regulator. But first someone had to sell it.

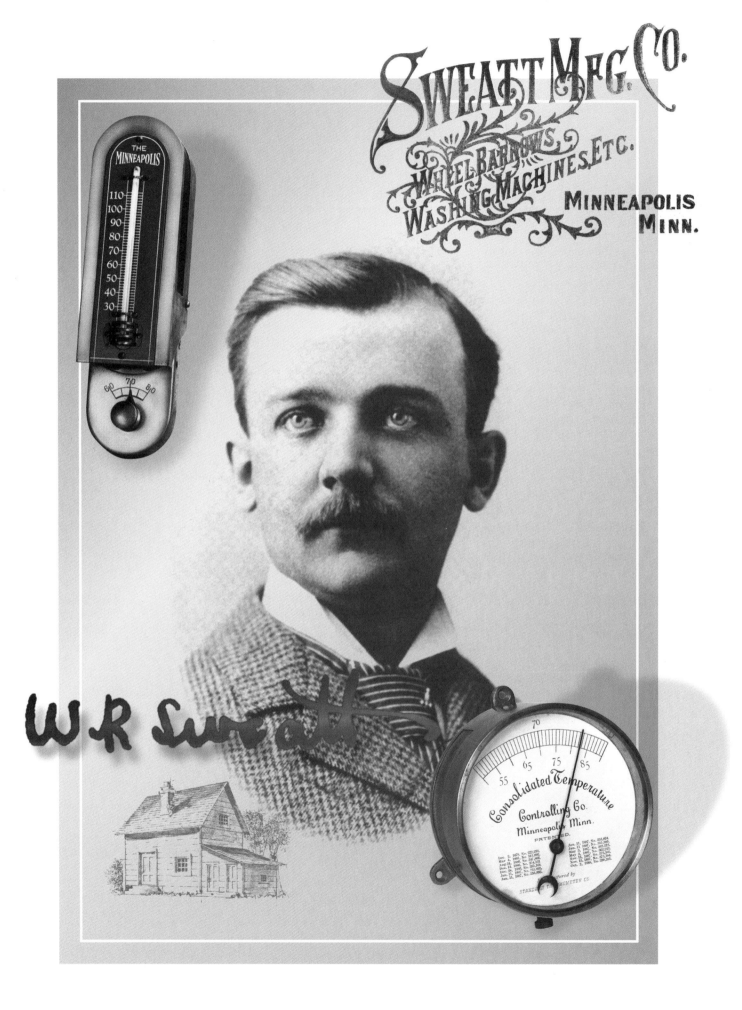

CHAPTER TWO

SURVIVAL AND SUCCESS

W.R. Sweatt was fed up, he had "writer's cramp from signing bank notes and his vest buttons were 'worn smooth from rubbing against bank counters.'"

—C.W. Nessell, *Honeywell The Early Years*

lbert Butz was the first president of the Butz Thermo-Electric Regulator Company, while W.R. McCormick and I.M. Hay, two investors from the Hay group, became vice–president and secretary–treasurer. In reality, however, Albert Butz was probably the Butz Company's only employee. Though Butz announced the formation of his company in several Minneapolis–Saint Paul newspapers, there is no evidence that he advertised his invention.[1] Butz apparently never placed a single advertisement for his damper flapper, and may not have begun production, for there are no remaining thermostats, motors, catalogues, or records from this period. If Butz generated any sales of his invention, they could not have been numerous. In general the historical record portrays Albert Butz as a tinkerer who preferred inventing to marketing. Butz filed several additional patent improvements between 1886 and 1889, assigning them to his company.

Butz's attorneys seem to have played a significant role in the survival of the company. As early as 1887, the legal firm of Paul, Sanford, and Merwin secured Julien Bradford's 1879 heat governor patent, lending much greater authority to the Butz invention.[2]

In 1888, Albert Butz abandoned his business and moved to Chicago. The law firm, however, retained the Butz and Bradford patents relating to heat regulation. It's unclear why Albert Butz left Minneapolis, and why he transferred his patents to the law firm. It seems that he experienced a falling out with the Minneapolis group, and may have sold all interest in his company to dissolve the relationship.

Though no longer directly involved in the business he had founded in Minneapolis, Butz acted for a short time as a distributor for the products he had invented.[3] The earliest known advertisement for the company that would eventually become Honeywell promoted Albert Butz's damper–flapper system in 1888. Published in *Century* and *Harper's*, the ad featured "Automatic Regulators For Steam Heaters, Hot Water Heaters, Hot Air Furnaces, and all other kinds of Heating Apparatus." Albert Butz is identified in the ad as the proprietor of a "local company" located on Lake Street in Chicago.

By 1888, Butz's attorneys had renamed the business the Consolidated Temperature Controlling Company, and had secured even more patents relating to heat regulation. The oldest known artifact from Honeywell's earliest days is a thermostat from around 1888, engraved with the trademark of the Consolidated Temperature Controlling Co. The *Harper's* ad also announced that the group controlled "all patents of Bradford, Butz, Sternberg, Draper, and Thompson," and that "these are the foundation patents and cover broadly Automatic Heat Regulators." The new name of the company reflected this consolidation of related patents and interests, and the ad cautioned readers, saying, "Do not buy, sell, or use any infringing apparatus." This admonishment most likely referred to a heat regulator produced and sold by The Guion Automatic Heat Regulating Company of Elmira, New York, which had been advertised a year earlier. By 1889, Consolidated purchased Guion outright, eliminating an early competitor.[4]

Among the holdings of the Guion Automatic Heat Regulating Co. was a damper motor

1892. Robbins was a successful entrepreneur and civic leader who was honored in the naming of the first suburb of Minneapolis, Robbinsdale. Other members of the first board of directors included John Ames and Oscar Green, employees of the Northern Pacific Railway Company, and Joseph Pyle, an editor of the *Saint Paul Pioneer Press* and close friend of railroad magnate James J. Hill.[8]

Manufacture and sale of the Consolidated heat regulator began in earnest, and by the end of 1891 the company's factory had moved into larger quarters, and employed five men. During this period, the directors continued to seek investors by encouraging friends and family to buy Consolidated stock.

W.R. Sweatt and his 3-year-old son Harold in 1894, a year after W.R. took over management of the company. Father and son together would be responsible for 75 years of uninterrupted leadership at Honeywell.

in which the Minneapolis company was interested. The Butz system depended upon some sort of motor which could open and close the damper door, and the 1919 *Minneapolis Sales Book,* published by the company, indicates that the Guion motor was the key to success of heat regulators.[5] Before 1916 and the wiring of American homes to line voltage, any motor providing sufficient torque needed to be hand wound or weight activated, the same way a grandfather clock is powered. In recent years, the early spring motor built for the Minneapolis system has been characterized by knowledgeable clock collectors as a superb clockwork mechanism.[6]

By 1889, the Consolidated Temperature Controlling Company owned 14 patents and had acquired a company manufacturing a competing product. While Paul, Sanford, and Merwin sought investors for the promising young company, "survival seemed to depend on acquiring technology rather than on dedicated management."[7] It didn't take long for the solicitors to interest five investors, several of whom would loom large in the history of the growing city of Minneapolis.

City Fathers, Regulator Investors

Charles Palmer, who had organized the *New York Morning Journal,* was elected president of Consolidated in 1888. Andrew Robbins succeeded him, holding the position from 1889 until

Jessie Wilson Sweatt with sons Harold and Charles in 1893.

This was the state of the company that would become Honeywell when an eager young man by the name of W.R. Sweatt arrived in Minneapolis. Sweatt was the son of Charles Sweatt, a Vermont banker and hardware merchant who had sought greater opportunities in the West.[9] Charles and his family had moved from New England to Iowa, where W.R. was born in 1867. Soon the Sweatts moved again, this time to Fargo, North Dakota. At 24, a few years after graduation from military school, W.R. moved to Minneapolis.[10]

In 1891, the city across the Mississippi from Saint Paul was a busy metropolis of 167,000 inhabitants. It was said to be the lumber and flour capital of the country, with mills lining the great river shoulder to shoulder.

George P. Wilson, who encouraged his son–in–law W.R. Sweatt to buy stock in the Consolidated Temperature Control Company. Wilson's law partner, John Van Derlip, was secretary of the company's board.

Soon after W.R. Sweatt arrived in the city, he met and married Jessie Wilson, a young woman who had moved in 1888 with her family from Winona, Minnesota to Minneapolis. Shortly after the marriage, Jessie's father, George P. Wilson, formed a law partnership with John Van Derlip, who by chance was the secretary of Consolidated Temperature Controlling Co. board of directors. Wilson undoubtedly introduced his young son–in–law to both Van Derlip and Andrew Robbins. The historical record clearly implies that Robbins had quite an influence on the young W.R. Sweatt.

Sweatt was encouraged by his father–in–law to buy stock in Consolidated, which he did in the amount of $5,300—52 shares for himself and one for his wife. As secretary, Van Derlip's signature appears on the original stock certificates. Two months later, Sweatt purchased a manufacturing company with which Robbins was also associated.[11] The Hubbard Specialty Company was an established business which manufactured woodenware such as wheelbarrows, grocery crates, and washboards. Robbins served as president of this venture as well. "W.R. was attracted to both of the businesses," a Honeywell document suggests. "Consolidated damper flapper hadn't found widespread public demand yet, but W.R. recognized its potential. The Hubbard company, more stable than the heat control business, offered immediate return."[12] W.R. renamed it The Sweatt Manufacturing Company. He thus had interests in two businesses – one with a stable, already-established market and limited potential for growth, the other a risky unknown, with potential for considerable success.

At this juncture, the Consolidated Temperature Controlling Co. still lacked full time management.[13] Every member of Consolidated's board of directors was involved with other ventures, most with full–time positions and responsibilities. As a result, the company languished. Consolidated needed aggressive planning and marketing, and it needed full-time management. In 1892, the name of the company was changed to the Electric Thermostat Company, with Andrew Robbins continuing as president and John Van Derlip as secretary.

Slow Times

The debts quickly grew to $7,500 in 1893, and several stockholders responded by agreeing to cover the losses.[14] The situation worsened over the summer, and the directors reduced employment to just two individuals. At a special stockholders' meeting on August 15, a decision was made: Unless the board could find someone to actively direct the company, it would discontinue the operation. The hope was to find a trustee willing to assume the liability and insure the debts of the company. The following day, on August 16, the stockholders of Electric Thermostat Company agreed to sell "an extensive list of patents" to W.R. Sweatt for the diminutive sum of $1.[15]

On October 5, the directors changed the name of the company to the Electric Heat Regulator Company, re–capitalized it, and elected Sweatt secretary–treasurer. Later that month, the "new" company's stockholders agreed to accept the assets of the Electric Thermostat Company, and to "assume the liabilities of Sweatt as trustee."[16]

A Young Volunteer

Honeywell lore has held that the directors simply asked W.R. to operate the company without pay. Another oral tradition has Sweatt leaving his home in Minneapolis to attend the 1893 World's Columbian Exposition in Chicago for a brief vacation. As the story goes, the board of directors voted to give Sweatt the responsibility without his knowledge or consent.[17] At a meeting of the directors on May 31, 1894, Sweatt requested and was given

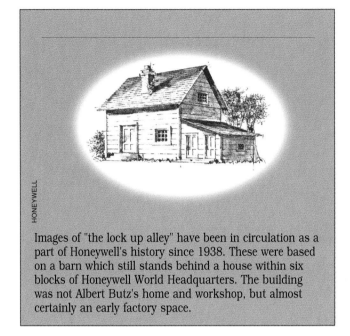

Images of "the lock up alley" have been in circulation as a part of Honeywell's history since 1938. These were based on a barn which still stands behind a house within six blocks of Honeywell World Headquarters. The building was not Albert Butz's home and workshop, but almost certainly an early factory space.

authority to order 600 motors and 500 thermostats. He was also authorized to contract for advertising at an estimated cost of $300 per month, and to continue advertising in such national publications as *Scribner's*, *Harper's*, *Century*, and *Cosmopolitan*. A few months later, Sweatt was authorized to borrow $3,000 from a bank in order to meet bills of purchase. Though Sweatt secured the loan, each director agreed to assume an equal portion of the debt.

In early 1895, Sweatt presented his annual report to the directors. The picture was grim, reflecting the general economic malaise resulting from The Panic of 1893–1894. Sweatt contended that the company simply needed more funds—funds not forthcoming from sales limited almost entirely to "door–to–door canvassing in Minneapolis–Saint Paul."[18] The damper flapper was still something of a novelty which resisted public acceptance.

By 1895, the company showed a profit for the first time. In 1896, W.R. Sweatt was given a salary of $1,200 for the year, and a retroactive salary of $1,200 for 1895 – for meeting the board's stipulation that the company clear $2,500 above expenses for the year. Despite this progress, the board of directors grew impatient, and Sweatt most likely became discouraged himself, as he was still engaged in the full–time management of his woodenware concern. "The company had struggled for a decade under four names to sell a product that was slightly ahead of its time."[19] A watershed was finally reached at a stockholders' meeting February 23, 1898, as W.R.

This recently discovered dial is Honeywell's oldest known artifact, dating from no earlier than 1888. Even the oldest existing damper-flappers are from the period of 1893-1900, after the company became the Electric Heat Regulator Company.

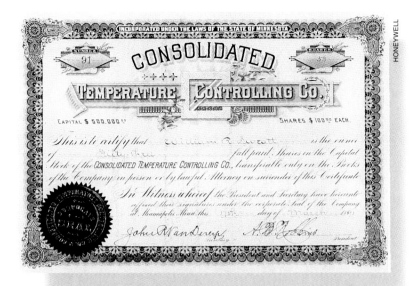

The stock certificate (above) from Consolidated Temperature Controlling Company was issued to W.R. Sweatt shortly after he arrived in Minneapolis from Fargo in 1891. The certificate is signed by John Van Derlip, company secretary, and A.B. Robbins, president. Van Derlip concurrently established a law office with W.R.'s father-in-law.

This stock certificate (below) was issued to W.R. Sweatt in 1892 during the brief period in which the company was called Electric Thermostat Company. Several months later, after W.R. took over the management of the company, it was renamed the Electric Heat Regulator Company.

Sweatt purchased the entire company from the other stockholders.

One popular account of the stockholders' meeting describes a discouraged W.R. Sweatt, distraught over the arduous business of keeping Electric Heat Regulator afloat. Sweatt explained that he was fed up, that he had "writer's cramp from signing bank notes and his vest buttons were 'worn smooth from rubbing against bank counters.'"[20] This account suggests that the board of directors hedged their bets against a possible loss of Sweatt's leadership, and offered to sell all the company's assets to him, to which a stunned Sweatt agreed. The actual minutes of the meeting are obscure, noting that Sweatt "proposed at the request of all [stockholders] present to run the company for another year, and to purchase the entire stock of the company at a rate of 12.5 cents on the dollar."[21] The total purchase price was $5,000, and an agreement was reached to allow Sweatt to pay the amount from earnings at $25 per month.

By 1900 Sweatt held all 400 shares of stock, and by 1902 he had paid off the company's outstanding debts. The young businessman

AUTOMATIC REGULATORS

For Steam Heaters, Hot Water Heaters, Hot Air Furnaces, and all other kinds of Heating Apparatus.

Perfect Control of Temperature in Private Residences, Public Buildings, School Houses, Churches, Railway Cars, Greenhouses, etc.

The Automatic Electric Heat Regulator controls the Furnace or Heater by the temperature of the living-rooms of the house. If the temperature of the room rises above the desired degree, the Regulator instantly closes the drafts of the Furnace and opens a check-damper in the smoke-pipe. If the temperature drops below the desired degree, the Regulator instantly closes the check-damper and opens the drafts of the Furnace. The Regulator can be set for any desired temperature, and thus the house can be kept at a lower temperature at night, or the same uniform temperature may be maintained day and night. Can be applied to any kind of heating apparatus.

We wish to establish a local company in each State, to whom exclusive privileges under all our patents will be guaranteed. This company controls all the patents of Bradford, Butz, Sternberg, Draper and Thompson. These are foundation patents and cover broadly Automatic Electric Heat Regulators. **Do not buy, sell or use any infringing apparatus.** Write for illustrated catalogue.

Consolidated Temperature Controlling Co.

309 Hennepin Avenue, Minneapolis, Minnesota.

Local Companies; A. M. BUTZ & CO. 154 Lake St. Chicago, Ill.; N. E. HEAT REGULATOR CO. 61 Bromfield St. Boston, Mass.

1888 Century & Harpers

The earliest known advertisement for the company that would become Honeywell promoted Albert Butz's damper-flapper system in 1888.

sold his woodenware company in 1901, which may have enabled him to complete the transaction.[22] Friends and colleagues noted that "in later years W.R. was very proud of his company's history of success. He was an astute manager and he'd proved it—from the time he began managing Electric Heat Regulator Co. in 1893, it never suffered a losing financial year."[23] In the fall of 1902, W.R. distributed his 400 shares of stock among his family, and oversaw the selection of a new board of directors including himself, his wife Jessie Wilson Sweatt, his brothers–in–law Wirt and Walter Wilson, and his father–in–law George Wilson. The participation of the entire family was an important element of the company's survival in its earliest and most difficult period. "W.R. would take his work and his typewriter home with him and night after night answer correspondence and complaints that he could not complete at the office. When necessary he pressed the family into assistance. They spent hours addressing envelopes when a new catalogue was to be mailed, and those too young to write sealed envelopes and licked postage stamps."[24]

A New Old Location

In 1891, the old Consolidated company had rented factory space in southeast Minneapolis. In May 1892, fire destroyed the Sweatt Manufacturing Company facilities in Robbinsdale, and Sweatt moved the woodenware business in with the heat regulator business. Once Sweatt Manufacturing was sold, he searched for a new location for Electric Heat Regulator. Sweatt rented an office in downtown Minneapolis, and a makeshift factory was established in a barn behind the house of Wellington DeVoe, the company foreman and the first known rank–and–file employee. A small, two–story barn still stands behind 3027 Columbus Avenue in south Minneapolis, only six blocks from Honeywell World Headquarters. Company artists since about 1937 have erroneously represented this structure as Albert Butz's home and workshop, where he invented the damper flapper.[25]

The barn was a temporary arrangement. By 1903, Electric Heat Regulator had moved to a new factory a block north on Lake Street, and three years later to an odd little building which has been variously described as a roller skating rink and a bowling alley. This long, narrow structure is the location at which the oldest surviving photographs were taken of factory operations. It consisted of one large room heated by two stoves.[26] The building was so poorly designed that it actually swayed with the wind, and one account purports that in a strong wind the walls had

The Sweatt Manufacturing Company manufactured woodenware of many types, including this wheelbarrow called "Sweatt's Barrel Tray" patented by Arthur Hubbard, superintendent of the factory, and advertised in the Sweatt catalogue of 1894.

Interior and exterior views of the former bowling alley show the first building Sweatt purchased for Electric Heat Regulator Company in 1908-1909. The building was in such disrepair that it was said the walls had to be braced in a strong wind to keep production pulleys and belts in alignment.

to be braced to keep the production pulleys and belts in alignment.[27] Erik Wistrand, who worked for Honeywell and its predecessor companies including Electric Heat Regulator from 1909–1950, recalled that even if wind wasn't a problem, there were times when the power cut out in the bowling alley. "We had a funny way of making do. My motorcycle was used to run machinery when the power went off," by running the bike on a treadmill.[28]

By 1910, Electric Heat Regulator Company employed 12 men in the bowling alley factory, where two types of motors were assembled: the original spring–wound motor which required periodic winding, and a newer, gravity–type motor which used an iron weight for power. In addition to the motors, the company assembled thermostats from parts purchased from Standard Thermostat Company of Boston.[29]

A New Thermostat Brings A Lawsuit

Around 1908, W.R. Sweatt and factory supervisor Joel Kersteter began experiments on a new product to further refine the automatic damper flapper control. The idea was simple. Modify an alarm clock, adapting the alarming mechanism in such a way that, instead of ringing a bell, it would mechanically change the setting on the thermostat. Through a clever arrangement of levers and catches, the clock would be mounted directly on the thermostat. The "alarm" could be set to go off at, say, 7 o'clock. And when 7 o'clock arrived, the device would turn the thermostat up automatically. In this fashion, a homeowner could manually turn the heat down at night—when one enjoys a lower household temperature for sleeping—and the clock thermostat would automatically turn up the heat in the morning by opening the damper on the furnace.

The idea of clock–based automation had been around for some time, so it was natural for Sweatt and Kersteter to consider combining thermostatic and chronologic automation. The idea of applying a clock to automatically perform work is nearly as old as the clock itself, and certainly predates the damper flapper. For example, earlier in the 19th Century the great naturalist John Muir invented a device which

Above Left: An early advertisement of the clock attachment for a more refined automatic control, 1908.

Lower Left: The first Sweatt and Kersteter Clock Thermostat was enclosed in a mahogany case and reportedly hung in Sweatt's home as early as 1905.

Mark Honeywell and company in front of his plumbing shop in Wabash, Indiana, about 1906.

automatically stood a bed upright on its footboard at a preselected time on an alarm clock, providing substantial impetus for a reluctant sleeper to wake up.[30]

By late 1908, Electric Heat Regulator Co. was advertising its Minneapolis Heat Regulator "with or without time attachment," and in 1911, the company landed in court in opposition to another company over a patent relating to the clock thermostat. The Jewell Manufacturing Company of Elmira, New York brought suit against Electric Heat Regulator for manufacturing a clock thermostat similar in design to a patent purchased from inventor Schuyler Post in early 1908.

Jewell had strong circumstantial evidence of infringement. First, there was a handwritten letter from Joel Kersteter to Jewell dated February 7, 1908, saying, "Gentlemen, I recently purchased a house in which there is one of your controllers but it is all disconnected and does not work. Please send me directions for connecting it up and making it work." The letter gave Kersteter's home address. Another letter was sent by Wirt Wilson, W.R.'s brother-in-law and Electric Heat Regulator board member, dated September 20, 1907, executed on

Wilson's insurance firm letterhead. It read," Please send me full particulars regarding your Heat Regulator. The cost of same and whether it can be installed readily by a novice. Please give full particulars."[31]   W.R. claimed that a prototype clock thermostat had been in use in his own home since

Starting in about 1902, W.R. Sweatt promoted Electric Heat Regulator's product as "The Minneapolis." This may have been a result of customers referring to the damper-flapper system as "The Minneapolis Heat Regulator" to distinguish it from regulators manufactured elsewhere.

1906.[32] His only proof, though, was his wife, who claimed that she recalled a conversation between W.R. and a friend from Fargo regarding the clock thermostat, and that she had recorded the date in her diary as September 16th, 1906. The matter was settled out of court, however, as Sweatt agreed to pay Jewell $3,000 for a license to manufacture thermostats of the Jewell design, along with a royalty of $10 for each thermostat manufactured prior to the settlement. Several years later, Jewell was acquired by Honeywell Heating Specialties of Wabash, Indiana, and in 1927, Jewell became a part of Sweatt's company when the Minneapolis and Wabash concerns merged.

Mark Honeywell

In 1906, Mark Honeywell, a young inventor in Wabash, Indiana was setting up shop as a plumber and heating mechanic. Honeywell was born in Florida and had become involved in the citrus industry at an early age. However, he was more interested in the invention of mechanical devices. He invented a very specialized device which launched his career, and led to the incorporation of the Honeywell Heating Specialty Company. The Honeywell Heat Generator, also called a mercury seal generator, created a revolution in the home heating industry.

Water and steam heating systems had been in use for more than a half–century before Honeywell's in-

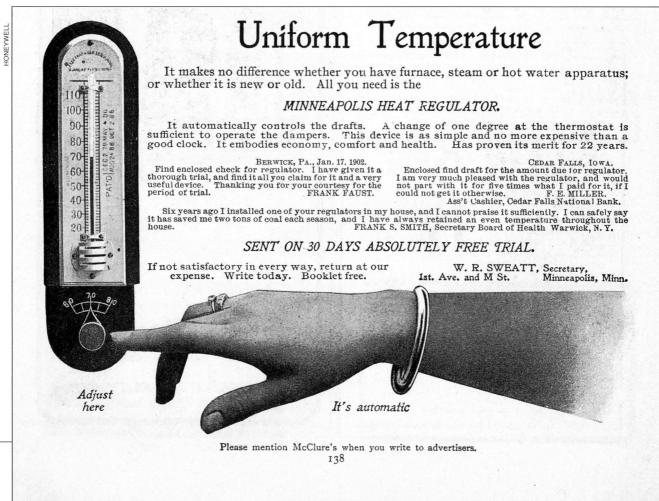

In 1912, W.R. Sweatt built a new factory and office space at 28th Street and 4th Avenue South in Minneapolis. The original building is a cornerstone of current Honeywell World Headquarters. Sweatt shrewdly designed the factory so it could be easily converted to apartments, if the regulator business failed.

vention. Most were gravity circulation systems which directed heated water throughout a building, the circulation resulting from the difference in weight between hot and cold water. This type of system was notorious for both poor circulation and unsatisfactory heat transfer. The system also incorporated an expansion tank to accommodate the overflow of heated water, but the tank often spilled. Honeywell's invention revolutionized the water heating system by allowing it to operate closed and pressurized. The heat generator featured a column of mercury which would not permit heated water to overflow until the system exceeded 10 psi. Pressurized water systems had greatly improved circulation, required smaller pipes and radiators, and allowed for superheating the water to about 212 degrees Fahrenheit.[33] Mark Honeywell's invention established him as an important player in the field of home heating. "It was natural for this type of development to lead into the temperature control field, and soon the company was designing a line of instruments that somewhat paralleled the Minneapolis line."[34]

The Dawn of Advertising

The Minneapolis company would soon take notice of Mark Honeywell's company, as they competed for market share in the growing field of automatic control and home heating. In the first decade of the new century, manufacturers of automatic controls shared the challenge of convincing American homeowners that their products were more than just novelties. Electric Heat Regulator had begun regular national advertising under the direction of W.R. Sweatt. From around 1905, advertisements placed in national magazines, along with aggressive door to door sales efforts in cities from Boston to St. Louis, had introduced the country to a heat

regulator called "The Minneapolis." Early thermostats were stamped "Electric Heat Regulator Co." in a semi-circle around the top of the unit, with "Minneapolis, Minn." stamped in the center. By about 1910 the thermostats were actually stamped "The Minneapolis" in bold face across the top of the cover. The cover itself had been developed by 1892, and protected the bi-metal strip and electrical switches. On the outside of the cover was the company's trademark and a convenient thermometer by which to read ambient temperature.[35] Before 1892, the thermostat was simply an exposed bi-metal strip mounted of a plate with bare electrical contacts.

Company lore suggests that W.R.—when not actually knocking on doors himself—would personally drive his salesmen around Minneapolis and Saint Paul in his horse and carriage, and would work on the company books while he waited.[36] On the other hand, his salesmen

W. G. Jennings
Chicago Sales

H. W. Sweatt
Vice-President

F. S. Stimson
Asst. Treasurer

1913
Wm. R. Sweatt
President

J. C. Kersteter
Superintendent

Minneapolis Heat Regulator's management, shortly after the company took on a new name in 1912 and moved to new facilities at 28th Street and 4th Avenue — where Honeywell World Headquarters is located today.

often spent time in the factory, sharing insights gathered from customers. This responsiveness to customers would be an enduring resource for the young company.

Letters from customers were consistently addressed to "The Minneapolis Heat Regulator Company,"—so W.R. took the cue. In 1912 he renamed his company to reflect the popular perception.

In 1912, the same year the name was changed, the company completed an impressive new factory and office complex on the corner of 4th Avenue and 28th Street in south Minneapolis. Though the complex has since undergone many expansions and now occupies nearly a square city block, that original building still forms the cornerstone of Honeywell World Headquarters. A trade publication called *Sheet Metal Worker* announced that W.R. had constructed a 6,000 square–foot building which was "Modern in every feature" to "accommodate [the company's] constantly increasing business in the manufacture of Minneapolis Heat Regulators."[37] Sweatt was so shrewd, he had actually built the factory so that it could be converted into apartments if the heat regulator business failed.[38]

Another indication of substantial growth occurred in 1913, when the capital stock of Minneapolis Heat Regulator Company was increased to $200,000. Company management was also more precisely defined, with W.R. president and treasurer, Fred Stimson assistant treasurer, Walter Wilson secretary in charge of sales, and J.C. Kersteter shop superintendent.

The competition for share of a growing market was heating up fast, and W.R. Sweatt's careful management had ensured that Minneapolis Heat Regulator was well–positioned as sales offices had been established in Boston, Syracuse, Cleveland, and St. Louis for "The Minneapolis." *Sheet Metal Worker* identified 14 manufacturers of heat regulators in 1913, including the Minneapolis Heat Regulator Company,[39] which then manufactured and sold four models of thermostats and two motors.

The public was on the verge of widespread acceptance of automatic control by 1913, when H.W. Sweatt, W.R.'s oldest son, graduated from the University of Minnesota and was appointed a vice president of the company. He would oversee the growth of a small Midwestern cottage industry into a worldwide leader in automation.

ANNOUNCEMENT
is made of the organization of
MINNEAPOLIS-HONEYWELL
REGULATOR CO.

ANNOUNCEMENT is made of the organization of the Minneapolis-Honeywell Regulator Co., for the purpose of acquiring and carrying on the businesses of the Minneapolis Heat Regulator Co., of Minneapolis, Minnesota, and the Honeywell Heating Specialties Co., of Wabash, Indiana.

Management of the new corporation will be vested in the former executives of the two companies.

Executive offices of the new corporation will be located at Minneapolis, Minnesota, and Oil Burner Sales Headquarters at Wabash, Indiana. There will be no interruption in service to the trade, and factories will be maintained and operated both at Minneapolis and Wabash.

Customers may, for the present and until further notice, address all communications, as has been their previous custom, to the Minneapolis-Honeywell Regulator Co., either at Minneapolis or Wabash.

News that stunned the heating industry was formally announced in 1927.

CHAPTER THREE

DIVIDE AND CONQUER

"We like the spirit of cooperation prevailing among our people at Minneapolis–Honeywell. We think it is grand. Disturbances, which at the worst are minor, are few and far between. The loyalty shown by the employees is not of the forced variety. It comes of a free will engendered by a desire on the part of a far–seeing management to treat the employees with the fullest measure of human understanding...Management was correct in its judgement which years ago prompted them to adopt the policy that we should all be just one big, happy family!"[1]

—*Minneapolis-Honeywell News Circulator*, 1938

Saves
Coal
Saves
Nerves
Saves
Lives

We have something to regulate heat for all kinds of heaters. Free information for a postal.

WM. R. SWEATT, Sec'y.
ELECTRIC HEAT REGULATOR CO.,
26th St. and K Ave., S., Minneapolis, Minn.

In 1913, W.R. Sweatt named his 22 year–old son Harold vice president of his promising heat regulator company. "H.W." had been born in 1891, the same year W.R. and Jessie moved to Minneapolis and become stockholders in Consolidated Temperature Controlling Company. From a very young age, he had been put to work on weekends and vacations, pushing a broom or boxing shipments. H.W. had been exposed to every facet of the business, and he was most likely the only 1913 graduate of the University of Minnesota who had already been named vice president of a company.

Apparently W.R. had given his son the title for practical reasons, for H.W. later commented, "Records show that before I got out of college and went to work full–time, I was a vice president. This was so that I could sign the papers in the absence of my father. I was a minor in those days, and I'm sure the legality of those signatures could have been questioned."[2] Though he was at least nominally an officer of his father's company, H.W. apparently considered pursuing a degree in law.[3] There were a number of lawyers on his mother's side of the family, including his uncle Wirt and his grandfather George. But H.W. also had a desire to get married and settle down. Shortly after receiving his B.A., he gave his childhood sweetheart, Mary Buchanan, an engagement ring. H.W. decided to forego his interest in the legal profession in favor of getting married and joining the newly–named Minneapolis Heat Regulator Company.

Though a vice president, H.W. was directed to assist Fred Dennison, the company's engineer, in improving product design, and this early assignment led to a lifetime of interest in the engineering process. In 1916, he was made the general manager of the factory,[4] and in later years, his name would even appear on a number of patents assigned to the company.

In 1913, the company had grown to 50 people and had sales of about $200,000 per year.[5] It was about to enter into a period of exponential growth. This was an era of awesome technological advance, as the Industrial Revolution evolved into the refined mass–marketing of comfort and convenience. These advances made automatic control increasingly attractive for a wide variety of applications.

Minneapolis Heat Regulator was busy developing the technologies, as well as the markets in which to sell them.

Selling Control

From the earliest days of the Butz patent, the primary challenge was sales. W.R. Sweatt understood the importance of getting his product in front of the public, and invested substantially in advertising. He wanted consumers, along with stove and furnace manufacturers, to know there was a spectacular new device promising to revolutionize home heating.

"It was W.R. who laid the foundation for the advertising policy of the company. He advertised in the trade publications to let the heating indus-

try know that selling and installing heat regulators could be profitable. The heaviest advertising, however, was in the magazines that were read by homeowners, and to a limited degree in newspapers, because W.R. realized that there was an educational job to be done before the sales volume could build up. In 1915, for example, the company ran advertisements of 1/4 to 1/2 page each in magazines with national circulation, including such as Saturday Evening Post, Harper's, Scribner's, McClure's, House Beautiful, National Geographic, and Good Housekeeping.[6]

The earliest advertising policy of the company was to stretch the budget as far as possible by concentrating on the months be-

tween October and February, when customers might be most receptive to advertising concerning their home heating plants.

Sweatt had some difficulty convincing manufacturers of stoves and furnaces that automatic controls could be profitable additions to their products. One problem was that many stoves and furnaces were equipped with dampers that could not accommodate the Butz system. C.W. Nessell wrote that "appeals to manufacturers brought scant results, and since the manufacturers would not come to him, [W.R.] went to them. He clamped his hat on his head and called on them with the result that in a few years they were all providing dampers suitable for regulators."[7]

HONEYWELL

In 1916, the executives, directors and staff of Minneapolis Heat Regulator posed for a summertime photograph behind their new facility at 28th Street and 4th Avenue in South Minneapolis. W.R. Sweatt is seated third from left. 25-year-old Vice President Harold (H.W.) is standing second from the right.

"Flapper" style was clearly in evidence among the executive office staff of Minneapolis Heat Regulator Company in 1923, including the bobs and bangs popular during the era of speakeasys and Clara Bow.

In addition, the advertising directed to homeowners began to work. As customers began requesting home heating controls, manufacturers quickly changed their minds about their potential profitability. It would not have been difficult for Sweatt to manufacture furnaces as well, selling the complete home heating system with his heat regulator as the crowning jewel. Instead, he made the decision to concentrate on the controls themselves. Thus was born the guiding principle that Honeywell would never enter into competition with its customers. A 1937 company profile in *Fortune* pointed out this important facet of Sweatt and his firm. "It would have been quite easy for [W.R.] Sweatt to have branched out into furnace manufacture and cashed in on the growing demand for furnace installations ...But long before 1913, when he brought Harold Sweatt into the company, William the founder realized that he had something that was good in itself, and he understood that to stray after will–o'–the–wisps would very quickly destroy its value."[8]

Advertising from the earliest period of the heat regulator emphasized the many advantages of the damper–flapper system. The most obvious was the convenience of not having to manually adjust the damper down in the cellar; all one had to do was change the setting on the thermostat right there in the living quarters. And because of the precision of the thermostat, the homeowner could save coal, stretching his heating dollar. With fewer trips to the basement to stoke the fire, there was less

chance of overheating or explosion. Several ad campaigns went to great lengths to establish the menace of overheating, tying it to medical pathologies from the common cold to emotional malaise, as a 1927 sales pamphlet indicates.

"Public health authorities everywhere are attempting to educate us all to the danger of overheated rooms, which very often occurs during the winter months. This overheating produces all sorts of ill effects upon the heat regulating and circulatory systems of the body. It reduces our resistance to disease, especially to cold and catarrhal affections and is even suspected of considerable responsibility in the development of tuberculosis. At any rate it is well known that it produces laziness and mental dullness, loss of appetite and low spirits...The ideal temperature

C.B. Sweatt, second son of W.R., served in the U.S. Cavalry during World War I. When he returned, he went to work for his father at Minneapolis Heat Regulator Company, following his brother H.W.

which all of us should strive to enjoy is 68 degrees, but it is impossible to maintain this temperature or any other without automatic control."[9]

This link between health and the home heating system was cleverly incorporated in literature calling automatic control "the heart of the heating plant."[10] One of the most seductive approaches emphasized novelty, an earmark of the Modernist age. By 1920, a Minneapolis Heat Regulator advertising campaign was asking, "Are you living in the [18]80s?"

As homeowners became familiar with automatic control, it became easier for Sweatt to urge manufacturers and installers to "sell the job complete." When customers requested automatic control, he noted, it would reflect well

JUST SET THE INDICATOR!
Forget About Drafts, Dampers or Valves

THE MINNEAPOLIS HEAT REGULATOR
ESTABLISHED 1885

For Coal · Coke · Gas · Oil

In 1926 W.R. Sweatt commissioned artist Philip Lyford to paint several canvasses incorporating the Minneapolis thermostat. These colorful oil paintings were used in numerous advertisements throughout the 20s.

on these firms to have the Minneapolis right there and ready to install.

Sweatt's company stayed in the vanguard of marketing innovation through the Thirties. In 1926 W.R. commissioned a well-known Chicago artist named Philip Lyford to create several large oil paintings incorporating the Minneapolis thermostat in domestic settings. These paintings were reproduced in four-color direct mail circulars believed to be the first of their kind.[11] Four years later the company sponsored a nationally broadcast radio show featuring the Minneapolis Symphony Orchestra. For 13 weeks, more than 22 CBS affiliates, listeners across the country heard live orchestra performances through the sponsorship of the automatic controls firm from Minnesota. This was the first time an American company sponsored a symphony orchestra for a radio program.[12]

Results from this aggressive marketing were soon forthcoming. In 1919, sales were close to $1 million, having nearly quintupled in less than a decade. The 1919 *Minneapolis Sales Information Book* boasted that "the first nationally advertised heat regulator was the Minneapolis—whose total advertising lineage would undoubtedly be several thousand percent greater than all others put together."[13] The sales book was equally hyperbolic about total sales, claiming that "approximately a million Minneapolis Heat Regulators are in use in the United States, Canada, and Foreign countries...While it is very difficult to estimate the number of competing machines installed, we do not believe there are over 100,000 to 150,000 of all other makes in use."[14] Even without the exaggeration, sales of the damper-flapper were impressive, and Minneapolis Heat Regulator was well ahead of its competition. C.W. Nessell estimated that by 1920, 300,000 Minneapolis systems had been sold, almost four times the combined total of all competitive units sold to that date.[15]

A New Director, A New Approach

In 1920, W.R. announced that his second son, Charles "C.B." Sweatt, would be the advertising manager and treasurer of Minneapolis Heat Regulator. Like his brother H.W., C.B. had been named a director of the company in 1916 while still in school, at the age of 18. He had graduated from the University of Minnesota the following year, and served in the cavalry in World War I. After his tour of duty, he returned to Minneapolis and began working for his father as a payroll clerk. When he was named advertising manager, he was given a budget of $60,000 for marketing the complete Minneapolis Heat Regulator line.

C.B. concentrated his ads in nine national consumer magazines, advertising year–round in five of them. This was augmented by an extra push during the heating season. About 75 percent of the budget went to consumer advertising, while the remainder was spent on trade publications and advertising to manufacturers, dealers and jobbers.

Door-To-Door Sales

When C.B. Sweatt was named advertising manager, there were 250 employees in the home office and factory, with 100 more in sales and distribution offices throughout the country. By 1926, there were branch offices in 9 cities, complemented by 15 authorized distributors. The damper flapper was still being marketed directly to homeowners who owned hand–fired coal furnaces.[16] At the peak period of door–to–door sales, Minneapolis Heat Regulator had offices in New York, Philadelphia, and Chicago, manned by some 50 to 75 sales professionals. They typically sold control systems ranging in cost from $60 to $180, which might include a clock thermostat, a limit control (which provided a high–end safety valve to prevent accidental overheating), and a damper motor.

The company's products were also beginning to cross international borders. Years before establishing international subsidiaries, the company was a well–known source of controls for discriminating customers abroad. By World War II, installations would be made in the diamond mines of South Africa and the Chinese National Museum. A letter from London in 1938 bore news of royal significance.

"Did you know that due to your engineering, tooling, testing and inspection being of such a high standard the King of England sleeps in comfort at Balmoral Castle, his Scottish residence? The Stoker Company, which made the installation, had always used competitive controls but when this very important job came along they realized only the very best would do."

The English monarch wasn't the only king to request the assistance of the company from Minneapolis, as a correspondent in the Amsterdam office wrote.

"His Majesty, the Sultan of Morocco, asked us, through his technical advisor, to solve for him the following control problem. In his bathroom

While the balance of Minneapolis–Honeywell advertising was directed toward consumers, automatic controls were also pitched directly to fuel and furnace companies throughout the 1930s.

there are three bath tubs, side by side. It seems that he uses the center one. H.M. now desired to be able to control the water temperature of the other two tubs while sitting in his own. The inquiry not giving us more details, we were left to our own imagination as to the reasons and the occupants of the other two tubs."[17]

Automatic Fuel & Automatic Control

The hand–fired coal furnace was nearly universally used during this period of rapid growth. As a result, for 35 years W.R. Sweatt and his company developed and sold damper–flappers for this type of system. But by the Twenties, oil and gas became viable options as technology made their use more practical. "When Minneapolis Heat Regulator and Honeywell merged [in 1927] fewer than 10 per cent of homes had been converted to automatic heat. By 1942, when business was slowed by World War II, 4.5 million U.S. homes had been converted, most of them to oil burners, the rest to gas and stokers."[18] (A stoker was a device which automatically fed coal into a furnace through a system of hoppers and conveyors.) Because methods of burning these fuels in a controlled manner had not yet been devised, these fuels were previously considered worthless for home heating.

When Oil Was Worthless

There is evidence that oil was used as a fuel some 6,000 years ago. However, until the present century it was used primarily to caulk and waterproof watercraft.[19]

Most oils have qualities that lend themselves to ignition. The widespread use of petroleum oil occurred in part because of a shortage of whale oil in 1860.[20] Whale oil had been prized for its luminous qualities when burned in decorative lamps, and when whaling nearly rendered the animals extinct, a method of distilling kerosene from petroleum oil was developed. The first oil burners in Europe were fashioned in Russia, and probably adapted from whale–oil lamps.

The first oil well in the U.S. was drilled in 1859, by Edwin Drake. Of course, oil had often popped up on its own,

Colonel Drake first drilled for oil in Titusville, Pennsylvania in 1859. Since oil occurs naturally throughout the world, it had been discovered in earliest prehistory. Oil floods often ruined ancient salt mines. Until refining methods could be developed, oil was thought to be worthless except as a patent medicine.

sometimes in salt mines. About the only use for it until that time was in patent medicines and some specious products marketed from the back of "snake–oil" wagons.[21] In the 1850s, a report by Dr. Benjamin Stillman of Yale described the easy distillation of oil into a profitable product. This report caught the eye of a group of investors in Titusville, Pennsylvania. Nearby was a large natural oil reserve, and these investors retained Edwin Drake to drill it.

"He did, although he knew nothing about drilling for anything, and kept at it for about

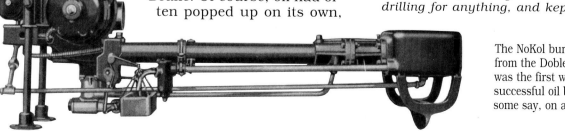

The NoKol burner was developed from the Doble Steam Automobile. It was the first widely produced and successful oil burner, and was born, some say, on a coal-less Monday.

two years with nothing much to show for his labors. The town people thought he was slightly off his rocker and called the well drilling process 'Drake's Folly,' but he kept on. Then on a Saturday evening, August 27, 1859, the drillers stopped work for the weekend at a depth of 70-feet. The next morning one of the drill crew took another look at the well and discovered it was filled almost to the top with oil. The battle was won, and with that little well a new industry was born."[22]

The Chicago World's Fair of 1893 introduced oil burners as an important new technology capable of being used for space heating. The exposition buildings were themselves heated by 54 oil–burning furnaces. By the 1933 Chicago World's Fair, more than 100,000 Chicago homes were burning oil for heat, and more than 300 retailers were selling oil burners for home heating.[23] During the 1893 Fair, insurance companies sent a representatives to classify the electrical and heat-ing equipment with respect to safety. He ended up doing such an impressive job that his employers formed the Underwriters' Laboratories.

Home heating with petroleum oil in the U.S. really began in earnest around 1917, when Minneapolis Heat Regulator Co. received its first substantial orders for oil burner controls.[24] The first oil burner

HONEYWELL

A late-19th century gusher. Oil did not come into wide use as a home heating fuel until several developments took place. First, methods of refining petroleum from raw oil had to be devised. Second, coal remained the fuel of choice until shortages and rations occurred during World War I. Finally, methods of automatic ignition and control had to be developed, because oil could not be lit by hand like coal or wood.

had been approved by Underwriters' Laboratories in 1912, and the second in 1919. At the peak of oil usage several decades later, more than 200 burners were listed by the testing and approval organization, and industry officials estimated there were more than 1,000 manufacturers. However, the diversity of suppliers and equipment generated problems as the demand for oil and oil burners increased.

Coal-less Mondays and a Steam Automobile

In times of national crisis, coal was reserved for production and defense alone. During World War I, the War Priorities Board declared "coal–less Mondays." But there were no restrictions on the use of petroleum oil, since it wasn't widely used. Although oil burners had been developed, they were still in the prototype stage. One had been developed for the Doble Steam automobile, on the verge of production when war began. The War Priorities Board's restriction on most metals prevented the Doble from going into production. So, its manufacturer began looking for other uses for its technologies, perhaps to assist the war effort in some way. In light of coal restrictions, someone envisioned the potential of an oil burner for the home heating front. Thus was born the first mass–marketed oil burner, appropriately named The NoKol. It was a burner of a kind that remained in use throughout the 1920s. Oil burned in a pot installed directly into the old coal furnace, so the furnace required only a simple conversion.

Ironically, the coal industry contributed to its own demise. In 1923, a bitter coal strike took place in the dead of winter. As a result, many Americans were forced to consider alternative ways of heating their homes.[25]

Automatic Ignition

Among the biggest challenges faced by manufacturers of burners and controls in adapting petroleum to home heating was the requirement for an efficient, safe method of automatic oil ignition.

"Oil can be a tempestuous and obstreperous fuel and gives vent to its anger in ways that are disconcerting to the homeowner. Consequently an oil burner must be constantly supervised while it is in operation and properly started when heat is wanted."[26]

The first oil burners required various controls, to provide for the introduction and ignition of oil, and safety measures to prevent fire and explosion. Consequently, the company was asked to adapt its damper–flapper system to heating oil. The first solution was to simply adapt the damper motor to open and close the main oil valve. This system, however, did not provide for ignition or repression of fire. If the pilot or burner flames went out, there was the very real possibility that oil would flood the furnace and even the cellar. A mechanical device was quickly devised to act as a safety shut–off valve, actually a bucket fed by a spill tube in the combustion chamber. If flame was not present, the oil filled the combustion chamber and then flowed through the spill tube into a bucket. The bucket was connected to the main shut-off valve so that if it filled, the valve would close. Unfortunately, obstructions could interfere with the spill tube, or the bucket could be bumped by a pet or careless worker. And when the fire failed, the basement would flood with oil.

In fact, there were many problems with fuel oil. Early burners were "tricky, capricious and temperamental," Nessell wrote, "and given to such shenanigans as filling the house with oily soot and blowing the furnace door through the basement wall into the front yard of the neighbor next door."[27] The development of more sophisticated controls began to remedy this situation by the mid–1920s. But the central

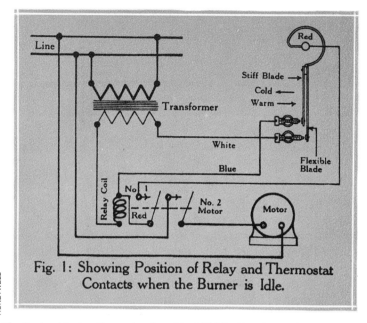

Fig. 1: Showing Position of Relay and Thermostat Contacts when the Burner is Idle.

The Series 10 circuit was developed in 1923 by Ben Cyr and H.W. Sweatt. As a low-voltage control circuit, the Series 10 stopped the system if anything failed. This was particularly important to the development of automatic fuel technologies, making it possible to burn oil and natural gas.

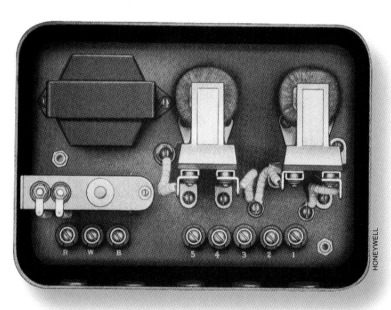

The Protectorelay was the first control designed to be universally applicable to the hundreds of oil burners manufactured in the 1920s and 1930s. The Protectorelay sequenced the ignition and combustion of nearly any oil burner. This standardization of controls was a boon for the oil heating industry which had been plagued by too many different burners.

problem remained: The development of a burner that could return the entire system to a stop position, with no danger of accidental flooding or ignition, should any component malfunction.

Minneapolis–Honeywell products helped turn the unreliable trip bucket to a historical footnote. The Pyrostat, for example, was developed as a proximity switch in the furnace. Employing a small bi–metal strip similar to that in the thermostat, it maintained a closed electric circuit as long as flame was present. If the flame was accidentally extinguished, the switch responded by opening the circuit, shutting down the electric motor which pumped oil into the burner. Another control that made fuel oil safer was the Protectostat, mounted in the chimney. This switch measured the temperature of the furnace exhaust, and if the temperature did not increase after the furnace was to have fired, the burner was shut down.

But the really revolutionary control was developed in 1923 by Ben Cyr and H.W. Sweatt.[28] Called the Series 10, it was a low-voltage control circuit which put everything "back dead center" if anything failed. Later, Honeywell developed the Protectorelay, the first control suited to the hundreds of models of oil–burners then manufactured. The standardization of controls was a significant boon for the oil heating industry.[29]

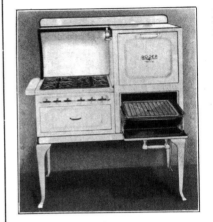

An early gas-burning range appeared in 1930. Gas was not used widely in home applications until adequate methods of transporting the fuel were devised in the late 1920s. Until that time natural gas was used primarily in areas where it naturally occured. Beacon Hill in Boston still boasts its Nineteenth Century gas street lamps.

A Ghost Story

Gas is one of the most common fuel used in home heating today. But it was relatively scarce in the early years of automatic heating, as technologies were not yet developed to pipe it great distances or to process it from coal. Until the 1920s gas was available only in certain areas.

The Chinese used natural gas 2,000 years ago, piping it in bamboo to their sacred temples to provide light and heat.[30] The term "gas," is actually a derivative of the Dutch word for ghost ("geist"), which evolved following the 1609 experiments of a Dutch scientist who discovered "wild spirits" in coal.[31]

Gas was discovered in America in 1776, on land George Washington wanted to use for a public park. This natural vent had caught fire and was called a "burning spring."[32]

An attempt to harness natural gas occurred near Rochester, New York, in 1863. Workmen drilling for oil struck a pocket of gas instead. When further drilling didn't produce oil, the well was abandoned. When the escaping gas caught fire, the owners of the property saw a way to turn disappointment into profit. They turned the fire into an attraction, calling it "The Old Burning Well," and setting up a restaurant at the site. In 1870 the well was bought by a company organized for the purpose of piping the gas 25 miles to Rochester, using a pipeline made from 12–inch hollowed pine boughs laid end to end. By the end of the decade, iron pipes made high–pressure transmission possible.[33]

In 1912, there were 547 companies in the U.S. supplying natural gas, mostly on a regional basis and limited to the coasts, where gas occurred naturally. With the expansion of gas transmission lines into the interior of the continent, the number increased dramatically.[34] This expansion culminated in 1948 with the completion of a gas line more than 2,000 miles long, extending from West Texas to New York.

Back in 1792, William Murdock, "the father of the gas industry," had pioneered a method of generating natural gas by processing coal. "It was manufactured gas that gave the gas industry its real start. Natural gas was fine when it was available, but the gas wells were usually remote from the major population centers."[35]

Manufactured gas made this fuel available in major urban centers not service-able by pipeline. Seattle, for

HONEYWELL

1915

example, was too remote to be reached by gas pipelines. Instead, a huge gas processing plant was constructed there. It still stands, preserved as a public park called "The Gas Works."

Until the early Twentieth Century, gas had been used primarily for lighting. Many Nineteenth Century buildings on the East Coast still have gas lamps and cocks in place in bedrooms and hallways.

One of the earliest modern uses of gas to generate heat came with the Bunsen Burner, developed in 1855 for use in the laboratory. At the same time, gas came into use in room and space heaters. A common sight in 1860s Boston was the portable room heater, a small gas burner with no exhaust vent. The heater was linked by hose to a gas cock in the room and could be moved anywhere there was a supply of gas. But for reasons of safety, it was limited in use.

Even after methods of locating and drilling natural gas were refined, gas was still used primarily for lighting and cooking. Coal remained the universal fuel for heating, as it was so plentiful. And it remained the primary fuel until fully automatic central heating with oil was pioneered in the Twenties.[36] C.W. Nessell claims that gas didn't take off as a fuel for home heating because gas companies were somewhat apathetic. "It was only when electricity began to make serious inroads on the amount of gas used for both cooking and lighting that they started to look for new markets," he wrote. "This began in a feeble way about 1924."[37] By 1933, gas companies in Chicago felt threatened enough to embark on an aggressive

new marketing campaign for home heating. By midsummer, they had made 10,000 installations, all of which were conversions of coal furnaces. Like the early oil burners, gas burners were designed for easy installation directly into the old coalburner.[38] Before long the public's interest in gas as a possible home heating fuel had enticed furnace manufacturers to make models specifically designed to burn it.[39]

Both oil and gas require automatic control, and both are somewhat unpredictable as fuels.[40] When first used for home heating, the only controls were old damper–flapper–type systems. Honeywell received its first orders for gas controls about 1915, and again was asked to adapt the Butz system to the new fuel.[41] Initially, the company arranged the system so that a damper motor simply opened and closed the main gas supply to the burner. A large pilot light was kept burning at all times, so large that in mild weather it could heat the house all by itself. This was a concern in areas where gas was manufactured from coal, because manufactured gas was expensive. Another concern was that the pilot would blow out, which could lead to the natural gas equivalent of a basement flooded with fuel oil: The house could fill with poisonous gas which might explode with a single spark. Troy, New York was the first city to pass laws in the 1880s requiring that an odorant be added to gas, to indicate its presence.[42]

It quickly became evident that the old damper–flapper system was not an adequate control for the gas–fired furnace. One problem was that the system depended on power from batteries or line voltage. If there

was an interruption or loss of current, the system would remain open or closed.

Sweatt's company began experimentation on automatic pilot protection that would stop the flow of gas if there was a failure. One early device was a mechanical switch similar to that developed for oil burners. A small bi–metal strip was placed in close proximity to the pilot flame, and if the flame went out, the strip would activate an electric circuit which would close the main gas supply. However, this protection proved insufficient, as it was vulnerable to mechanical failure, and its operation depended upon an uninterrupted outside source of electricity.

A breakthrough came with a special kind of circuit, a thermocouple that translated heat directly into electricity. The company's thermocouples made it possible to have a completely closed, self–sufficient system. The electricity generated by the pilot light was sufficient not only to keep an electrical switch closed, but to actually operate the main gas valve.[43] With dependable automatic pilot protection and an available source of fuel, the gas home heating system became a viable alternative to oil and coal.

The Door Closes on Door-To-Door Sales

Until the 1930s, when hand–fired coal furnaces were rapidly becoming obsolete, door–to–door sales and direct advertising were responsible for the bulk of controls sales. "But," *Fortune* wrote in a 1937 company profile, "by degrees merchandising interest shifted from consumers to dealers, jobbers, and manufacturers. The chief reason for the shift was that a man could scarcely buy automatic heat without automatic controls, and as the oil and gas burner and coal stoker business increased, the control industry teamed up with it more and more closely."[44]

Companies manufacturing controls increasingly sold their wares directly to furnace manufacturers, dealers, and installers. As oil and gas became the new universal fuels, automatic controls became a mandatory part of the system, and Honeywell found itself in the enviable position of having an indispensable product.

Even so, the declining need for the door–to-door salespeople did not necessarily prove their demise. Ever since the stove had been moved to the basement and the damper–flapper rigged up, homeowners depended on salespeople to help out with the technical aspects of installation, repair, and instruction. These complexities only multiplied with automatic central heating, and in a sense the salespeople of the early 1900s became the service staff of later years.

1926

Divide and Conquer Part One: The Strategy of Diversification

W.R. Sweatt and his sons remained true to the philosophy of avoiding competition with their customers. Instead, they developed a strategy that would eventually bring them to a position of preeminence in the controls industry. While avoiding the manufacture of finished products, the Sweatts wanted their company to "expand and diversify until ultimately it would supply controls for every purpose...and sometimes if your competitor has a gadget that you need to fill out part of your line it is expedient to buy out your competitor."[45]

Diversification was a natural response to market changes resulting from the introduction of automatic fuels. A commitment to research and development had been conceived in the earliest days of the company, when W.R. would ride along with his door-to-door sales personnel. Information on customer concerns and insights was regularly brought back to the shop. This responsiveness remained somewhat casual in the early days. The company didn't have a formal engineering department prior to 1925. Incredibly, there were not even any shop drawings of the company's products. "Two men in the shop acted as engineers and together they worked out new ideas," C.W. Nessell said, "and within 24 hours usually had a working model made and in production within 60 days. However the day came when they wanted to make some drawings and a long drawn-out howl came from the front office when the requisition for a drafting board went in. However, the drafting board was provided and the engineering department was started with two or three engineers in 1925."[46]

Product development grew rapidly from 1900 to 1937. During this period, the company evolved from manufacturing one thermostat and one motor to producing more than 3,000 control devices, and its engineers received more than 1,000 patents.[47] As was the case with many consumer goods in those days, the diversity of the company's controls was often exaggerated by the fanci-

1929

ful and sometimes tongue–twisting appellations invented for them. *Fortune* commented on this uniquely American phenomenon, and fingered Honeywell as one of the culprits: "As the company has accumulated more and more patents and gadgets, it has also been accumulating one of the most outlandish terminologies in all industry – the food industry not excepted." This "outlandish terminology" referred to such products as the Chronotherm and Acratherm; the Protectorelay and Protectoglo; the Aquastat, Weatherstat, Modustat, and Airstat, to name just a few. Though the names were fanciful, the products were not; Honeywell engineers were consistently pushing the limits of what was thought possible.

The damper–flapper motor itself went through several generations of improvement before it was ultimately made obsolete by automatic fuel. The first motor had been a hand–wound spring motor, and, before the turn of the century, Sweatt's company had developed a gravity motor as an alternative, utilizing an iron weight on a chain for power. In 1915 a third motor was added, powered by direct current (DC) electricity from batteries.[48] The following year, the company anticipated the breakthrough of line voltage, by bringing out an alter-

Until 1925, Minneapolis Heat Regulator had no drafting or engineering department. Production simply kept a pegboard updated with samples of each component hanging upon it. By 1944, a full drafting department bustled with activity.

nating current (AC) motor which could run directly off the 'lighting circuits.'

The thermostat, perhaps the most visible component of the home heating system and therefore something of an icon, was in constant metamorphosis.[49] The clock attachment developed by W.R. Sweatt and Joel Kersteter around 1908 evolved into a line of clock thermostats. In 1912, the Model 47 was introduced as the standard clock thermostat, with a one-day clock that required winding once a day. This could be set to raise the temperature at an hour determined by the homeowner. It was usually set to open the dampers and fire up the coal furnace early in the morning. In 1917, the company introduced a substantial improvement with the Model 55. Called a "Duplex Thermostat," it both raised *and* lowered the temperature settings at predetermined times. And it used a clock that required winding only once every eight days. The Model 55 represented state–of–the–art automation. At the same time, the company had begun building thermostats from scratch, all under one roof. (Until then it had secured some components from other companies.)

The facilities of Honeywell could barely keep pace with the company's rapid expansion. Numerous additions, renovations and annexations transformed the original building into a sprawling complex.

The increasing popularity of the clock thermostat also made it important as a timepiece. "In many homes the thermostat clock had become an important time–teller in addition to performing its basic function," Anthony Gohl wrote.[50] The "Deluxe Model 55" was introduced in 1920, after the company received complaints that the regular 55 clock, purchased from the Salem Clock Company, was plagued with inaccuracy. A new clock was secured from the Boston Clock Company, and was jewelled for accuracy and durability.

As automatic fuels grew in popularity throughout the Twenties, the subsequent demand for clock thermostats resulted in a critical shortage of reliable jewelled 8–day clocks.[51] In 1922 the Minneapolis Heat Regulator Co.

made the stunning decision to manufacture its own clocks. It seemed a tremendous risk for a company specializing in thermostats and damper–flappers, hardly models of delicate precision. But the clock had become an integral part of home heating controls, and early damper motors were clockwork mechanisms of a sort. Since the Boston Clock Co. unit had been successful, the company decided to base its own design upon it, and proceeded to establish a complete clock–making shop.

With this new effort, the Minneapolis Heat Regulator Co. crossed the line into the domain of time management. In an article about the

In 1927, Minneapolis Heat Regulator was justifiably proud of both its product and the production line for the Model 77 Clock Thermostat. The company built its own high-quality clock shop from scratch, and by 1927 was producing 40,000 clocks per year.

company's clock thermostats, Anthony Gohl pointed out that "for centuries, clocks and clock–mechanisms have controlled man's actions—when to arise, when to eat, when to pray, when to open and close his shop doors."[52]

Thus was born the "Minneapolis 77," which came to be called "the best 8–day, 7–jewel clock ever made for heating equipment." In actuality, however, it may have been one of the best clocks ever built *of any kind.* Up until the 77, the company's thermostats had been given names reflecting their prices when purchased with damper motors. The 77, however, was a light-hearted departure from this practice: 77 was the number of Red Grange, the University of Illinois' legendary halfback. A new motor for the 77 was known officially as Model 24, but in practice as the football motor. The Minneapolis 77 was celebrated in *The Bulletin of the National Association of Watch and Clock Collectors,* where its "polished perfection" was detailed.[53] In 1927, when Minneapolis Heat Regulator Company and Honeywell Heating Specialties merged, the company was producing 40,000 clocks annually.

Sweatt and his sons were well aware of their company's growing accomplishment, and they weren't afraid to boast. In the 1926 *Minneapolis Sales Information Book*, descriptions of the clock department glowed with pride.

"Along practically the whole length of the building and extending for about one fourth of its width, is the famous Minneapolis Clock Depart-

ment, where the Model 77 7-jewel 8-day clocks are built and assembled. This department is most interesting; in it are tiny lathes and drill presses so fine and accurate in their construction that it was necessary to send abroad to get them, as they were nowhere obtainable in the United States. There are tiny scales for weighing and little screws which go into the movement of the clock and which are so small that you can hardly see them without the aid of a magnifying glass."[54]

Production of the Model 77 continued until 1931, when the Chronotherm was introduced as the first electric clock thermostat. A company advertisement showed a frustrated man hand-cranking his automobile, an image designed to suggest obsolescence. The ad wondered, "You wouldn't keep a car you had to crank, but is your heating plant up to date?" It described the new clock thermostat as "almost human, this marvelous new invention, equipped with an electric clock." Originally called the Thermochron, it provoked a copyright dispute with the Telechron Clock Company, which apparently felt that the name would cause confusion among its customers. Andy Jones, who was employed at Minneapolis-Honeywell for forty years, recalls his first day in 1933: "My first job was to destroy hundreds of brochures which read 'thermo-chron'...I sat at a paper-cutter every day for more than a week cutting up those 'misprinted' brochures."[55]

The internal assembly of the Model 77 7-Jewel 8-day clock.

Many new products require some time to get the bugs out. However, in the case of the Chronotherm, that expression could sometimes be taken literally:

"Honeywell's first electric clock thermostat used a clock motor with a rotor that was not enclosed. When we received the first returned model that wasn't working, we discovered the reason. A cockroach had climbed into the clock for warmth, got caught in the rotating part, and died. An executive wrote the customer: 'No wonder the clock wouldn't run—the engineer was dead.'"[56]

The Chronotherm was just one of several electric clock thermostats, and it was not the only one with problems. Acratherms were also introduced, some of which had digital clock mechanisms designed to automatically adjust temperatures at pre-selected times. Some were equipped with a time control that could only be set directly on the hour. In some neighborhoods, every household would call for more gas at precisely the same moment in the morning, creating a tremendous drop in pressure in the gas lines. In cold weather the gas company would be besieged with calls to come and re-light pilots.[57]

The limit control, developed in 1910, was a simple little device mounted directly on the furnace. When the temperature exceeded safe

limits, the limit control would shut the system down, acting as the last line of defense against malfunction. Originally developed for the damper–flapper–equipped, hand–fired coal furnace, a limit control was eventually produced that was interchangeable between hot water and warm air systems, whether fired by coal, oil, or gas burners. The final system to which the limit control was adapted was the steam boiler, which rounded out the line for residential heating plants.[58] The company could now provide limit controls for the safe operation of any heating system built anywhere. And to this day, the limit control has remained integral to the safe operation of the home heating plant.

Early in the century, Minneapolis Heat Regulator had also expanded into the field of valves for natural gas and street steam. After the company had adapted the damper–flapper system to alternative fuels and heating systems, its engineers designed and manufactured a lever–type valve of their own. This was a significant development, as the company was now testing the waters beyond the realm of residential heating, and branching out into controls which could be applied specifically to industry. Gas and steam valves were needed for bake ovens, vulcanizers, and forges, among other industrial applications.[59]

From 1913 to 1939, Honeywell added to its product lines virtually every month.

Divide and Conquer Part Two: The Strategy of Acquisition

In 1927, Minneapolis Heat Regulator Company, 40 some years old, merged with 20-year-old Honeywell Heating Specialties of Wabash, Indiana, and both companies were officially dissolved. They became a new company twice the size, and no longer privately held.

Mark Honeywell had built his company into a small but serious competitor, mostly through the success of his heat generator, which used a column of mercury to create a closed hot–water system that could operate under pressure. World War I, however, had seriously limited the quantities of mercury available to private industry, and Honeywell had been forced to diversify in order to survive.[60] This diversification was reflected in a change of name. In 1916, Honeywell Heating Spe-

cialty Company, named for the mercury heat generator, became Honeywell Heating Specialties. This slight variation reflected a commitment to enter into the field of home heating controls in general, and into direct competition with W.R. Sweatt.

The rivalry really began to heat up in 1922, when Honeywell acquired the Jewell Manufacturing Company's instrument line. Jewell was the company which had filed suit against Minneapolis Heat Regulator in 1911 over patents relating to the clock thermostat. Sweatt had agreed in the out–of–court settlement to pay the New York firm for a license to use its patents, and a royalty on products which did not give notice of this license.[61] When Honeywell Heating Specialties, a more substantial and diversified competitor, acquired Jewell, W.R. Sweatt found himself in an awkward predicament. He either had to advertise for his competitors by stamping his own products with their patent–licensing information, or pay them cash for each unit sold.

Mark Honeywell had also made inroads into the lucrative market of automatic burner manufacturers. The company "pioneered in securing contracts with oil burner manufacturers whereby controls could be sold as original equipment with heating units, and it possessed the lion's share of this business."[62] As the demand for oil burners increased, Honeywell Heating Specialties would be in an advantageous position. Even though Minneapolis Heat Regulator was nearly twice its size, Honeywell Heating Specialties was becoming a very serious obstacle to further market domination.

"Not that the two companies, each bearing the stamp of its leader's personality, were very evenly matched. In 1927 the Minneapolis Heat Regulator Company generated annual sales of $3.25 million against only $1.5 for Honeywell.

The Honeywell Heat Generator (above) used a column of mercury to seal hot water heating systems. Invented by Mark Honeywell in 1909, the device allowed such systems to operate under pressure for the first time, greatly increasing efficiency and effectiveness. When World War I put a pinch on mercury supplies and made it costly to produce, Mark Honeywell expanded into other product lines, (opposite page right) including several damper motors which competed directly with Minneapolis Heat Regulator's damper-flapper.

The market was big enough for them both. And yet each had patents and products the other needed for domination of the market, and each spent time and money duplicating some of the other's product line and sales effort in order to stay competitive. It made sense that the two become one, if only the obstacle of personalities could be overcome."[63]

The merger was certainly a surprise to industry experts, many of whom were employed by one or the other, given the historical intensity of the rivalry. Supposedly this rivalry even extended to a personal level between W.R. Sweatt and Mark Honeywell. It has been reported that the two men avoided each other assiduously, even crossing the street to avoid one another at industry conferences and trade shows.

Exactly who was responsible for first proposing a merger is unknown. However, both Sweatt and Honeywell were highly skilled and prudent managers, and both would have understood the potential advantages their combined firms would have in the heating controls market.

Honeywell employees insisted that the merger was proposed by Mark Honeywell or his assistant, Willard Huff. Veterans from the Minneapolis Heat Regulator Co., on the other hand, claimed the idea had been proposed by Earl Bailie, an old school chum of H.W. Sweatt. One company anecdote relates the story of H.W. and Bailie accidentally meeting while vacationing on a Florida beach, where Bailie casually proposed the idea.[64] However it originated, once the idea was formally presented to Sweatt, Honeywell, and other top management, the process moved swiftly.

The new organization was to be a public company, with its stock first offered on the Chicago Stock Exchange and later on the New York exchange. Headquarters were to be in Minneapolis, with W.R. Sweatt serving as chairman of the board of directors. Mark Honeywell was named president, and his offices were to remain in Wabash, which became "the oil burner headquarters of Minneapolis–Honeywell."[65] H.W. Sweatt was vice president and general manager, while his brother C.B. was vice president in charge of sales. Willard Huff became treasurer, and Ben Boalt, who had married W.R.'s daughter Beatrice, was named secretary. Both W.R. and Mark Honeywell were approaching retirement age by the time their companies merged; Sweatt had been in the business for 35 years, Honeywell for 20.

The stock market crash of October, 1929 made Sweatt and Honeywell look like geniuses. Though the economic currents of the day were turbulent, Minneapolis–Honeywell was in excellent position to weather the storm. It had become a public corporation capitalized at $2 million of 7 percent preferred stock and 130,000 shares of common stock. The cost of preferred stock was $99.50 per share and the price of common stock was $32.50, with company officers and executives owning 60 percent of the shares. The combined assets of the two predecessor companies totaled over $3.5 million, while liabilities were less than $1 million. The 1928 Annual Report came out just a few months before Black Monday. "The results for the first year of operation of the company are very gratifying," it noted. "Sales and net earnings were the largest for any year in the history of the company or its predecessors combined." This pattern of success and growth continued despite the Depression. In the ten years following the merger, company sales tripled.[66]

The merger ensured Minneapolis–Honeywell's position as the undisputed leader in home heating controls. But the prospect of going public must have been unsettling to the two gentlemen who had successfully controlled the market with private companies. Over the

The Honeywell Type D Electric
Regulator Motor

The Honeywell Spring Motor

The Honeywell Gravity Motor

years, Sweatt had shown his books only to the company's bankers, and the more sensitive information relating to profits and assets he passed along only "by word of mouth as a matter of conference convenience."[67] And Mark Honeywell apparently never even kept records on paper, or they remained well hidden, for none have ever been found for his company.[68]

A Decade of Acquisitions

The next 10 years were a period of spectacular growth and diversification. As a result of the merger, the company could provide controls for any home heating system.

In 1931, Minneapolis–Honeywell acquired the Time–O–Stat Controls Company. Time–O–Stat had been formed in 1928 by the merger of four Midwestern controls companies. In 1929 the company netted $370,000, 20 percent more than the combined totals of its four predecessor companies a year earlier. However, Time–O–Stat was hit hard by the stock market crash, and 1930 earnings plunged to $17,000.[69] In buying the company, Minneapolis–Honeywell gained access to a number of important patents, designs, and products.

One of the most significant acquisitions occurred in 1934, with the purchase of the Brown Instrument Company. This was Minneapolis-Honeywell's first major entry into the field of industrial process control, and extended its product line and engineering well beyond the realm of home heating.[70] Minneapolis–Honeywell already had a full line of residential controls, but only a limited line of industrial controls. Brown Instruments, on the other hand, manu-

factured a full line, which was then complemented by Honeywell's accessories.

Brown Instruments took its name from Edward Brown, an engineer born in 1834 in Earith, England. Brown emigrated to Philadelphia around 1860,[71] and there studied ways to measure high temperatures of the type encountered in kilns and foundries. The most obvious challenge was meltdown, since any instrument designed to measure high temperatures has to withstand them. In 1869 Brown invented the first pyrometer, an instrument based on the expansion principle, just like the thermostats Albert Butz used 15 years later. The pyrometer operated by measuring the difference in expansion of iron and graphite rods, which registered on a calibrated dial. The young engineer built a business around his invention (the pyrometer is still widely used), and he continued to invent and patent devices such as speed and temperature indicators.

Brown won many awards for his inventions, and also built a reputation as a manufacturer of useful and durable measuring devices.[72] When he died in 1905, the business consisted of only one workman and himself, was housed in three rooms of a residence, and had total annual sales of $16,000.

Over the Years

From left to right: The Model 55 "Duplex" thermostat was developed in 1917. The famous Model 77 is shown before and after the merger. Introduced by the Minneapolis Heat Regulator Company in 1924, it was the best 8-day 7-jewel clock ever made for the heating industry. The Chronotherm was an electric clock thermostat developed in 1931 which eventually replaced the handwound Model 77. The Acratherm (far right) was developed with the Chronotherm in the 1930s. It became the new standard for thermostats and replaced the old coffin-shaped Minneapolis as an icon of automatically-controlled home heating.

The Model 55 "Duplex"

The Model 77 before Minneapolis-Honeywell merger

Brown's son, Richard, took over and the business underwent a rapid expansion. The company pioneered numerous thermo–electric instruments, and by World War I, as the demand for ceramics and metal alloys exploded, it encompassed an entire city block. When Brown was acquired by Minneapolis–Honeywell some 30 years after Edward's death, the company had 500 employees who produced $2 million worth of instruments annually. Like his father, Richard was a gifted engineer and inventor, and personally received over 40 patents. At the time of the purchase, Brown made 500 different instruments, and had branch offices or distributors in most American cities.[73] Though small by Minneapolis–Honeywell standards, it had an unimpeachable reputation, as "one of the best makers of the... instruments which are at the heart of the industrial processes."[74]

Brown's instruments were in constant demand in industrial centers all over the world. The company had initiated a very early presence in the Pacific Rim, through a close relationship with the Yamatake Company of Tokyo. Founded in 1906, Yamatake began distributing Brown Instruments in the Far East in 1920. Minneapolis–Honeywell inherited the relationship with Yamatake, and the Japanese firm came to be considered its first international partner.[75]

The acquisition of Brown Instruments was actually a fortuitous historical quirk, evolving out of a chance conversation between two executives who happened to sit next to each other on a train. Willard Huff, treasurer of Minneapolis-Honeywell, had attended a National Recovery Act meeting in Washington, D.C., and met Richard Brown on the Congressional Limited from Washington to New York.

"They struck up a conversation," according to one account, "and each soon became intrigued by the complementary nature of the businesses they represented. Minneapolis–Honeywell's instruments and controls were designed to control relatively low temperatures, and except for motorized valves, Minneapolis–Honeywell offered nothing for controlling high temperatures found in many industrial processes. Brown, on the other hand, made products only for the high temp industrial market and bought accessories."[76]

The two men were so intrigued, in fact, that they wasted no time proposing the purchase to their respective boards. The companies began negotiations immediately, and on the last day of 1934, Minneapolis–Honeywell acquired Brown

The Model 77 after Minneapolis-Honeywell merger

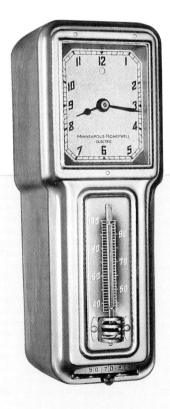

The Chronotherm electric clock thermostat

The Acratherm thermostat

Instruments Company for $2.3 million. Richard Brown, who became a Minneapolis–Honeywell vice president, felt that the Brown name was a valuable asset and insisted that it be retained. Thus the company was run as a subsidiary of Minneapolis–Honeywell until it became a division in 1949. Eventually it would be called Philadelphia Division and Process Control Division.

But the early years of the merger were somewhat difficult. C.W. Nessell asserted that it was an association of two companies with strong, well-established personalities. The Philadelphia people "resented the Minneapolis influence," according to Nessell.[77] Some of the friction may have originated from the fact that Brown was a union shop, while Minneapolis–Honeywell was not.

A Heated Controversy

In the Thirties, a dispute about heating large commercial buildings helped propel Minneapolis–

Honeywell into a line of controls which it had formerly considered substandard.

The company had always maintained that the best way to provide automatic heat control in large buildings was to apply the same electro–static controls used in single family dwellings, using an electric motor at the radiator that was activated by an electric thermostat. Each room could then have its own electric circuit from thermostat to valve motor. Manufacturers of commercial heating systems, on the other hand, maintained that pneumatic systems, usually applied to large space heating systems like steam radiators,

Edward Brown (above left) invented the Pyrometer in 1869. Born in 1835 in Earith England, Brown immigrated to Philadelphia in 1858 or 1860. He founded Brown Instruments, later acquired by Minneapolis-Honeywell.

Richard Brown (above center) was the son of Edward Brown. He became president of Brown Instruments when his father died, and oversaw the company's tremendous growth through the first three decades of the 20th century. He became a vice president of Minneapolis-Honeywell in 1935, when Brown was acquired by the Minneapolis firm.

Takehiko Yamaguchi (above right), founder of Yamatake Trading Company. Yamatake became a distributor of Brown Instruments in 1920. When Brown was acquired by Minneapolis-Honeywell, the controls company counted the Japanese firm its earliest international partner.

The Brown Instrument Company (left) in 1914, in Philadelphia, long before the acquisition by Minneapolis-Honeywell.

were more effective and more cost–efficient. The pneumatic system centralized the motive power for the steam by using a single large compressor to pressurize the entire system, with bellows at each radiator which simply opened or closed a diaphragm to regulate the steam. *Fortune* wrote:

> *"To regulate a control valve on a radiator, admitting more or less steam, either an electric motor or a simple flexible bellows diaphragm is equally efficient, but in an office building with hundreds or thousands of rooms it is obviously cheaper to install one central air compressor with pipes running to the diaphragms on the control valves than to place a separate electric motor on each valve. In the pneumatic system the compressed–air tank is kept at a constant pressure of about thirty pounds, pipes run first from the tank to the thermostats, and from the thermostats to the diaphragms. The thermostats used in the pneumatic system do not differ from the electric ones in principle, except that instead of making and breaking circuits the heat sensitive element controls the amount of pressure on the bellows by blocking or opening the pneumatic line."[78]*

Minneapolis–Honeywell's continued assertions that electric controls were superior became something of a joke in the industry. The company publicly ridiculed pneumatic manufacturers and patrons as corner–cutters, proclaiming loudly that electric control was more expensive only because it was better. Despite their rhetoric, they were rapidly losing what little commercial business they may have hoped to gain. The *Fortune* profile called the pneumatic controversy the company's only *bona fide* fiasco. "Presently," the article suggested, "it became obvious that electric controls could not successfully compete with pneumatic systems at least on a price basis."[79]

Honeywell responded by acquiring two companies that overnight made it both a manufacturer and supplier of pneumatic controls. Customers and competitors alike were stunned.

One of the two big names in pneumatic systems in the 1930s was the Bishop & Babcock Manufacturing Company. In 1936, Minneapolis–Honeywell bought the company's heat regu-

lator division in Cleveland. While it was a relatively small acquisition, finalized for $50,000, it was important for Honeywell. The company could then offer either electric or pneumatic systems to space heating contractors.

The other big name in pneumatics was National Regulator of Chicago. In 1937 Minneapolis–Honeywell bought this company, developer of the Metaphragm, a simple metal diaphragm that governed the flow of steam, improving the valve mechanism in pneumatic systems, and making them even more cost effective than electric systems. Honeywell gained only 100 employees when it purchased National Regulator, but it was a dramatic demonstration of the company's willingness to purchase competing technologies even if the acquired technologies had been the focus of expensive negative advertising campaigns.

Remarkably, Minneapolis–Honeywell made most of its major acquisitions during the Depression, when its size enabled it to purchase smaller companies struggling to survive. By 1937, sales were nearly $16 million annually, and employment had ballooned to 3,000.

One of those employees was Lawrence Bird, of Wabash, Indiana, whose story illustrates the furious pace of acquisition. Bird became a perennially displaced person during this period of acquisitions, a sort of Honeywell refugee.

> *"I went to work for Honeywell Heating Specialties in 1923. After the merger with Minneapolis Heat Regulator, I was transferred to Minneapolis. I only stayed a few months 'cause I didn't like it. So I resigned, headed back to*

The Pyrometer became the symbol of Brown Instruments' worldwide reputation as a leader in the field of industrial controls and indicators. Until Edward Brown invented the carbon-rod pyrometer in the mid-nineteenth century, there was no accurate way to measure the extremly high temperatures in foundries and kilns. The Brown Instrument Company was acquired in 1935, and retained its name for many years as a division of Minneapolis-Honeywell.

Indiana and went down the road to Elkhart, where I got a job with Time–O–Stat Controls. A couple years later, Minneapolis–Honeywell bought Time–O–Stat. I couldn't believe it. I still didn't want to move, so I quit and went home."[80]

The pattern continued in such a way that Bird actually had to retire from the controls industry altogether to avoid working for the Minneapolis–Honeywell Company.

Upward and Outward:
The Expansion of Facilities

The spectacular growth of the company before World War II could also be gauged by expansions of the plant in Minneapolis. Built to be easily converted into apartments if the business failed, the facility underwent several major modifications. In 1916, 10,000 square feet were added, and three years later another 25,000. In 1926, just before Minneapolis Heat Regulator and Honeywell Heating Specialties merged, W.R. Sweatt oversaw the construction of an eight–story tower, 70,000 square feet, annexed to the north end of the structure. This tower featured a limestone facade engraved with the immediately outdated "Minneapolis Heat Regulator Co."[81]

The headquarters grew so fast that it apparently caught the eye of a few interested groups beside contractors and inspectors. In 1937, when the Minnesota State Legislature was considering a tax bill which would substantially increase corporate taxes, the company was in the midst of yet another major expansion, which would add an additional 200,000 square feet. H.W. Sweatt, then president, was deeply troubled by the potential tax liability, and suspended work on the addition as an implied threat that the company might consider moving to a location where the tax climate was more favorable. Not surprisingly, the tax bill didn't pass.[82]

A World Citizen

Minneapolis–Honeywell's expansion during and after the Depression was not limited to the United States. Sweatt and his sons had been quick to realize the potential of international sales of home heating controls. By 1919, when the menu of products consisted of little more than the Butz damper-flapper system, the *Sales Book* optimistically asserted: "There is scarcely a foreign country, including the tropics, where regulators have not been shipped."[83]

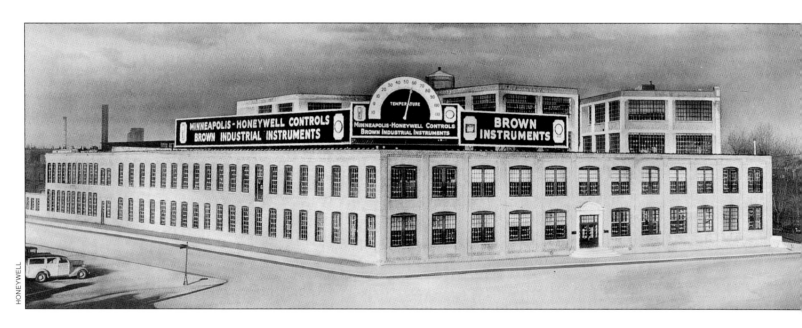

HONEYWELL

Located in Philadelphia, Brown Instruments Company had established a worldwide reputation as a manufacturer of devices for measuring and indicating industrial processes. Honeywell acquired the company in 1935, and retained the name, capitalizing on Brown's sterling reputation.

The first international office had actually been acquired with the 1930 purchase of Time–O–Stat Controls Corporation. Time–O–Stat had established a distribution office in Toronto, manned by a young entrepreneur named Tom McDonald. When Honeywell purchased the firm, it established the Toronto office as a subsidiary, and retained McDonald to run it. By 1934, Canadian distributorships included Calgary and Montreal. Though these offices initially handled only controls manufactured in the U.S., factories were eventually built in Canada to enable the subsidiary to market products built in Canada.

Prior to 1934, most overseas sales had been handled through the New York office. That year, however, Minneapolis–Honeywell established its first European subsidiary in The Netherlands. N.V. Nederlandsche Minneapolis–Honeywell was an ideal locale for export distribution because of Amsterdam's free port facilities, where goods could be stored in bonded warehouses and shipped abroad without incurring a duty fee.[84] Other European subsidiaries followed in quick succession. One was created in London in 1936, and another in Stockholm two years later. Despite the clouds of war gathering over Europe, Honeywell was determined to establish a foothold on the Continent.

In May 1939, the company acquired a plant and warehouse in London and began factory operations there, while augmenting the staff of its Swedish subsidiary. By the end of the summer, H.W. Sweatt had traveled to Europe to visit the new offices, and to scout prospects

exact information regarding the present position of our English and Holland companies, but 'business as usual' appears to be their slogan and while we sympathize with them, we believe that they are capable of handling the difficult and unusual problem with which they are confronted."[86]

Depression Years: Waiting For The Market to Return

Minneapolis–Honeywell prospered during the first years of the Depression. But reality caught up in 1932, when sales plunged from $5.5 million to $3.5 million. The Sweatts reacted by cutting employment from 1150 to 647, but consistently tried to minimize the blow to the workforce.[87]

When similar economic conditions had plagued the company in the early Twenties, W.R. had sought temporary contracts for piecework, to try to keep production workers with less seniority on the floor. Cutter & Washington radios were built in Minneapolis during this period. In 1932, Sweatt resorted to similar measures by contracting with the Pillsbury Company to produce flour sifters that Pillsbury used as a premium to promote sales. Minneapolis–Honeywell produced some

for further expansion. His report was "optimistic over foreign business." An article in the company newspaper, *The M–H News Circulator*, noted that Sweatt was "very favorably impressed with our European operations."[85]

But, as the article also implied, Europe was on the brink of war: "We do not have

A factory was secured for Honeywell's operations (above left) in the United Kingdom in May 1939. It was to become an important point of contact between Minneapolis-Honeywell and the Allies during World War II. A factory was established outside of Toronto (above right) by 1932. Until full manufacturing operations began, Minneapolis sent parts for assembly by Canadian Honeywellers.

2 million sifters, at a cost of 7.5 cents each, and this temporary arrangement kept a few extra toolmakers on the line. The company also produced gear trains for water meters for the City of Minneapolis. This vigorous pursuit of outside contracts proved essential to the company's survival during those lean and discouraging years.

Even in 1932, Honeywell's worst year, the company still somehow managed to stay in the black. The speed of its recovery to sales in excess of $9 million by 1935 is graphic evidence of a manufacturer with the ability to withstand misfortune. "Minneapolis-Honeywell" commented *Fortune*, "was completely Depression-proof."[88]

HONEYWELL WORKERS

ATTENTION

A Meeting Is Being Held At
305 EAST LAKE ST.

WEDNESDAY, MARCH 17, 1937
At 8 P. M.

To Discuss the Organization
Of Your Plant

Honeywell is the last large unorganized plant in the city. Let's try to get every worker in the union, both men and women.

Every worker in the country has come to realize that his lot can be made better by a bona fide union. Let the International Association of Machinists represent you for the betterment of your conditions.

 15

Handbills were distributed and posted around the plant and in the neighborhood urging Honeywell workers to attend organizational meetings in 1937.

Growing Unionization

The same article noted that the company did not seem to suffer the labor–management strife that had victimized so many other plants across the country. Unions were doing their best to organize labor into powerful collectives for bargaining. But the situation at Minneapolis–Honeywell, at least on the surface, seemed somewhat less contentious:

> *"The big happy family psychology pervades Minneapolis–Honeywell so completely that President Sweatt's professed ignorance of any labor problem is credible—although it is distinctly an oddity in the Twin Cities. The company has no official attitude toward unionization—possibly because no union has ever gained a foothold in the plant. But over in Philadelphia the CIO points to its contract with Brown Instrument Co., and claims that the plant is 97 percent organized. There are no indications, however, that an explosion of Lewisite [a reference to labor leader John L. Lewis,] in Minneapolis is imminent. Altogether the labor policy—or, better, unpolicy—is liberal, informal, and satisfactory all around."[89]*

Even so, this "unpolicy" was not quite the insulation from problems that the Sweatts might have hoped. At almost precisely the same moment the magazine article appeared, notices were posted urging Honeywell workers to help the International Association of Machinists organize "the last large unorganized plant in the city." Union organizers began setting up their soapboxes outside the plant.

Charles Hoyt, who worked in the home office, recalls an incident involving one of these streetcorner orators. "There was an agitator across the street from the plant loudly talking to the workers as they left," he says. "W.R. came to my desk on the sixth floor, opened the window, and heard the speaker say: 'Mr. Sweatt has a better garage than your homes.' W.R. turned to me and said, 'I hope Henry [his chauffeur] hears that.'"[90]

In actuality, the company's first union already existed at Brown Instruments. When Honeywell acquired Brown in 1935, most of the Philadelphia workers were members of the local chapter of United Electrical Workers. Editorials in *The M–H News Circulator* walked lightly around the issue of union organization, but their position was unmistakable. The editors were complimentary to Sweatt's avowed commitment to "the family of Honeywellers," and critical of anything that suggested unionization. A June 1938 editorial was entitled "Just One Big Happy Family," and echoed the familiar idealism of the *Fortune* article.

"We like the spirit of cooperation prevailing among our people at Minneapolis–Honeywell. We think it is grand. Disturbances, which at the worst are minor, are few and far between. The loyalty shown by the employees is not of the forced variety. It comes of a free will engendered by a desire on the part of a far–seeing management to treat the employees with the fullest measure of human understanding ...Management was correct in its judgement which years ago prompted them to adopt the policy that we should all be just one big, happy family!"[91]

A year later, though, sentiments between management and union organizers had deteriorated considerably. In the midst of the violent demonstrations of the 1939 WPA Strike, *Circulator* editorials became blunt.

"Free speech and free thought in America are a common heritage...Disloyalty, bordering on treason, is not among the rights guaranteed our peoples. Disturbances affecting operation of laws enacted for welfare of the whole are not among such inalienable rights. Strikes of the common garden variety have been condoned by the courts as a reasonable means of bringing opposing groups into agreement, but strikes of the WPA variety are far from being the common garden variety. In fact, it is even a misnomer to refer to them as strikes...If analyzed, even only superficially, one can but come to the conclusion that the WPA walkouts with their attendant disorder, and even loss of life and liberty (for those who wish to work) amount to a declaration of defiance, with threats, by a small minority, against a government of the people, by the people and for the people. Such a condition is intolerable."

The article concluded, "We can think of nothing more disconcerting to our peace and happiness than the possibility of unstifled open revolt against law and order directed by undercover individuals pledged to disturb the sanctity of our Constitution."[92]

An April editorial described "the elevation of the place of man in society," and demonstrated exactly how Honeywell had participated in this elevation.

"New social relations, not governmental, but coming from within the business organizations themselves, have created the sense of satisfaction in jobs and a sense of individuals personally contributing to a satisfied society from the knowledge of a job well done. This has been brought about largely by employers and managements who have put the same zeal into solving human problems that they have put into searches for new efficiencies ...We need only reflect on the many privileges created for employees by 'W.R.' These, plus others added, are in existence today and help to create the atmosphere of a plant wherein men want to work."[93]

The editorial listed privileges including "group health and accident insurance, sickness and disability compensation; vacations with pay; safety instructions and guards; safety committees and inspectors," and many others. Indeed, Minneapolis–Honeywell did appear to take good care of its employees, especially in comparison to other companies. Even so, by 1941 there was trouble in the plant, as 19 employees were joined by Local 1145 of the United Electrical, Radio, and Machine Workers in serving a strike notice on Minneapolis–Honeywell. A commission from Minnesota's Division of Conciliation was called in by Governor Harold Stassen to oversee mediation and determine if the strike was preventable.

The efforts of the International Machine Workers in 1937 hadn't met with much success, perhaps because parts of the Honeywell plant had already been, by tradition, loosely organized among themselves. One of these organizations consisted of Tool Room employees, responsible for the manufacture and repair of tools and dies upon which the whole plant depended.

This informal organization was known as the "Shop Committee," and it "attempted to represent the machine shop employees on conditions of employment, grievances, etc."[94] In June 1939, Local 1145 received a charter, and that autumn filed charges with the National Labor Relations Board alleging that Minneapolis–Honeywell discriminated against its members. The board found in favor of the union, and the union gave notice of a possible strike while the company appealed the finding. The state commission, meanwhile, reviewed complaints of the 19 employees, most of whom claimed they had been discriminated against for being members of the union. In only one case was evidence of such discrimination found. Edward Larsen had been laid off in 1937 and rehired two years later, at a rate of 5 cents an hour less, "a result of prior organizational activities in the Tool Room."[95]

The commission did point out that there was a strong perception among employees that the company was less than enthusiastic about their organization.

"The commission is satisfied that many of those employees who testified honestly and sincerely believe that the company seeks to discourage all union activity in the plant, and the commission also feels that the company has never taken adequate steps to disabuse employees as a group of this belief. In short, the commission feels that a complex of persecution exists between a substantial group of employees on the

MINNEAPOLIS-HONEYWELL NEWS

| Volume 1 | MINNEAPOLIS, MINN. NOVEMBER 1937 | Number 1 |

WILLIAM RICHARD SWEATT

We have lost our old friend, W. R. Sweatt, but in memory he will never be lost. As long as old-timers get together his name will be frequently mentioned and the part he played will be the soul of their recollections.

He was a brilliant leader and a genius in the matter of building our organization, but we will remember him first of all as a friend, for everyone who knew him loved him and knew him as a very human person, interested in all who worked with him and ready to help them when they needed help.

Nothing that W. R. took part in was ever dull. Any project, however simple, was full of adventurous thrill and romance if he took a hand in it.

We will miss him all right, we will miss his vigorous manner of accomplishing things. We will miss his friendly advice and counsel, but we will always be thankful that we had the experience of knowing him, thankful for the memory of a truly great man.

one hand and the Management on the other, and that both sides have contributed to this situation and its continuance."[96]

The union's basic complaint was that the company refused to enter into a contract with it. The company responded that it was in no way obligated to "make any contract with any union which does not represent a majority...of its employees by a proper election."[97]

Minneapolis-Honeywell, in a plant which employed 2,000 workers, had never had a personnel department. The challenge of responding to grievances had always fallen to Deke Foster and George DuToit, plant superintendent and vice president of production. According to the commission,

> *"Superintendent Foster has been unusually cooperative and sympathetic to the problems of individual employees, but no one was charged with the group problems of employees generally...The principle function of both Superintendent Foster and Vice President DuToit is production, and it is obvious that the burden of such duties allowed little time for handling relations with employees."[98]*

Foster and a foreman named Harry Long had drafted an "Employee Policy in Regard to Job Preference Rights in the Production Machine Shop," which the commission said indicated the company's "clear acceptance of the basic principle of collective bargaining." The commission ultimately found insufficient cause for a strike, but made detailed recommendations that the company "publish and declare fixed policy governing its relations with *all* plant employees."[99]

The company had simply grown too large to continue operating as "one big happy family." And this growth made it inevitable that formal measures and offices be established to govern relations between labor and management.

End of an Era

When Mark Honeywell became chairman of the executive committee in 1934, H.W. Sweatt was elected president of the company. Three years later, the first issue of the *M–H News Circulator* (later renamed the *Circulator*) appeared. The issue was dedicated to W.R. Sweatt, who had taken a tiny enterprise with a novelty item invented by an emigrant and turned it into "the company that controls the controls industry."

The company bears the imprint of W.R. to this day, as it continues to apply his double–edged strategy of diversification through technology development and acquisition. And it also bears the imprints of his sons, C.B. and H.W., who transformed Honeywell into a multi–national blue–chip institution. The Sweatt sons were to guide Honeywell through the important years of World War II, which yet again redefined the company and brought spectacular success.

A 1942 advertisement made the company's commitment to war production explicit. It also asserted that Honeywell products could help production facilities across the country better serve the war effort.

CHAPTER FOUR

THE WAR YEARS

"In the mad rush of these war days, the spot light of attention and effort is rightfully focused on the combat devices that M-H makes for the Armed Forces. But there is another group of important products, which in times of peace brought M-H to world prominence, that have also gone to war".

—H.W. Sweatt, *President*

The 1930s were watershed years for American business. Emerging from the ruins of the Great Depression, many corporations began to experience significant growth once again.

The sense of renewed prosperity and recovery contributed to a growing political and cultural isolationism in the United States. This political provincialism did not necessarily extend to business, and forward-looking companies like Minneapolis-Honeywell had already taken the first tentative steps to a global marketplace.

On September 1, 1939, Germany invaded Poland, and polarized Europe. Two months later, Congress reacted by approving the United States Neutrality Act, but war was coming closer nonetheless.

In June 1940, Hitler's troops marched into Paris. The following March, President Roosevelt approved the Lend-Lease program, in which the United States provided Britain with military equipment in exchange for access to British bases. It seemed inevitable that the United States would eventually enter the conflict.

Ideally Prepared For Production

As early as 1940, the *M-H News-Circulator* announced, "The equipment and facilities of the M-H plants are being placed squarely behind the expanding national defense plans of the United States Government. Practically the complete facilities of the Wabash plant have been put on government orders... Work being done or bid on ranges from piece parts worth less than a cent a piece to a gun pointer worth $2,100. Battery cups, bomb hangars, flare standards, gun sights, telescopes, howitzer discs, and airplane inclinometers are among the items being figured or made."[1]

The *M-H News-Circulator* went on to note: "Preparations are being rushed within the plant to take care of such defense contracts as may be awarded to Minneapolis-Honeywell. Everything possible is being done to fit work on government orders into the production program for the normally slack winter months."[2]

The possibility of significant government contracts caused management to renew the building program it had stalled in 1937 as the result of proposed changes in corporate taxation.

"With a quarter of a million dollars going into a new addition to the Minneapolis plant, the Minneapolis-Honeywell Regulator Company is taking care of normal expansion needs and providing room which can be used for the production of defense materials, if necessary," H.W. announced.[3]

By 1941, it was clear that Honeywell was going to be a mass–production facility for military instruments and equipment, and an entire issue of the *Circulator* was devoted to this topic. Military officials publicly visited the Minneapolis facility to meet with the Sweatts and tour the plant.[4] Though conflict in Europe and the Far East had been growing for some time, America's preparation for war suddenly seemed a frantic headlong rush. The spectacular military-industrial strength of Nazi Germany meant that the fast production of a huge volume of material was imperative. The *M-H News-Circulator* noted.

The board of directors of Minneapolis-Honeywell during the World War II, 1941-1945. The company jumped into war production with both feet, but kept an eye toward postwar markets at all times, thanks to the foresight of this group. Seated, left-right, Charles Buckland, W.L. Huff, George DuToit, Jr., C.B. Sweatt; Standing, left-right C.J.C. Quinn, H.W. Sweatt, R.P. Brown, Mark Honeywell.

"When it is realized that America must do in one and one-half or two years what a militarized nation under a dictator accomplished in seven years, then again the problem becomes clearer. This problem is to attain the most tremendous output of the necessary instruments of war ever achieved anywhere in the shortest time possible."[5]

Thus the conflict took on the character of industrial competition. All the major players in World War II were highly industrialized, and their militaries depended upon the technologies of industry.

Minneapolis-Honeywell eagerly assumed its new role on the front lines of war production.[6] It had pioneered the mass–production of precision instruments with the Minneapolis 77, the high quality 7-jewel 8-day clock produced in the Twenties.

"Because of the experience and knowledge gained through the half century or more of its existence, and the ability to produce intricate and

delicate instruments of high quality and precision workmanship, M-H was found to be ideally equipped to render aid to the nation's defense, and M-H is truly proud of the contribution it has already made and will continue to make to help America prepare."[7]

In the fall of 1941, construction was begun to complete the north end of the plant, eventually adding 65,000 square feet.[8]

Still At Home With Controls

Even as defense work expanded in the days before the Japanese attack on Pearl Harbor, the Sweatts were quick to point out that military contracts would in no way impede production of the traditional products. Moreover, an expanded national defense program also meant an expanded market for automatic heating controls.

"Not only has [Minneapolis-Honeywell] been directly engaged in the making of fire control de-

vices for tanks, trench mortars, aircraft and anti-aircraft guns and telescopes and inclinometers for airplanes; but also in the thousands of standard controls that go into army camps, navy yards, shipyards and defense housing to give comfort and health to the nation's defense forces."[9]

H.W. Sweatt anticipated the pitfalls of super-accelerated production, and took steps to ensure the company's prosperity no matter what happened in the context of international politics. I.K. Foster, Superintendent of the Minneapolis plant, reported that to this end Sweatt had spoken to the company's association of veteran employees, the Minnregs. "He made a particular point of the fact that engineering development would be continued at full speed so that when conditions changed suddenly, we would have something new to offer, and so help keep volume from dropping off suddenly."[10] Above all else, it was important to H.W. that a fevered rush to war production didn't cause the company to lose sight of its long–term goals in the business of domestic heating controls. In fact, demand for

thermostats, limit controls, and damper motors continued to outpace defense contracts even through 1941. A *Circulator* editorial observed, "We must fulfill so far as possible the obligation to serve the steadily expanding volume of business, along ordinary lines, which at this writing is stiff and by far our greatest volume."[11]

Even after Pearl Harbor, H.W. Sweatt pointed out that the company's full line of products was important before the war, was important during the war, and would continue to be important after the war was won.

"In the mad rush of these war days, the spotlight of attention and effort is rightfully focused on the combat devices that M-H makes for the Armed Forces. But there is another group of important products, which in times of peace brought M-H to world prominence, that have also gone to war. In discussing this phase of the business, H.W. Sweatt, President, said, 'The essential uses to which the regular line of M-H products have been put since Pearl Harbor makes a long and impressive list, and that should not be lost sight of. Our plants...are serving a dual role

Special Products Manufacturing Division in 1947. The department became the basis of the company's Aero Division.

Above: Four women in the lens polishing department appeared in the company newspaper, the *M-H News-Circulator*. During the war, the company took on countless contracts for exacting optical devices such as tank periscopes and mortar sights. Honeywell was one of the first companies to apply mass production techniques to such sensitive instruments.
Below Right: Honeywell did things that optical experts said couldn't be done, like making lenses and reticles on a production line.

young men were to be called for military duty, and this meant dozens of military camps and bases would be required. Construction of thousands of barracks, hospitals, laundries, officers quarters, mess halls, and all the other assorted structures that make up a military establishment opened a tremendous market for temperature controls. Honeywell sought a share of that business and got it."[14]

Precision And Mass–Production

Before the Model 77 clock thermostat, experts would have dismissed as ridiculous the idea that an accurate 7-jewel 8-day clock could be designed and manufactured in a mass–production facility. As a result of its success with the Model 77, Minneapolis–Honeywell was asked to study the possible mass–production of many highly complex military instruments. Among the first contracts were orders for optical devices such as gun sights and tank periscopes, devices that required very small tolerances, and seemed to require production methods at odds with the assembly line.

today. They are not only servants of men for Victory, but 'keep alive' the markets and the channels of trade that will follow peace.'"[12]

Honeywell's line had been greatly expanded, particularly after the acquisitions and engineering breakthroughs of the 1930s. The company had fortuitously created domestic markets for controls that also aided the war effort. For example, controls for oil and gas heating systems were developed just in time for wartime restrictions on the use of coal. Minneapolis-Honeywell domestic controls had helped facilitate the widespread conversion of coal heating to automatic central systems using oil and gas. Even where coal furnaces had not been converted, the old damper-flapper system automated the firing, and this helped conserve coal.

"M-H automatic heating controls will help to stand between America and a coal shortage of 35 million tons during the winter. No fancy war-time gadgets, but our standard workaday prewar line of controls will step onto the 'firing' line."[13]

Honeywell automatic controls were also an important part of the government-initiated building projects that accompanied major defense programs. Passage of the Universal Military and Training Act in 1940 meant that "thousands of

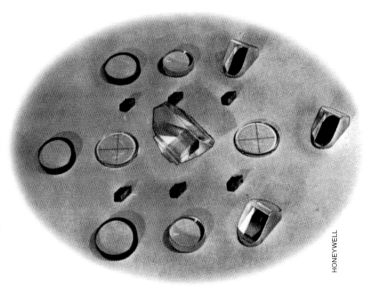

"[Minneapolis-Honeywell] was the only supplier of tank periscopes for the American and British armies," C.W. Nessell wrote. "...Since Honeywell knew nothing about the optical business, it did things that the optical people said couldn't be done. They said that telescope lenses and reticles had to be made one by one through time-consuming hand operations, but Honeywell naively and successfully made them on a production line."[15] In fact, when company engineers looked over government orders and specs, they often found easier methods and cheaper materials with which to fill orders.

"One of the first jobs was frames for tank periscopes," Nessell wrote. "The sample submitted was a carefully machined, costly affair weighing 100-150 pounds. M-H engineers looked it over, quickly decided sheet steel and a little spot-welding would do the job cheaper and faster. It did. Since then M-H has carried the bulk of the tank periscope program—and tanks have 12 periscopes, some models even more."[16]

Another example of this approach was the etching of the cross–hairs on optical devices like periscopes and telescopes. Such an operation was usually very exacting and expensive, with a high rate of rejection of the end product. Before Honeywell took on the problem, a machine called a pantograph was used to etch "reticles." The machine cost $15,000, and produced only 10 etchings at a time, with a 50 percent rejection rate. Honeywell engineers developed a simplified device costing only $600, achieving higher output, and producing rejections only about a quarter of the time.[17] Popular legend has it that an

Above: The M-1 gunner's quadrant was among the first items that Minneapolis-Honeywell produced under contract for the U.S. armed forces at the outset of World War II. Honeywell surprised many procurement officials by applying mass production techniques to precision instruments with stunning success.

At Right: Another important Honeywell product during the second World War was the M-4 Tank Periscope.

Army general, asked how Honeywell had managed such an innovation, responded, "Well, all I can say is they were so damn dumb down there they didn't know it couldn't be done, so they went ahead and did it."[18]

Security Badges And Merit Pins

By mid–1941, work on defense contracts had grown to the point where the company thought it prudent to increase security at its plants and offices. Honeywell employed guards 24 hours a day at company entrances and exits, and began checking identification badges of workers and visitors. Employees considered the identification badge a privilege. One asserted, "This badge we proudly wear because it identifies us as one who is doing his part in helping America prepare."[19]

After December 7, 1941, preparation turned into production. As America entered the war, an *M–H News–Circulator* editorial noted: "We are all war workers...Just as the soldier cannot fight without arms, he is ineffective without other supplies. So we who are busily fastening leads to mercury switches may take pleasure in knowing that switch we have just completed will help

The Honeywell-produced tank periscope in action in the European theater. The device is mounted on the tank's hatch door.

refrigerate the food supply for many of our men in Australia, or we who make valves can know that a valve we made is functioning as an essential part of a destroyer in the Atlantic..."[20]

Minneapolis-Honeywell wasted no time in distinguishing itself among war production plants. Just ten months after Pearl Harbor, within the company's first period of eligibility, it received the coveted Army-Navy "E" Award, "the highest of industrial awards" conferred by the government. On August 17, 1942, Brigadier General Donald Armstrong presented H.W. Sweatt with the "E" flag, to be flown with pride on the company flagpole, along with "E" Award blazer pins for every employee. General Armstrong said Minneapolis-Honeywell had produced "far in excess of what the Army anticipated," and had thus distinguished itself by earning this rare military decoration.[21]

The presentation program noted, "when the rising tide of war in Europe placed a premium on the production of war equipment, the Army–Navy 'E' award was extended to embrace those plants and organizations which showed excellence in producing ships, weapons, and equipment." [22]

Only 3 percent of the nation's war plants ever received an "E" during World War II,[23] but by V-J Day in 1945, Minneapolis–Honeywell had managed to win fifteen more.

From The Thermostat To The Pickle Barrel

During the Thirties, the company had begun to research possible applications of Honeywell temperature controls in cars, trains,

ships, and planes. Heating or cooling a moving vehicle presents a much different problem than heating a home or office building, and airplanes were particularly tricky, since they typically experienced violent changes in temperature as they climbed or dropped thousands of feet in a few moments. In late 1940, Minneapolis-Honeywell engineers developed a servo/amplifier system for controlling ambient temperature in aircraft cabins, based on the Modutrol system they had designed in the 1930s for accurate temperature control in residential and commercial buildings.

The basic idea of Modutrol was to control environmental conditions through a system of multiple, proportional settings and constant output, constantly regulated. By contrast, the old damper-flapper system was either open or closed. A proportioning system, on the other hand, would always be running, simply by mixing varying amounts of heated and unheated air to attain the desired temperature.

With airplanes this type of control would be of particular advantage. In the summer and fall of 1939, Willis Gille, chief test engineer, and John Sigford, test engineer, began work-

ing with Thomas Harrison of Brown Division in Philadelphia to perfect the Modutrol system, in an effort to market the results to the airline industry. The three men worked with a two–phase reversible motor developed by Lewis Cunningham. They attempted to control the torque and direction of the motor by using an amplifier so that the motor would respond instantaneously to signal changes. The challenge was to develop an amplifier to perform the job. By mid-June, the men had developed the G-58 amplifier, and two months later, an application-ready improvement, imaginatively named the G-59.

At the same time, the Sweatt brothers had asked Chief Engineer Bill McGoldrick to determine the company's ability to contribute to the imminent defense programs. McGoldrick organized an elite engineering group including Gille and Sigford, with Bob Kutzler, Hub Sparrow, Gil Taylor, Russ Whempner and Al Baak. McGoldrick's group quickly recognized the remote proportional positioning system developed by Gille, Sigford, and Harrison as something the military would find interesting. The group built a demonstrator model displaying their amplifier

The original M-H nameplate on the trusty heater valve that assured the "Old 59's" pilot and crew normal cabin temperature as they soared over the Himalayas.

in use with a Cunningham motor, and McGoldrick made some calls in an effort to arrange demonstrations. Ultimately he made contact with Mel Lammers, the civilian head of Army Air Force Materiel Command at Wright Field in Dayton, Ohio. In January 1941, Gille, McGoldrick, and Russ Whempner made the trip to Dayton to demonstrate the amplifier, along with some mercury switches, to a group of AAF technicians and scientists.

> Whempner remembered the trip: "We gave them our 'dog and pony' show which involved the cabin temperature control demonstrator, a remote position demonstrator and some pressure switches. I remember getting some 'ohs' and 'ahs' but that was it."[24]

No one at Wright Field had seemed terribly impressed with the demonstration, and it occurred to company officials that perhaps cabin temperature control seemed like an unnecessary extravagance to the military with war looming on the horizon.

On The Level: Reconnaissance Photography

A month after the demonstration, however, the Photographic Division at Wright Field asked to meet with company representatives again. They were impressed by the demonstration, and they wondered if the company could adapt its proportioning motor to a problem with their Fairchild reconnaissance camera.

On August 17, 1942, Minneapolis-Honeywell was honored by the government and the military by receiving the Army-Navy "E" Award, the highest commendation given to war production plants. Only about 3 percent of all production facilities in the nation were recognized in this manner.

HONEYWELL

HONEYWELL

HONEYWELL

Fairchild cameras used in reconnaissance flights to photograph large areas, horizon to horizon, were plagued by inaccuracy. Serial photographs of vast areas of the earth's surface were needed, but if the camera was not perfectly parallel to the surface the photographs could not be easily assembled. Because planes in flight experience turbulence, it was difficult to keep the cameras level. The Photographic Section at Wright Field believed that the proportioning motor developed by Gille, Sigford, and Harrison might be used in some type of camera–leveling device.

Honeywell engineers had a functioning prototype within a few weeks. Wright Field personnel were pleased with the results, and by early February, Photographic Section ordered six amplifier systems designed for ready modification of six camera mounts. The system was designed to incorporate engineer Waldo Kliever's pendulum-like sensors on two of the plane's axes, the roll and pitch (side-to-side and front-to-back). The sensors responded to motion by centering on gravity, sending an electronic signal through a G-59 amplifier which positioned a Cunningham motor in the same proportion as the signal received from the sensor. The motor positioned the Fairchild camera mount. Thus the motion of the sensors was transferred through the amplifier and motor directly to the camera mount.

Russ Whempner delivered the systems to Wright Field in April. They proved spectacularly successful. Not only had they solved the leveling problem, they had also achieved remote control of the camera, so that it could be mounted in the tail of the airplane. After hearing of the successful camera mount, Armament Branch immediately contacted Minneapolis-Honeywell. They were somewhat secretive about what they needed, but they made it clear that they were interested in the electronic transfer of motion from one place to another, such as had been demonstrated with the camera leveler. Armament Branch had been working for some time on a mechanism that would provide a stable bombing platform for its top–secret, state-of-the-art bombsight, the Norden Mark XV.

The Norden Bombsight

For nearly ten years prior to World War II, the U.S. Navy and Army had been working to

In 1940, Minneapolis-Honeywell engineers applied Modutrol proportioning technology to help solve the Army Air Force's problem of how to keep a reconnaissance camera level while photographing the surface geography below. Honeywell's innovation eventually led to the development of the automatic pilot.

increase the precision of bombing from the air. More precise bombing could reduce the risk to airmen, by reducing the return bombing runs needed to knock out a target. It could also make it possible to fly at a higher altitude, significantly reducing the risk from enemy ground fire. And it could serve to reduce resource-intensive saturation bombing.

In the early 1930s, a major breakthrough occurred. A man named Carl Norden invented a revolutionary new bombsight, and founded a company in New York solely for the purpose of developing and manufacturing it. The U.S. Navy contracted to purchase his bombsights.[25] It was said that the Norden bombsight could drop a bomb in a pickle barrel from 20,000 feet. Once, when asked if this was true, Norden himself responded, "Which pickle would you like to hit?" Slightly more conservative estimates of the bombsight's capabilities suggested it could drop a bomb within a 100-foot circle from 4 miles up.[26]

The Navy had traditionally been assigned to bomb moving targets from relatively low altitudes. However, this bombsight seemed more suited to the high altitude bombing of stationary targets, the domain of the Army Air Force. The Norden bombsight had actually become standard equipment on both Army and Navy bombers well before the war. By the end of the war, some 25,000 bombsights had been built by the Norden Company alone, and thousands more were manufactured by other contractors. The bombsights cost $10,000 each, and were called "the only truly accurate bombsight in existence during the Second World War." Each sight was 12" by 19", weighed 45 pounds, and contained more than 2,000 parts.[27] The sight not only calculated the exact moment to release the bombs, it automatically released them as well.[28] A 1943 *Popular Science* article noted that "the bombardier is pitching the bomb toward the target as a pitcher throws a curve across home plate, but he is pitching with plenty of mechanical aid."[29]

It was public knowledge that the Navy and Army had highly sophisticated bombsights which were removed from the plane by armed guards when the crew deplaned, and then secreted away in canvas bags. Ladislas Farago, in *The Game of The Foxes*, pointed out that American popular culture had made something of a fetish of the Norden bombsight. And so, apparently, did Germany, as the Nazis probably had some detailed knowledge of the Norden bombsight even before Pearl Harbor.[30]

Prime Minister Neville Chamberlain of Great Britain had knowledge of it, too. In August 1939, he wrote a personal letter to President Roosevelt asking that the Royal Air Force be given access to the Norden sight.

> *"The secretary of State for Air informs me that the United States Navy Department has developed a new type of automatic air bombsight known as the Norden bombsight, and I understand that this sight is the most efficient instrument of its kind in existence. We are therefore most anxious to obtain details of the sight...In normal times I should not make a direct approach to you in such a matter, but in the present grave situation I venture to ask you whether you could help us to obtain the information we desire...Should the war which threatens break out, my advisors tell me that we would obtain a greater immediate increase in our effective power if we had the Norden bombsight at our disposal than by any other means we can foresee."[31]*

Roosevelt responded that it would not be possible, due to legal barriers which would require the U.S. to make such information available to *all* foreign requests, an obviously unwise course of action.[32]

One goal of precision bombing was to make war more humane and less costly through more effective bombing. General Edgar Sorenson, USAF Assistant Chief of Staff for Air Intelligence in 1943, explained this seeming contradiction:

The Norden bombsight was top secret for much of the war, though its capabilities were publicly celebrated. In conjunction with the Minneapolis-Honeywell C-1 automatic pilot, the system made precision bombing possible, giving Allied Forces a tremendous advantage in air power.

"To put an automobile out of commission, you don't have to destroy the whole automobile. All you have to do is to take out the rotating contact in the ignition distributor. Similarly, to destroy the capacity of an enemy country to fight, you don't have to destroy the whole country, or even its armies. You knock out the heart of enemy production capacity. ...Gradually, and not at all spectacularly, you so disintegrate the enemy's internal economy that he is able to fight no more. It is to make war cheaper in terms of casualties and mass destruction, that precision bombing aims. Because of it, the task of our troops invading enemy territory is to be quicker of accomplishment, and accompanied by fewer losses. Because of it, we may be able to diminish the postwar hatreds which come to populations that have suffered too grievously. Because of it, we may have a smaller task of postwar rebuilding, and the nations now our enemies, with whom we some day shall have to trade, will more quickly get back onto a sound economic footing..."[33]

The Norden bombsight contributed immensely to the process of making more effective weapons. And in the process, it ultimately helped to shorten the war.

Precision Bombing
Requires Precision Flying

The basic problem of precision bombing was controlling the many variables encountered in

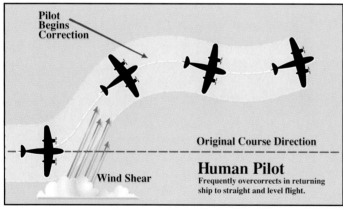

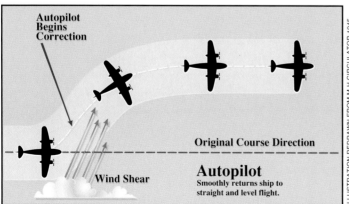

ILLUSTRATION REDRAWN FROM M-H CIRCULATOR 1945

The automatic pilot corrected for inevitable human error by precisely compensating for wind and other factors.

releasing a bomb from a moving airplane. The Norden bombsight was effective in its computation of the relationship between these variables, but only if they could be stabilized during the period of targeting and bombing in flight. The airplane itself needed to be as steady as possible, a seemingly insurmountable challenge, since aircraft routinely experience pockets of turbulence, changed wind directions, and varying air speeds. A human pilot has some very formidable limitations when it comes to stabilizing against these inevitable shifts.

"Probably the most important single element in precise bombing is accurate flying. Yet even alert pilots have difficulty holding a course within 2 or 3 degrees while at the same time maintaining exactly constant air speed and altitude. To exploit the capabilities of the bombsight to the full it is essential that flying on the bombing run be as automatic and precise as is the operation of the bombsight."[34]

Just a single degree of oscillation during the release of a bomb at 25,000 feet could throw the bomb over 400 feet from its target.[35] Because a pilot often cannot detect such oscillations, much less correct for them, it became apparent that precision bombing depended on the development of technologies that would make precision *flying* possible.

Army And Navy Efforts

The Navy had originally developed the Norden bombsight in conjunction with the Norden company, and they continued to work together to stabilize the bombing platform. The Army Air Force, because of its specialized bombing needs, was allowed to procure Norden equipment through the Navy.[36] However, the Navy was apparently protective of its relationship with Norden, and refused to allow direct transactions between the Army and the company. This caused considerable friction between the two services. After the U.S. finally entered the war, and each branch was receiving fewer bombsights than it felt necessary, this friction escalated further.[37]

Army Modifications

The Norden Company and the Navy had already developed a stabilizing system to be used in conjunction with their bombsight, called Stabilized Bombing Approach Equipment (SBAE). The people at Wright Field, however, were unhappy with the SBAE, and began working on extensive modifications to it; they wanted a system for the automatic control of flight.

The *210* flew more than 1800 hours for Honeywell, testing the C-1 autopilot, turbo regulator, formation stick, and other aeronautical equipment during the war. The stripped-down B-17 saw no actual combat, but made numerous bombing runs on a small and remote lake in northern Minnesota, where the company had built a bombing platform.

They also renamed it the Automatic Flight Control Equipment (AFCE).[38] Their goal was stunning in its scope. They wanted to develop a mechanism that would be capable of flying a bomber automatically, an "automatic pilot."

Norden's automatic pilot was entirely mechanical: Gyroscopes were connected to servo motors by long copper cables that moved in housings similar to bicycle brakes. However, as the plane climbed several thousand feet and experienced a drop in temperature, the cables and airframe would contract in different degrees, and the whole system became sloppy, or simply ceased to work. Moreover, the electrical components of the system were all direct current (DC), which made it somewhat unstable as well. Army engineers believed that the system developed by Gille, Sigford, and Harrison could have an application in their automatic pilot program.

In mid–1941, Armaments Chief Master Sergeant Don Hamilton met with McGoldrick, Gille, Kutzler, and Taylor. Hamilton showed the Minneapolis-Honeywell men a device mostly covered by a white sheet, and asked if they could adapt potentiometers to an exposed gyroscope, creating an electronic transference of motion from the potentiometers through a G-59 amplifier to a servo motor. The Honeywell engineers believed they could; they took a few measurements and then went home. Ten days later, they were done. Production manager Mel Fedders returned with Gille and Kutzler, and installed their Modutrol–inspired mechanism on the pitch axis of a mock-up auto pilot system. The system worked fine,

except for one thing. The small G-59 amplifier was not powerful enough to drive the huge flight surface of a Flying Fortress.

McGoldrick, Gille, Kutzler, and Taylor returned to Wright Field with a larger amplifier. Once again, the device was installed on a mockup in a locked vault. When the mechanism worked perfectly, Wright Field technicians immediately took it out and installed it in on the pitch axis of an operational B-17. Captain Don Diehl, pilot of the test plane, was apparently somewhat skeptical, for he asked technician George Borell to sit in the tail of the plane with a pair of bolt cutters and cut the servo line if it failed to work.[39] The Honeywell system automatically controlled the pitch axis of the test plane so effectively, however, that Wright Field wasted no time in ordering a complete set of controls for all three axes of the AFCE. A month later the Army Air Force loaned Minneapolis-Honeywell a B-17, so the company could install and test equipment at Wold-Chamberlain field in Minneapolis.

In just a few months, Honeywell had gone from being the leader in home heating controls to being a leader in aeronautical engineering.

Bombing With Feed Sacks Of Lime

The Army Air Force was eager to test the new system with the Norden bombsight. Feed sacks filled with lime were released from a B-17 using the AFCE and the Norden sight. The lime would burst and scatter upon the ground and be visible from the bomber, so the crew would know imme-

HONEYWELL

Turbo equipped for high altitude flying, this heavy B–17 bomber has just hit a Focke–Wulf aircraft factory at Marienburg, Germany. Honeywell's regulator for the turbo supercharger became standard equipment for all U.S. heavy bombers, the B–17, B–24 and B–29.

the Boeing plant. The team of Gille, Kutzler, and Taylor took the instrument sets on a private railroad car under armed guard from Minneapolis to Seattle.

The first installation of what came to be called the C-1 automatic pilot took place at Boeing in a brand new B-17, on New Year's Day, 1942. After testing the autopilots for only 160 hours, the Army Air Force was convinced. It drafted a contract with Minneapolis-Honeywell for the electronic modification of 600 Norden SBAE units, including the installation of potentiometers on the gyroscope pickups, the G-59-type amplifier system, and conversion of the whole system to alternating current (AC), which has significant advantages in applications that involve sensitive, precision operations, since it provides a smoother signal.

In the fall of 1942, Colonel Robert Jarmon, chief of the Bombardment Branch at Wright Field's Armament Lab, flew to Washington, D.C. in a fully-equipped Flying Fortress. The system was approved by the military for all bombing missions and became standardized in May 1943 through the intensive work of Army personnel and Minneapolis-Honeywell engineers at Wright Field. At the same time, work on the old SBAE system was suspended, and the Minneapolis-

diately whether they had hit their target. Earl Bower, an engineer with Minneapolis-Honeywell, remembers testing the AFCE and bombsight on Thanksgiving Day in 1941.

"On the first run, the bombing was so accurate the AAF personnel on board figured it must have been just luck. So the plane was landed, reloaded with another set of feed sacks, and this entire load was also delivered on target. They were very impressed."[40]

At about this time, the Army Air Force and Minneapolis-Honeywell built a 24 square–foot bombing platform and anchored it in a small lake in Northern Minnesota. Subsequent testing of the AFCE and Norden bombsight yielded such promising results that the AAF soon ordered 23 more units.

The War Is On

After Pearl Harbor, Army officials at Wright Field ordered the removal of all automatic pilot equipment, and the return of the B-17 Flying Fortress they had loaned to Minneapolis-Honeywell. When the first six sets of modified AFCE were completed, Wright Field ordered the company to ship them to Seattle, where they were to be installed directly in heavy bombers at

Honeywell C-1 Automatic Pilot went into production in October.

Though the system was approved, there remained some question as to who would be responsible for the bulk of production of the new AFCE. The Navy continued to insist that Norden be granted manufacturing contracts for the modified system, and requested that Minneapolis-Honeywell provide them and the Norden Company with plans and specifications.[41] Army Air Force personnel considered this recommendation unjust to Minneapolis-Honeywell. Ironically, the Norden Company was neither prepared nor willing to produce the modified automatic pilot. Minneapolis-Honeywell had many assets recommending it for full production of the AFCE, including the fact that it had recently added thousands of square feet to its production plant. The Army pointed out that Minneapolis-Honeywell "had facilities for greater production rate" than Norden and an "effective field organization."[42]

From the very beginning of Honeywell's autopilot work, the company had organized a trained group of field representatives to attend to C-1 maintenance, and provide instruction in adjustment and operation. Eventually, Minneapolis-Honeywell's field organization included more than 75 men all over the world who were basically civilian soldiers, sleeping

in the same barracks and wearing the same uniforms as Army Air Force personnel. They wore "Tech Rep" insignia, and were given the rank of Captain in case they were taken prisoner.[43] The 12th Air Force in Egypt, and Lt. Gen. George Kinney's 5th Air Force, were the first combat units to demonstrate successful use of the autopilot system.

Aero: A Division And A Cat

In July 1942, Minneapolis-Honeywell leased a building on Cicero Avenue in Chicago for the purpose of modifying the SBAE and then manufacturing the AFCE from scratch. The company sent a group of recruits in to check out the facility. They "rushed out for brooms... for all the building consisted of was empty space except for a cat that was soon dubbed 'Aero.'"[44]

But the plant didn't remain empty for long. H.W. Sweatt announced its opening on October 5, 1942, noting that he expected the newly created division to employ over 2000 people. Sweatt named Tom McDonald, former head of the Toronto office, to take the helm. Aero Division's challenge, he said, was the unprecedented mass production of highly sophisticated "electronic instruments."

Performance Of The C–1

The performance of the automatic pilot was usually measured by the degree of precision the Norden sight was able to achieve, and reports from the theaters of combat indicated that the C-1 and the Norden sight were performing above even the highest expectations. Conversely, however, there were some indications from testing units back in the States that the sight was not performing as well as hoped. This contradiction escalated to the point where test engineers actually recommended that the automatic pilot system be discontinued, while officers conducting combat missions emphatically rejected their findings. Finally Robert Lovett, the Assistant Secretary of War, stepped in to resolve the issue.

"The VIII Air Force planes are not concerned with theoretical conditions," he wrote, "but with actual and, as they have used both, it seems to me that their distinct preference should be conclusive evidence to us as to what is needed. If, therefore, there is any tendency to delay the project on the

The C-1 autpilot became one of the most famous Honeywell products during World War II. Like the Butz damper-flapper before it, the C-1 was actually a system of integrated components rather than a single invention. Pictured here is the vertical flight gyro, the largest of three gyros in the system. One gyroscope was needed for each axis of flight.

basis of statistics which show that an unmodified sight is theoretically more accurate than one equipped with the mercury erector, I suggest that such discussions be postponed until after the German targets have been hit and destroyed by the use of equipment which the combat units have found most effective for this purpose."[45]

By November 1942, an Army Air Force report noted that 90 percent of bombing done in qualifying training was done on the C-1 autopilot, and that personnel were "highly in favor of the C-1 pilot." Furthermore, the autopilot came to be "considered a morale factor and an inducement to do better bombing."[46] In terms of sheer numbers, it may have been even more successful than the Norden bombsight itself. In April of 1944, the Strategic Air Forces in Europe requested that AFCE be installed on every plane, while it requested Norden bombsights on only about every third craft.[47]

Pilot Reception Of The C-1

Lt. Col. William Stark, Operations Officer at AAF Headquarters in the India-Burma Sector, explained that pilots were at first reluctant to use the new device.

"Most pilots are skeptical of new gadgets, particularly those that take the controls out of their hands. Barely three years ago when anyone ventured to suggest that a gadget could handle the controls and fly better bombing runs than the pilot, despite heavy bursts of flak and attacks by enemy fighters, any man with the wings would declare indignantly that no mechanical robot was going to fly his plane when the going got tough. We arrived in Burma in the summer of 1942 with automatic gadgets on our B–24s. But with such heavily defended areas as Rangoon, Bangkok, and Mandalay for our targets, we were afraid to entrust the success of our missions to this mechanical robot."[48]

The control panel formed the interface between the human pilot and the C-1 automatic pilot in the cockpit. The human pilot was able to make small or large adjustments in flight by a simple turn of the knob, flying the plane through the C-1's powerful servo motors. In this way many bombers were flown home despite having their manual controls damaged or destroyed. It was a process described to be as "easy as tuning in W-G-N on the radio."

The crews began to reconsider, Stark said, when a Minneapolis-Honeywell field engineer named Ted Frystak arrived in 1942. He moved right in with them, saying his job was to "keep the equipment in A-1 condition, an extremely simple task since we had never used it anyway." But Frystak prevailed in the end.

"By the spring of 1943," Lt. Col. Stark said, "he had enabled us to fly practically all of our missions and about 85 per cent of our bombing approaches and target runs on the autopilot. Not only did his work enable us to improve bombing accuracy from 25 to 50 per cent, but it also reduced the mean error 50 per cent. This means that if the mean error is cut from 1,000 to 500 feet, the effect of the bombing is quadrupled. It follows that nine planes can do the work of 36. It follows also that return trips over the target are cut to a minimum, fewer lives are risked, less effort is expended, and less equipment is needed to accomplish a mission."

Pilots used the AFCE for relief from the fatigue of long flights, especially in rough weather, when the controls of a heavy bomber could turn

Don Hamilton (right) and Willis Gille in April 1970. The two were members of the "brain trust" group that developed the automatic pilot in 1941. Hamilton, a Master Sergeant in the Air Corps, defined the problem, and Gille, a company engineer, worked out many of the engineering details.

a flight into a wrestling match. The longest run which the India-Burma group made was to Bangkok and back, 16.5 hours, 2700 miles, but even after a flight that long, crews were in much better shape if they had used the AFCE.

Still, pilots remained reluctant to utilize the AFCE during the actual bombing. "No one was anxious to be the first to try a raid with a robot at the controls," Stark said. "By the turn of the year the autopilot was being used to and from most targets with such success that crews felt fresh enough to fly more and more combat missions. If this had been the only advantage gained, the device would have been a real contribution to our raids."

Eventually the squadron realized that the autopilot was just as effective during the actual bombing, and that it substantially increased results. On one raid to Bangkok made in rough weather, the mission took 16 hours and 30 minutes. After a successful bombing, the group returned, having been on autopilot for 16 hours and 10 minutes, except for 20 minutes of manual control during takeoff and landing. Navigators loved the automatic pilot, too, because it could hold an extremely steady course.

"Successful use of the device on complete missions was a gift from the gods for the navigators," Stark noted. "Nowadays, if the pilot starts to fly his ship manually, he usually will hear a loud gripe over the interphone from the navigator in short order: 'Throw it back on the autopilot so we can keep a straight course.' Never without an answer, the pilot snaps back, 'Just wanted to see if you were awake.' And both enjoy the free ride on AFCE."[49]

The automatic pilot revolutionized flight. The record attests to its unimpeachable performance, and to the fact that it saved thousands of lives.

Amazing Stories

Months before the government allowed disclosure of the automatic pilot, strange stories began appearing about huge bombers flying themselves for thousands of miles after their crews had bailed out. At least two such episodes occurred on training flights over American airspace. In early 1943, a crew bailed out of a B-24 Liberator over the

East Coast, and the plane flew 2,000 miles to Mexico without anyone aboard.[50] On November 22, 1944, the *Chicago Daily News* reported such an incident under the headline "Wild B-17 Heads Here." A B–17 Flying Fortress had developed control problems, and the crew had parachuted to safety in Marion, South Dakota. The pilotless plane had made a run in the direction of Chicago before crashing in Isabella, Minnesota.[51]

Even more amazing stories were published after disclosure of the automatic pilot. In December of 1944, the *M-H News-Circulator* reported a "Fortress Saga" in which a normal bombing run was cut short by enemy attack planes. A crew bailed out of its flak-damaged B-17 with the plane on autopilot, and flying a diversionary course away from the rest of the squadron. German Messerschmidts followed what they thought to be easy prey, unaware they were wasting their ammunition on an abandoned bomber.[52]

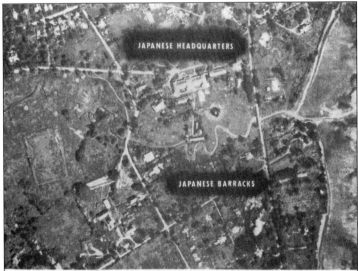

The success of the Norden bombsight in conjunction with the C-1 automatic pilot was dramatic. This bombing run took place at 16,000-feet over Burma. The accuracy of the electronic targeting equipment meant that American bombers could remain at relatively safe altitudes, out of range of many anti-aircraft weapons, and still achieve surgical precision.

HONEYWELL

Still other stories related the safe returns of severely damaged planes through the automatic pilot. In many cases, enemy fire or even mid-air collisions had completely destroyed the manual controls, yet pilots were able to bring the planes back using the autopilot controls. In one case, a Messerschmidt collided with a B-17, severing most of the fuselage and the manual control cables for the rudder and elevators. But because the electronic controls were located in the tail of the plane, the autopilot was able to retain control of the craft and bring it home.

Another famous story appeared in the *Saturday Evening Post*. Sergeant George Perlin related the "Incident Over the Sphinx," in which a Flying Fortress called *Benancye II*, stationed in North Africa, was returning to base after a bombing run. Fuel was running out just as a blinding sandstorm kicked up on the surface, effectively preventing the plane from landing at Payne Field. Orders were given to abandon ship.

> *"When all fuel gauges showed 'empty' all around, the pilot ordered the crew to bail, with each man carrying a knife to cut himself free of his chute when he hit the ground. At their altitude, the sandstorm below showed up as a mad brown boiling cloud, stretching to the circular horizon. One after another, the minute black specks whirled down into the storm, until, reluctant to leave their ship, only the pilot and co-pilot remained aboard. Just before they bailed out, they set the automatic pilot to carry the ship on away from the ancient city [Cairo] and its inhabitants, intending for it to crash harmlessly out in the open desert."*

The tail of this B-17 was nearly severed by gunfire from a Messerschmidt, yet incredibly it was able to return to base by virtue of the C-1 autopilot.

The abandoned plane "made a 180 degree turn, she cleared treetops, landed in a wheat field, jumped a ten-foot irrigation ditch and came to a rest in a cotton field." Incredibly, *Benancye II* had run out of gas at the precise moment a human pilot would have cut the engines, and the plane suffered only bent propellers and a little sand in her engines. She had landed herself and survived. Unfortunately most crew members were unable to cut themselves away from their parachutes, and were dragged to their deaths in the violent sandstorm.[53]

The automatic pilot often held a damaged plane steady while its crew, some of whom may have been injured by flak, made preparations to bail out. For this reason, many soldiers credited it with saving their lives. Lt. Carlton Mills, a bombardier who was shot down making a bombing run from Italy to Munich, related what became a familiar story.

> *"The attack left two of our motors knocked out and the fuselage pretty badly shot up. One of the shells had exploded against my leg and torn up my side. A second later the order came to abandon ship. We were 24,000 feet up. With my foot, I*

Honeywell's important role in wartime production was manifest in the christening of this B-29 Superfortress. The "Honeywell Honey Frances Carl" was named for the winner of a beauty contest back at Minneapolis-Honeywell's Mercury Switch department. The bomber is decorated with decals which indicate that it made 42 bombing sorties, downed two enemy planes, dropped supplies to POWs in Japan, and made six trips "over the hump" from India to China.

The entire crew of Minneapolis-Honeywell flight research technicians and engineers in 1944. That year, they flew 1,106 hours on some 600 flights, testing such Honeywell devices as the C-1 autopilot and turbo regulator.

couldn't get back to the bomb bay, and to get out the escape hatch up front meant removing my chute, removing my flak vest, buckling the chute back on again (they built the escape hatches before they thought of the flak vests). That kind of thing takes time. And that's where the autopilot came in. It held that torn–up plane in a steady glide while I took off the chute, took off the vest, put on the chute, and jumped from the escape hatch. If there hadn't been any autopilot, or if it had suddenly stopped working, the plane would have turned wing over wing into a spin just like that."[54]

Another story in the *M-H News-Circulator* suggested that the autopilot could actually recover a plane that had gone out of control.

"Rudy Rudloff, a salesman in the Cleveland office, was lunching with several customers in a downtown restaurant in Columbus. During the conversation the name 'Minneapolis-Honeywell' was mentioned. At the table next to theirs was a Lieutenant of the Air Corps who wore a number of foreign service bars. No sooner had the name 'Minneapolis-Honeywell' been mentioned than this lieutenant got up from his table and came over to the table where Rudy was sitting and asked if there was anyone there from Minneapolis-Honeywell.' Rudy Rudloff identified himself. 'I was flying a bomber which was very badly shot up,' the man said, 'and went into a spin. Nothing I could do seemed to help. I was spinning to earth and felt sure it was my last moment when suddenly I thought to try the autopilot. I shoved the control over to the autopilot and immediately the plane straightened out and on the autopilot control I got back to my base safely.'"[55]

Herb Williams, a Chief Field Engineer for Minneapolis-Honeywell's Aero division, was stationed in England with the 8th and 9th Bomber Squadrons. He said that "more than 10,000 American and Allied fliers in the British theater

alone credit the C-1 automatic pilot with their lives and liberty...Until we stopped counting, more than a thousand of our planes came back and were landed safely on the automatic pilot."[56]

A Far Superior "It"

Minneapolis-Honeywell's incredible technological advances were generally kept secret until it was certain the enemy had already

In the autumn of 1944, Minneapolis-Honeywell technicians played host to several news reporters, including Sally Luther and Virgina Hofer (at right) from Honeywell's in-house papers, *The Circulator* and *Aero*. The editors were allowed to take control of the company's test-bed B-17 through the C-1 autopilot.

HONEYWELL

The Minneapolis-Honeywell Formation Stick installed in the cockpit of a B-29. This device allowed the pilot to fly a heavy bomber through the automatic pilot, greatly reducing fatigue by making use of a highly sensitive joystick-type control.

gained access to them. Employees were aware only of having a hand in creating some state-of-the-art instruments relying on electronic engineering. The *Circulator* acknowledged Minneapolis-Honeywell's important role as best it could while still maintaining discretion.

"Because of the importance of our product," the paper noted, *"we are prevented by the government from referring to it by name, so its history must refer only to 'It.' Some months back the Engineering Department at Minneapolis decided they could make a far superior 'It' with the use of electronics as only they had developed it. They made an 'It' and it worked. In fact, it worked so well that the U.S. Air Corps wanted more immediately. More 'Its' meant not dozens but hundreds, and at*

the same time thousands of problems. 'Its' in any form as well as other Electronic instruments had never been made on production machinery before or in production quantities, and the Air Corps wanted them yesterday, not tomorrow."[57]

The engineering and production of this "It" opened up a new age for Honeywell.

The Electronic Automatic Pilot Unveiled "Now It Can Be Told"

In September 1943, after rumors had circulated about a "robotic" device that could actually fly the Army Air Corps' Flying Fortress bombers, the public was finally informed of the electronic automatic pilot. The first published accounts appeared only after the enemy had gained access to it by salvaging downed American bombers. The idea of an automatic pilot seems commonplace today, but in 1943 it was stunning news indeed. The *News-Circulator* announced boldly, "Amazing M-H Control is Key to Pin-Point Bombing,"[58] indicating that the mechanism was integral to the Army Air Corps' secret program for precision bombing. Minneapolis-Honeywell had, in fact, established an entire division in Chicago for the production of the automatic pilot. Aero Division published its own employee newspaper, and in October the organ announced with pride, and perhaps a little relief, "Now It Can Be Told."[59]

In October 1944, full details were published in *Electronics* magazine by two Minneapolis-Honeywell engineers who had been part of the development team.

"The precision of even the most skillful human pilot is limited by such factors as his reaction time, susceptibility to fatigue, inability to detect slight variations the instant they occur, errors in judgment, and errors in muscle coordination. The autopilot, on the other hand, detects flight variations the instant they occur and makes the required correction of the airplane's controls quickly. When properly adjusted, the autopilot will smoothly return the plane to straight-and-level flight after an off-course deviation, without over-control or under-control."[60]

The automatic pilot consisted of gyroscopes which detected the normal changes in wind direction, turbulence, air pressure, etc. and responded by making adjustments in the ailerons, elevators, or rudder. In doing so, it helped create a new science of avionics. A company previously known for thermostats had invented, developed, and produced an amazing flight control instrument. It seemed a long way from the little gilt box on the walls of America's living rooms to the skies over Berlin and Tokyo. Yet, this instrument was not *totally* unrelated to

HONEYWELL

the company's prewar product line—the original Butz system, after all, was concerned with the automation of a tedious manual process. The automatic pilot represented the extension of basic technologies of automation to the control of flight.

As Easy As Tuning In WGN

With public interest in the device running so high, a group of newspaper editors traveled to Chicago in September 1944 to take a ride in a B-17 Flying Fortress, see the autopilot in action, and even take the controls. Sally Luther, editor of Honeywell's own *Circulator*, described "the excitement of turning a small knob and feeling the whole great weight of the Fortress's 30,000 pounds respond gently and obediently with a swing to the left or right."[61]

The cynical gang of reporters from the Chicago dailies was unabashedly impressed. Eugene Griffin wrote in the *Chicago Daily Tribune*, "It is as simple to fly a Flying Fortress as to tune in W-G-N on the radio with the recently disclosed automatic electronic pilot now used on the army's four engine bombers. A twist of a knob makes the big plane dip and roll or hold a table-steady course for a bombing run."

"Eight thousand feet above Chicago's south side, the Tribune reporter, who never had been up in an airplane before, was grabbing on to rods and ammunition frames to keep from rattling around in the waist of the Fortress. 'Are we shaking apart?' he asked. 'Oh, that's just one of the other reporters trying to sky-write,' said a crew member. 'Does he have to scribble like this?'"[62]

Wright Field began assigning more flight-related problems to the company, and M–H engineers found themselves developing and manufacturing a growing line of highly sophisticated instruments for flight.

The Turbo Supercharger

The Turbo Supercharger turned out to be nearly as universal as the automatic pilot. Like all internal combustion engines, those of a heavy bomber need air to run, a commodity in short supply at the high altitudes where the Flying Fortress flew. Usually, this was overcome by introducing compressed air into the carburetion of the engine via a supercharger. However, the pilot was required to constantly adjust the supercharger manually. Changes of altitude and air speed meant a corresponding adjustment of the supercharger, and if it wasn't properly adjusted, the engine could explode.

Minneapolis-Honeywell developed a turbo supercharger which diverted some of the engine's exhaust to provide the motive force for the compressed air, effectively governing the air intake of the huge engines in all conditions. The system would automatically adjust for altitude changes, or it could be manually operated by the pilot when he required greater power.

One Minneapolis-Honeywell field engineer stationed in the South Pacific said, "Every pilot I have flown with and others I have talked to refer to the Electronic Turbosupercharger Control System as 'The Pilot's Dream.'"

The turbo supercharger became stock equipment on B-17, B-24, and B-29 bombers. The system consisted of five control units.

A B-29 Superfortress, complete with Honeywell's autopilot and turbo supercharger, rolling out of Minneapolis-Honeywell's hangar at Wold-Chamberlain Field in Minneapolis in 1944.

The experimental facility was large enough to house five B-17 Flying Fortresses. The door of the hangar measured 180 x 130 feet, and was rumored to be the largest in the world.

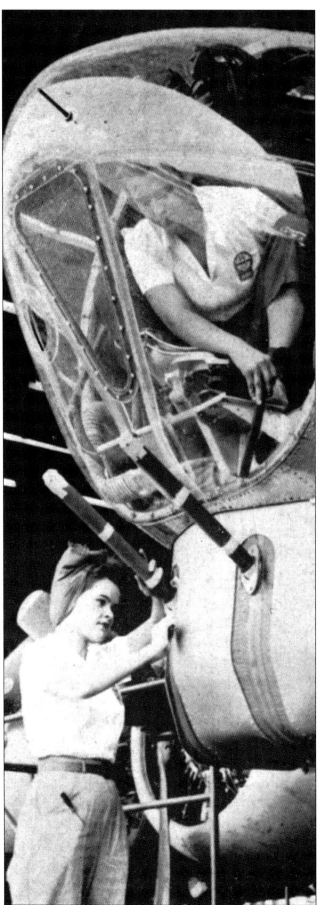

HONEYWELL

There was a motor which positioned "the waste gate" or damper in the exhaust stream, and a Pressuretrol which measured the air pressure at the supercharger and maintained it at the level selected by the pilot. There was also a governor which acted like a limit-control on a furnace, except that it prevented over-revving rather than overheating. Finally, an amplifier received all impulses and sent them to the waste gate.[63]

The Formation Stick

On April 11, 1945, America was introduced to a top secret accessory to the automatic pilot. The formation stick was a pistol–grip which ran through the autopilot and put the "services of the autopilot at the pilot's fingertips. The advantage is that where manual control of a heavy bomber requires a force of perhaps 100 pounds, electronic control through the Formation Stick requires less effort than a child uses in turning a bicycle." Holding a plane in tight formation could take every ounce of strength of both the pilot and co–pilot. The formation stick, however, was designed to assist the human pilot in holding the plane in a tight formation, by allowing him to "steer" the autopilot system with a joystick like device also called a "jinking stick," because it made evasive maneuvers very easy for the human pilot.[64]

The Pressure Transmitter

For many years prior to World War II, oil and fuel gauges were somewhat dangerous, because they required that raw flammables be piped through the cockpit to the indicators. Engineers at Minneapolis-Honeywell designed a pressure transmitter allowing flight crews to keep tabs on the machinery and fluid levels without this additional risk. There were other pressure transmitters, but Honeywell's was extremely simple, light, and inexpensive.[65] The transmitter was designed by Honeywell and manufactured elsewhere, and saved "hundreds of man-hours in the assembly of every plane," and "reduced the cost of pressure indicating equipment by more than $1000."[66]

The Gas Gauge

Another challenge with Army Air Force heavy bombers was how to effectively measure the

Women played an important role in war production, stepping into many production roles traditionally reserved for men. Pictured here are Patricia Rogers and Bea Alexander as they make adjustments on a B-17-G.

amount of fuel in their tanks. Fuel tanks are located in the wings, and the natural motion of flight causes waves in the fuel, which made standard mechanical indicators unreliable. To make matters worse, fuel has a tendency to "boil" or bubble at high altitudes, creating a froth on its surface which could corrupt accurate measurements. In addition, fuel contracts at the frigid temperatures encountered at high altitudes. All these factors could cause as much as a 15 percent error in fuel indicator readings. In a huge B-17, this could mean a difference of hundreds of gallons. A plane with less fuel than its gauge indicated could easily run out, while carrying more fuel than necessary meant that a bomber couldn't carry as great a payload. Minneapolis-Honeywell engineers developed an electronic capacitance gauge which solved the problem by measuring the weight of the fuel in the tanks rather than the volume. The gauge used multiple pickups throughout the fuel system to measure the electrical capacity of the fuel, which decreased in a ratio proportionate to its weight.[67]

Experimenting And Educating

Perhaps the most obvious symbol of Honeywell's new aeronautics work was a giant hangar built at Wold-Chamberlain field in Minneapolis. Dedicated on September 24, 1943, the experimental facility was large enough to house five B-17 Flying Fortresses. The *door* measured 180 x 130 feet, and was rumored to be the largest in the world.[68] This facility was impressive acknowledgment of the many contributions the company made to the entire field of avionics.[69] After the war, when demand for research space had decreased, most of the space was rented out to Northwest Airlines. The company did, however, retain a small area for experimental work and for corporate planes.[70]

The new hangar was home to a B-17 known only as "two-one-zero," for the last three digits of its tail number. This was the original Flying Fortress loaned to Minneapolis-Honeywell in the first days of the AFCE project, and it became the first aircraft to test many important instruments. Logging more than 1800 hours of test flight, "210" tested all the successful Minneapolis-Honeywell controls. The formation stick, autopilot, supercharger and fuel gauge. After the war, the Army Air Force declared "210" surplus, and Minneapolis-Honeywell donated the bomber to the University of Minnesota's engineering department.

The company's association with education was more than just philanthropic. The sophisticated nature of items like the C-1 autopilot meant that well-trained technical representatives were critical to the success of company products. From the very first contract with the Army Air Force for autopilots, the company offered a six-week educational course with the price of the modified AFCE. Eventually, it established an Aeronautical School at Wold-Chamberlain Field, where technical representatives and enlisted men alike learned the intricacies of the new devices. The company also established a branch of the school in Great Britain, to train overseas Army Air Force personnel in the use and maintenance of the C–1 autopilot. By mid–1944, the Minneapolis-Honeywell Aeronautical School had turned out 2500 graduates. This program was one of the first of its kind in the country, and was seen as a model for training in the fields of high tech engineering, manufacturing, and service. Minneapolis-Honeywell even went to Hollywood for assistance with the program, contracting with Walt Disney Productions to produce ten instructional films for the school.

At the height of World War II, Minneapolis-Honeywell women arranged a hosiery drive, collecting rayon, silk and nylon. Old hosiery was recycled for use in powder bags for the U.S. infantry. These women from the Welding and Coil Winding departments were "Victory Queens" during the war.

HONEYWELL

In October 1941, Bette Davis signed into the company's guest book during a visit to Minneapolis headquarters. Davis was married to Arthur Farnsworth, a West Coast representative of Minneapolis-Honeywell headquartered in Hollywood. The actress was presented with a unique gift from the company, a hand-engraved Chronotherm personalized for installation at "*Butternut,*" her country estate.

Storyboards were drawn up in January 1943, and filming soon followed.[71]

Minneapolis-Honeywell was, understandably, a substantial presence at the experimental laboratories at Wright Field in Dayton. In 1945, *M-H News-Circulator* editor Sally Luther made a trip to Wright Field to take stock of the Honeywell presence there.

> "On the walls of almost every building I saw the familiar little gilt thermostats and the tall letters M-H. M-H is there in other ways too. Almost every lab needs a high altitude chamber for testing guns or men or instruments or clothing under actual flight conditions. These igloo-like constructions can simulate atmospheric conditions of 40,000 feet above sea level, with temperatures as low as -60. Honeywell controls help regulate these low temperatures and Brown Instruments keep the running record of 'what cooks inside' or better, 'what freezes.'"[72]

The relationship had grown so close that two Honeywell employees were actually invited to participate in an Army tour of German scientific facilities following the war in the summer of 1945. Willis Gille and Hub Sparrow, who had developed the C-1 automatic pilot, helped con-

duct an "exhaustive survey of Nazi flight developments." This study turned up some shocking information, including "models and blue prints of German air secrets which, had the Allies been held off another six months, might have won the war for the Nazis." Gille and Sparrow were more than a little surprised at one particularly extensive facility, where they "learned of a whole roomful of Minneapolis-Honeywell autopilots and turbo regulators, gyros, amplifiers, motors, and other gadgets" all apparently salvaged from fallen bombers. And elsewhere in Germany, the group found a German JU-88 aircraft in which a complete C-1 autopilot had been installed.[73]

Honeywell Women During The War

Because so many men were called to active duty during the War, for the first time, women entered the labor force *en masse.* Minneapolis-Honeywell employed thousands during the war, in every position which men had occupied, with the exception of management. "Women entered the factories by the thousands to fill the jobs vacated by men who joined the armed services."[74] This unprecedented situation called for special attention by the company nurse, Marjorie Cowdin, R.N., who wrote in the *M-H News-Circulator,*

> "In these war days the women of our world are playing a stellar role not only in the natty uniforms of the WAVES, WACS, Coast Guard, Nurses, and the Red Cross, but also in the less dramatic uniforms of production, which are slacks, smocks, overalls, and aprons for farm, home and factory. We find you in many new and unbelievable tasks; welding, riveting, assembling, polishing, grinding, spraying, at drill presses, punch presses, in foundries and machine shops replacing men, in jobs that were considered exclusively theirs prior to this war."[75]

Kate Massee reported in the *Chicago Daily Tribune* that women constituted 30 percent of the workforce at Minneapolis-Honeywell's Aero division in Chicago.

These women "perform their jobs with great skill and dexterity," she wrote, "according to Thomas McDonald, vice president in charge of the Chicago plant. In fact, Mr. McDonald says he and the industrial relations department heads are constantly amazed at how well the women turn out their share of equipment vital to high precision bombing. At present the women...work two daily shifts, from 8:30 a.m. to 5 p.m. and from 9 p.m. to 6:30 a.m. six days a week. The women at Minneapolis-Honeywell come from all walks of life. Some were engaged in business before taking up war work, others had never worked before, and most of them have close relatives in the services."[76]

Minneapolis Heat Regulator had hired women for the production line as early as the 1920s, because it seemed that their smaller hands and fingers provided them with a distinct advantage in delicate assembly tasks.

Exemptions For Honeywellers

The Minneapolis-Honeywell Regulator Company's contributions to the war effort were such that many employees were exempt from military service. "Hundreds of male and female employees were in the service during the war, but a greater number were not allowed to enter the military. Their Honeywell jobs were deemed crucial to the war effort and the government wanted them to remain part of a company which was vital to the country's survival."[77] Of those Honeywellers who served in the armed forces, 26 were killed, many of them automatic pilot specialists.

Honeywell Keeps In Touch

Honeywell boosted the morale of American troops abroad in some ways other than just producing materiel. In 1944, the company received an interesting request from some GIs in France, who happened to see a Minneapolis-Honeywell advertisement in a copy of *Life*.

> "Our attention was arrested by your statement in Life magazine that your new Moduflow Control System was necessary to maximum heating comfort. We are entirely in agreement with you and feel that, with a few modifications, your system would satisfy our heating problem. Finding no dealer in the vicinity, we are taking the liberty of writing to your office as your advertisement suggested. Our six-man foxhole, 6x8x5 requires a heating unity which will keep the interior at an even 72 F despite sub-zero temperature and high winds, prevalent this time of year. It must be of rugged construction to withstand rough usage and occasional shelling. If you have a unit to fit above specifications, please ship COD immediately. It would do much to lift our morale and shorten the war considerably.
> Sincerely yours,
>
> Pfc. F Giordano, Pvt. Don Fitzpatrick, Pfc. Clarence Swartz, Pfc. John Overall, Pfc. John T. Smith, Sgt. J. Waligore."

The company published the letter in the *M-H News-Circulator*, along with a response:

> "Dear Mr. Fitzpatrick
>
> Your request for a heating control has been referred to our Foxhole, Outhouse, and Here's-a-chance-for-some-free-publicity department. Let me reiterate our statement that our Moduflow control system is necessary to, in fact, the essence of optimum heating comfort. Your particular need is an example of why our inventive genius labored and brought forth a mountain rather than a mouse. Our accent today is on Zoned Heating, and a foxhole is the ultimate example of this principle. To explain: your 6x8x5 rut with ends is a melting pot. You have an Italian, an Irishman, a German, and Englishman, besides a Waligore and an Overall. A temperature to suit the Italian taste would not necessarily be to the Englishman's liking. An Irishman, in common with the canine species, can and does acclimate himself easily. The German, on the other hand, perhaps would require the most consideration—more Lebensraum, and as a direct result, more control...
> Yours very truly,
> M-HRCo
>
> P.S. Due to upset economic conditions and restrictions imposed by War Export Board, payment is acceptable in cigarettes and Spam cans."[78]

The company also participated in a contest to name a B-29 bomber stationed in the Pacific. The *Honeywell Honey Frances Carl* made 42 combat sorties, downed two enemy aircraft, made six trips "over the hump" from India to China, and even made a mercy drop of supplies to American POW's in Japan. The *Honey* was named after Frances Carl, an employee in the mercury switch department who had won a company beauty contest.

As the war wound down, a ravaged Europe cried out for relief, and Honeywell workers organized a major program to help.

Four Honeywell women celebrate outside the factory on V-E Day, May 1945. When news was received that Germany had surrendered, managers blew the factory whistles, signaling a holiday for all employees.

"A big market for controls, but no dollars to pay with at the present time. That's the picture for M-H in Europe as seen by John Amand, one of the managers of the N.V. Nederlansche Minneapolis-Honeywell Co., Honeywell subsidiary in Amsterdam, Holland. The war-torn countries of France, Belgium, and Holland are eager for controls of all sorts. With the German control industry virtually wiped out, the demand for U.S. supplies is further augmented."[79]

Honeywell Celebrates V–E Day

On May 11, 1945, the *M-H News-Circulator* reported that "Early morning at the plant on V-E Day had been much like any other morning. Attendance on the first shift was close to 100 per cent; the same had been true of the preceding third shift. Honeywell people were prepared to work until the final proclamation was made. Then at 8:04 President Truman delivered his epoch-making official declaration. Immediately Factory Manager Paul Wishart called Maintenance Foreman Paul Cotea: 'Let 'er go!' On this signal, Cotea gave the word to ring the bells throughout all three plants for a period of thirty seconds. This was to announce the 24 hour shutdown."[80]

V-J Day followed several months later. The year of 1945 ended with sales of $85 million, the bulk of which were defense contracts.[81] "A total of 4,173,561 products for the Army, Navy and Air Forces, not one of which was commercially manufactured before the war, was produced by Minneapolis-Honeywell in the 1,347 days between Pearl Harbor and V-J Day," the *Circulator* noted. "These weapons had a value of $184,537,269."

The annual report for 1945 detailed a mind-boggling contribution to the war effort: 3 million periscopes, 300,000 telescopes, 100,000 mortar sights, 160,000 gunners' quadrants, 110,000 autopilots and associated devices, 800,000 turbo regulators. And over 35,000 4-engine bombers were equipped with Minneapolis-Honeywell C-1 automatic pilots and turbo superchargers.

The day after V-J Day, August 8, 1945, H.W. Sweatt called together his top executives to discuss the company's post-war strategies.

Technology and War:
The Dream of Humane Warfare

In January 1946, Lt. General L.H. Campbell, Chief of Ordnance at the War Department in Washington, wrote to commend Minneapolis-Honeywell for a job well done:

"Dear Mr. Sweatt: I want to take this occasion to thank you and your company with the warmest feeling of appreciation for the outstanding part you have played in producing war materiel for our troops. Your facility has been an outstanding producer of fire control instruments, and in many cases the sole producer of instruments without which field operations could not have been conducted as successfully."[82]

The autopilot in connection with the Norden bombsight, for example, had doubtless sped the end of the war by making precision bombing a reality. Colonel R.L. Finkenstaedt spoke to Aero Division employees on December 23, 1944, when the Chicago plant responsible for manufacturing the C-1 autopilot was awarded the Army-Navy "E".

"Think of what it would mean if increased production and increased supplies to our armed forces could shorten this war by one hour. In one hour a machine gun can fire 10,000 bullets. A battleship can hurl 500 tons of projectiles a distance of over 12 miles in the same time. In sixty minutes a fleet of bombers can bring untold damage and loss of life to a city. In one hour thousands of our soldiers, sailors, and marines can be killed."[83]

M–H News-Circulator editor Sally Luther gave eloquent voice to a worldwide dream in September, 1944, when she wrote, "We must find a way to use the marvels of electronic devices and all the other great scientific developments of this war for a brilliant and never-ending peace."[84]

NASA's Space Station Freedom, though temporarily on hold in the early 1990s, promises to be a source for many controls contracts for Honeywell.

CHAPTER FIVE

DEFENSE AND AERONAUTICS
1945-1985

*"Honeywell's obligation to the citizens of the
United States and the Free World is the production of materials for defense. For defense needs,
new plants, new equipment, and new personnel
have been added on a substantial basis."*

— *Contact Point*, (April 1951)

Minneapolis–Honeywell had converted a heating control business into a sizeable manufacturer of government requisitions, and the C–1 autopilot was
the symbol of the company's capacity to respond to changing times
and needs. Within just six months,
a demonstrator model of the
Moduflow temperature control system had been transformed into an automatic
flight controller ready for installation in the
country's heavy bombers. This startling trans-
formation was the result of Minneapolis–
Honeywell's tremendous endowment of scientific and engineering talent. H.W. Sweatt's foresight in seeking synergy between the corporate
resources and the nation's defense needs led
directly to the company's outstanding contributions to winning the war.

Years would pass before the full significance
of the wartime projects would be realized. But
some obvious advantages had accrued to the
company, and these were immediately converted
to civilian markets. For example, the new
Moduflow system of the post–war years required
a knowledgeable sales and service department,
so the company arranged an education program
modeled directly after the Minneapolis-Honeywell
Aeronautical School.[1]

This was a painful time for many employees
who had come to Honeywell in the midst of the
war, when company contracts were limited only
by production capacity. Now, thousands were
being laid off or "voluntarily terminated" as
government orders were slashed. The editor of
the company newspaper, Sally Luther, her own
job in jeopardy, posed the question, "What Lies
Ahead?" in a June 1945 editorial. She, too,
lamented the scarcity of raw materials necessary
to convert tank periscope production
lines into thermostat production lines.

*"Since V–E Day, cutbacks on
war production have been speedy and
severe... the unexpected speed of these
cutbacks has made it necessary to
lay off 1,000 persons. These plus
the voluntary terminations, have
meant a total reduction of 1,500
during June. We have absorbed the
first shock. And now naturally we're
asking what's ahead? What about MY job? Further cutbacks are anticipated in July although
not as extensive as in June, and by August 1 the
work force is expected to be pretty well levelled
off.... Had we been able, when periscope cutbacks came through, to put periscope assemblers
to work assembling thermostats, layoffs would
have been reduced to a minimum. We were not.
And this is why. The raw materials needed to
make thermostats are strictly rationed."[2]*

Cutbacks were worst after the Japanese
surrendered, when most remaining government contracts were cancelled. The company
had been forced to release another 1000 employees following V–J Day, August 15, 1945.
Even so, H.W.'s announcement was tinged
with pride. "Tuesday, 14 August 1945, marked
the end of a period of Minneapolis-Honeywell's
history which we can all well be proud of.
Friday, August 17, we received telegrams in
effect terminating all our remaining war contracts... Today for the first time we can turn
our thinking and efforts completely to the
peace–time problems that are confronting this
company." The remaining work force "embarked at once into vigorous production of
Honeywell's controls for the post–war world.
Within 30 days of the victory," he added, "M-H
expects to have achieved regular production at
a rate equivalent to its best pre–war year."[3]

Atomic Power
1945–1950

The Second World War had been fought in laboratories and on production lines as well as in trenches. With the devastation of Hiroshima and Nagasaki, the era of the atom dawned. Humankind had harnessed the vast power of the building block of matter itself, and had created a weapon of tremendous power. Minneapolis-Honeywell had been directly involved in the birth of the new atomic age, as the C-1 autopilot was in command of the two B-29s that dropped atomic bombs in August 1945. The C-1 also piloted several unmanned planes which flew through the Bikini Island tests in 1946.[4]

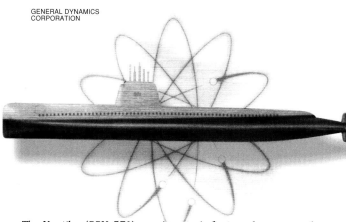

GENERAL DYNAMICS
CORPORATION

The Nautilus (SSN-571) was America's first nuclear powered submarine, launched on January 21, 1954. Honeywell supplied the air conditioning controls.

Honeywell's involvement in the nuclear age went beyond the autopilot. A 1955 article noted that "Honeywell's experience in the field dates back to the very beginning of the nuclear program, starting with the Manhattan Project which developed the atomic bomb. Many automatic controls, recorders and other instruments produced by the company were used in the Manhattan Project."[5] In addition, the company was involved in outfitting the facilities of the Atomic Energy Commission's testing sites and headquarters at Los Alamos, New Mexico. The AEC's 1950 order was the single largest order the Commercial Division had ever received.[6] Most of it, however, was comprised of traditional Honeywell products, like thermostats and valve controls. The company was also proud of its contract to supply the *Nautilus* (SSN-571), the first nuclear-powered submarine, and proudly proclaimed that Honeywell equipment was fully in control of the ship's 10 different "air conditioning zones."

Honeywell literature bubbled over with national pride.

> *"The fabulous power of the atom, harnessed in the Nautilus, gives the U.S. Navy a submarine which can circle the globe without refueling – or without resurfacing for weeks or even months. The only limit to her submergence is human endurance. To make conditions liveable below the sea for the crew, and to offset the intense heat of nuclear fission, the Nautilus, which was built by the Electric Boat Division of General Dynamics Corporation, contains a large air conditioning system. Ten air conditioning zones are included...And picked to control the air conditioning systems on this first atomic submarine, were Honeywell controls."[7]*

Honeywell's highly-regarded commercial products were a major factor in the company's involvement with the nuclear program. In 1955, the company joined Northern State Power and General Mills in forming a consortium of Minneapolis-based companies in order "to determine objectives and activities in the atomic energy field that will benefit the state and its industry...We are on the threshold of an age which undoubtedly will see great advances in the peaceful uses of atomic energy."[8] The assembly was called the Minnesota Nuclear Operations Group, and was designed to explore how the companies might further expand into new markets opened up by nuclear technology. "The company," said one report," chiefly through its Industrial division, has developed many special controls specifically for atomic reactors and other atomic energy installations, including the atomic-powered submarine *Nautilus*. Most of the reactors operating today are at least partially controlled by Honeywell equipment."[9] The Ordnance Division also would eventually accomplish work relating to advanced nuclear weaponry, including contracts for kits to adapt nuclear warheads to various missile systems.[10]

Aero Rises to the Top

The world had changed since 1940, and Honeywell was a more worldly company. It could no longer see itself as the quaint but aggressive leader of the home heating controls industry. The company had grown tremendously, for even with the cutbacks after V-J Day, it still carried twice its prewar payroll.

Sweatt and other directors were uncertain about the highly specialized technologies of the Aeronautical Division. While it seemed plausible that automatic pilots and turbo-regulators might find a niche in commercial markets, management was ambivalent about making a long-term commitment to an area which had germinated and matured during the war years. There was a discomfort of being perceived as having profited from war. To address the challenges and future of the Aeronautical Division, the directors convened in Chicago. Russ Whempner, who had been involved with Aero from the earliest days of the autopilot, recalls those uncertain days:

"Harold Sweatt was quite strong in his feelings that he didn't want the company to be referred to as a 'war monger.' A board meeting was held at the Seneca Hotel on 6 November 1945, and [Chief Engineer Bill] McGoldrick, Al Wilson, who was then head of our aeronautical operation, and I, were invited to the meeting to make a presentation on what we felt we could do with an aeronautical division in peace time. Upon the conclusion of the meeting, we were advised that $500,000 had been set aside to continue our effort along the lines proposed with the admonition that if we could not show some kind of profit within a period of time, the effort would be ended."[11]

Company executives kept returning to the residual assets of high technology which the Aero Division had developed during the war. Many years after the Chicago meeting, Al Wilson recalled that H.W.'s "imagination was roused by the promise Aero business offered in the way of developing technology."[12] Steve Keating, chairman of the board from 1974 to 1978, was hired in 1948 to administer contracts in the Aeronau-

tical Division. He remembered that Sweatt was intrigued by the "romance" of defense technologies. "It was a more romantic thing than the thermostat business."[13] Still, Sweatt was not one to be satisfied with abstract payoffs in an uncertain future. He required measurable profit from Aero's research and development.

Diminutive early profits caused concern among top management. In 1946, Aero profits were just $25,000, barely breaking even compared to other sections of the business. Al Wilson and several other managers were convinced that Aero Division should be judged on the basis of return on assets, rather than on gross sales, as it leased much of its equipment and facilities from the government. In time, Wilson was able to convince Sweatt and Willard Huff that, when evaluated in this way, Aero was competitive with other areas of the company.[14] (After the merger of Minneapolis and Honeywell, Huff was part of a triumvirate of top management that included H.W. and C.B. Sweatt.)

Fortunately, Aero Division was still swamped with government contracts that had not been cancelled. Six months after the Chicago meeting, Wilson reported to H.W. Sweatt that orders placed since the first of the year (1946) had exceeded $4,100,000. "Our Aero shop facilities were planned on the basis of a shop for $3,000,000 annual sales," Wilson pointed out.

Willard Huff was Vice President and Treasurer following the merger of Minneapolis and Honeywell in 1927.

Al Wilson headed the aeronautical operation in 1945, and was instrumental in allowing Aero to become a profitable division.

Steve Keating was hired in 1948 to administer contracts in the Aeronautical Division. He became Honeywell's sixth president serving from 1965-1974 and chairman of the board from 1974-1978.

"...Therefore no more sales can be accepted for 1946 delivery except in very limited quantities of items in production."[15]

Wilson's report was cautiously optimistic about Aero's future. He was especially interested in the automatic pilot and its possible application to commercial aviation. But the Aero shop had been so deluged with government requisitions that management had been slow to address this market. Worse, both Bendix and Sperry had already developed automatic flight controllers which were now being installed in commercial planes. These autopilots were heavier, but they were less expensive and they included compass interfaces, which most airlines required.[16] Meanwhile, Wilson and his engineers were testing a new "E-6" automatic pilot which would eventually serve the Air Force's next generation of heavy bombers, the B-36 and B-50. Before the E-6 went into production, Aero designers were at work on the E-11, the first automatic pilot for supersonic jets.[17]

Wilson's report focused on possible opportunities within commercial aviation. He indicated that the company's gas gauges and turbo regulators had an uncertain future in commercial markets because of developing jet engine technology. Cabin temperature and pressure controllers appeared to be strong products, he noted, but engineers had not yet updated or refined the dated systems already in production. The only exclusively military product the company then manufactured was an order for 50 Shoran recorders, a device for computing targets without a visual frame of reference. "This order for 50 recorders to map Japan grew out of Shoran work during the war," wrote Wilson. "It has no direct commercial application but does give us know-how in navigational techniques which may be useful.... We took this order to fill our shop when we thought orders would be slow."[18]

The Aero Division's best customer was the Army Air Force, and the division had to be content with government rather than commercial contracts. Wilson was not overly concerned about this dependence on defense-related business, however. He emphasized to Sweatt that

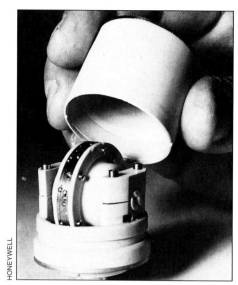

HONEYWELL

In the 1950s and 1960s, Honeywell constantly improved gyroscopes, making them more sensitive and precise while reducing their size and weight. The resulting miniaturization made it possible for the company to produce generic gyroscopes with a wide variety of specialized high-tech applications in space and missile programs.

what business the division *did* have was due to the strength of its engineers and scientists. The implication was that Aero would pay off only in direct proportion to the investment the company was willing to make in research and development. "How big should this [Aero] operation be? How profitable is it? One answer, of course, is that it should be as large as possible as long as it is profitable. I feel it is my major job to try to get the facts which will lead to the answers to these questions. The facts are not available yet because of our limited peacetime experience in this field."[19] He was optimistic that the division could reach $10 million in sales by 1950, depending upon "a considerable enlargement of our engineering activities."[20] However, Wilson wrote, "We do not know now to what extent we are living on our engineering capital built up at government expense during the war."[21]

The war years never did subside from the point of view of defense production, for as soon as World War II concluded, the nation plunged right into the arms race of the Cold War. For 40 years, there would be no shortage of funds for research and development of technologies for American defense. And with the introduction of nuclear submarines, jet fighters, and guided missile systems, there would be bountiful work for Honeywell's Aeronautical division.

Military Products Group

In accordance with management's desire to phase out of military projects following the war, the Ordnance division was discontinued. Ordnance had been producing materiel ranging from periscopes and gunner's quadrants to ammunition. After V-J Day, there was a "feeling of optimism" that the company's engineering and production skills could be successfully applied to peacetime civilian markets.[22] Unfortunately, world events worked against these plans. As tensions continued to grow between the United States and the Soviet Union, an unexpected demand for military equipment developed. Increased demand eventually caused Ordnance Division to be reborn and "essentially postponed Aero's attempt to focus on

HONEYWELL

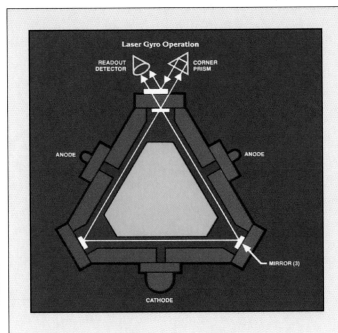

HONEYWELL

Pictured Above: Ring Laser Gyros in testing. Honeywell has been a leader in the field of Ring Laser Gyro research and development for over 25 years.

Diagram at Left: The Ring Laser Gyro consists of two concentrated light beams that have identical frequencies when the gyroscope is at rest. With a change of motion, one beam has a longer optical path to travel, and the result is a proportional change in frequency which is registered as a digital output. Thus, the Ring Laser Gyro does precisely what a mechanical gyroscope does, using completely different technology.

Above: The Boeing 757 and 767 aircraft of the 1980s incorporated Honeywell Laser Inertial Navigation systems.

Right: Honeywell Ring Laser Gyro equipment became standard on many business jets, like the British Aerospace BAe 800 business aircraft.

Below: The Air Force F-15 is among the world's most advanced all-weather fighters. Today these platforms carry key Honeywell components for flight integration and navigation.

civilian markets."[23] This continuing flow of government contracts helped fund development projects which diversified Aero's line, and items like gyros and navigational systems were re–engineered and designed as stand–alone products, with applications in several markets.

"Gyros became a very important part of additional work in auto pilots and space guidance systems," said Ed Lund, who worked in Aero's production department at the time.[24] Aero gradually began to move away from components and into systems. The "autopilot" became an "automatic flight control system."[25]

The outbreak of the Korean War in 1951 caused Honeywell to re–activate the Ordnance Division, and missile projects acquired increasing importance over the next few years.

"Honeywell's obligation to the citizens of the United States and the Free World is the production of materials for defense," the company explained. "For defense needs, new plants, new equipment, and new personnel have been added on a substantial basis."[26]

In 1957, Honeywell reorganized its defense-related businesses into the "Military Products Group," a unit including Aero, Ordnance, and a new Boston division involved in gyro-related projects. Headed by Steve Keating, who would become CEO in 1974, Military Products Group aggressively developed an expanding product line and advanced the technologies of power systems, lasers and radiation, and training simulators. [27]

The rapid growth and diversification of the group's business was a direct result of government contracts, particularly in missile systems. By the time the Military Products Group was formed, Honeywell had "played an important

Above: The M739 point-detonating fuse was a staple of Honeywell's ordnance business until the late 1980s.

Below: From 20mm to 120mm calibers, Honeywell Ordnance Division mass produced a wide variety of ammunition. By 1981, the division had developed and produced over 200 million fuses.

role in nearly every missile project from weapons to atmospheric research."[28]

Honeywell continued to win government contracts, for it had a strong reputation that grew with every project, bolstered by an explicit commitment to research and development. In 1958, Honeywell established a Research Center in a former county poorhouse in Hopkins, Minnesota. In an article for *Missiles and Rockets*, Raymond Nolan reported that scientists at the new Hopkins facility were guided by only one rule: Their research must always be relevant to improvements in the field of automatic control.[29] The center supported basic research for all areas of the business, and employed 150 people. Once research had developed identifiable applications to a Honeywell business, it was turned over to the research section of the appropriate division. This commitment to research helped to ensure the continued health of the Military Products Group and by 1958 it had gross sales of $110 million, or one-third of the company's annual revenues. Most of this work concerned inertial guidance and missiles, along with development of improved gyroscopes. Nolan pointed out that "the subject of space flight and M-H participation in future programs has also been given considerable attention. Company planners see something around $22 million by 1962."[30]

The new group was well–positioned for the imminent space programs,[31] historian J. Michael Stapp noted: "The launch in October 1957 of the Soviet *Sputnik* caught America essentially by surprise: it signalled the beginning of the space race, and also pointed out to the American military that the USSR possessed intercontinental ballistic missile capability. In the U.S., immediate attention was placed upon military and space research and science education. Missile work, already in progress, was intensified." [32]

Gyroscopes

Honeywell engineers continued to work intensively on gyroscopes, since these precision instruments were at the heart of many of the company's navigational guidance systems and automatic controls. Throughout the 1950s, technicians experimented with a new device which came to be known as the Electrically Suspended Gyro (ESG). The idea was to create a gyroscope at the highest level of accuracy and durability, features important to preventing gyro "drift" or error over time. The ESG consisted "of a rotating ball suspended within a shell by means of electric fields. The absence of any wearing surfaces suggests extremely long and reliable operation, and the drift rate is so low that it makes testing difficult because the gyros must be operated for extremely long periods of time before the drift is great enough to be detectable."[33]

Design work began in 1957, and the Electrically Suspended Gyro was first built in 1959. The company hoped to develop the gyro for azimuth navigational systems in guided missiles like the Navy's Polaris system.[34]

By the early 1960s, Aero researcher Joe Kilpatrick was working to bring gyroscopes into yet another generation of development. Kilpatrick worked with beams of light in opposing directions. These light beams were sensitive to movement, like the spinning iron spheres in a traditional or Electrically Suspended Gyro. His work resulted in the invention of the Ring Laser Gyro (RLG), which went into production in 1966 with a laser gyro navigation system presented to the Navy at China Lake, California. The Ring Laser Gyro continued to undergo intensive de-

HONEYWELL

Honeywell's sonar technologies were state-of-the-art in 1970. This "Scanar 11-F Sonar" was used for oceanographic surveying, salvaging, and fishing.

velopment through the 1970s. "The RLG went though one of the longest and most complex cycles in Honeywell's history. But perfecting the concept has made Honeywell the world leader in new-generation gyro technology."[35] By the late 1970s, the RLG was ready for the commercial market. In 1978, Boeing awarded Honeywell a multi-million dollar contract for RLG navigational equipment for its 757 and 767 aircraft, and the Ring Laser Gyro became the center of the aircrafts' flight management system.[36]

Defense Systems Division was established in 1977 in response to a general trend toward increased government investment in ordnance and aviation products. This trend was a reversal of what had been a consistent decline in the appropriations that Congress had allocated for defense. Electrically Suspended Gyros were increasingly in demand, and Honeywell was awarded a contract to retrofit the nation's aging B-52 bombers with contemporary navigational and automatic flight controls.[37] In the 1980s, Honeywell Ring Laser Gyro equipment became standard equipment on many business jets. What most recommended the new technology was its low maintenance, coupled with its effectiveness. An RLG navigational system helped make it possible to reduce the

normal crew on a Boeing 757 by one, which reportedly caused a problem between airlines and unions.[38]

Throughout the Seventies, laser gyros were thought suitable only for short–range guided missile systems. They were eventually recognized as desirable for very long–range intercontinental ballistic missile (ICBM) systems as well, because of their rapid response time, insensitivity to shock, vibrations, and g-forces, and their ability to survive long periods of dormancy without any special environmental control. Honeywell believed laser gyros were capable of seriously competing with conventional ones by the 1990s. When executives proposed them for general use in most major ICBM guidance systems, the Air Force agreed. Unfortunately for Honeywell, the Air Force contracted with Litton, Raytheon, and Rockwell to further develop the idea.[39]

Ordnance: Applied Technologies And Military Contracts

When reactivated in the early Fifties for the Korean War, the Ordnance Division "basically picked up where its predecessor left off in 1945," producing fire control products, periscopes, ammunition, and fuses.[40] As the company expanded in all areas, Ordnance also grew, especially as the result of several acquisitions which diversified the company's defense interests.

In 1951, Minneapolis-Honeywell acquired the Intervox Company in Seattle, a small manufacturer of ship-to-ship telemetry and ultrasonic underwater systems. Executives felt the acquisition of Intervox positioned the company to enter the field of sonar, which would prove useful in future military contracts. Intervox eventually became Honeywell's Marine Equipment Division (MED). In 1955, corporate restructuring placed MED under the direction of Ordnance as a development laboratory specializing in military applications of radiation, sonar, ultrasonics, and telemetry.[41] In 1960, MED established a deep ocean research unit designed to study ocean mechanics, acoustics, magnetics, and thermodynamics.

Growth and diversification characterized the Ordnance Division through the Fifties, and by mid–decade, components for missiles, anti-aircraft gun controls, and underseas warfare equipment were added to production. Many highly-sensitive government programs were also awarded to the division during the decade. For example, the top–secret Wag Tail project for the Navy and Air Force involved a low–altitude bombing system, a predecessor to the sophisticated technology of the cruise missile.

Right: Honeywell's MK-46 torpedo, an efficient and reliable product for over three decades, in production in 1985.

Below: Honeywell's MK-46 torpedo was called "the world's most widely used torpedo" in 1986. Here, one is launched from a Honeywell test craft.

Perhaps Ordnance's most important contract, however, began in 1956. The Anti-Submarine Rocket (ASROC) was a prime contract for the Navy, for the development and production of a rocket-assisted anti-submarine weapon with sonar for detecting targets. It reached full production in 1959 and was fleet–operational by 1961. The success of ASROC led directly to other important military contracts, such as the Polaris MK–11 sub-launched missile in 1962.[42] Four years later, Honeywell won prime contracts with the Navy for the lightweight torpedo MK-46, one of the longest-running weapons programs in company history, continuing in production for more than 20 years. "They considered, always, in the Navy, the Mark 46 as the mark of reliability," Ed Lund recalled with pride. "The best thing for the buck."[43]

By 1967, as elements of its work were seen to have commercial applications, Marine Systems once again received full division status. One exciting new product was a ship positioning system that combined underwater technologies with the familiar field of navigation and inertial reference, using acoustics to help a ship maintain position at sea. The system quickly became standard equipment on thousands of vessels worldwide, and led to a more refined system of the same nature—The Automatic Station Keeping system (ASK), developed by 1970.

Aerospace And Defense Group

In 1966, Military Products Group business accounted for a quarter of all Honeywell sales. A number of key government programs had begun to wind down, and Ordnance materiel orders had begun to slacken due to the possible cessation of hostilities in Vietnam. But the commercial facets of the company's defense and aerospace business remained lucrative nonetheless, especially in avionics and marine products. The Military Products Group was renamed the Aerospace and Defense Group in 1967, to reflect evolving technologies and changing markets. At the same time, the Aeronautical division became the Aerospace division. This section of the company continued developing and

For many decades Honeywell was a leading developer and manufacturer of simulators for the military. These systems provided training in aircraft maintenance, sonar procedures, submarine operation and strategy, and many other technologically sophisticated environments.

In 1972, Honeywell's Government and Aeronautical Products Division developed a helmet-mounted targeting sight which allowed pilots to take aim by simply looking at their target. A computer processed head movements of the pilot and translated them into electronic fire control commands.

marketing flight controls, gauges, engine controls, altimeters, and proximity–warning equipment. Commercial sales of avionics equipment showed marked improvement in the late Sixties. In 1969 Honeywell contracted with Douglas to provide for the first major commercial installation of digital avionics in the new DC-10, and Boeing placed a substantial order for altitude alert indicators for its 727 and 737 aircraft.

In the area of marine systems, the company continued to excel throughout the 1970s. In 1967, the Marine Systems Center had been formed from the company's Seattle and West Covina, California operations, and acoustics and sonar research continued. However, an important new business was also developing. For some time, Honeywell had been designing and manufacturing training simulators like the Space Cabin, along with many other avionics-oriented trainers, and navigation training complexes were prepared and sold to the Navy. Sonar signal processor operations were the subject of another training simulator, giving the company entree into the air anti-submarine market. Marine Systems Center experienced rapid growth in the late Sixties, and reached divisional status in 1973.

In the early Seventies, the Systems and Research Division became a center for inquiry. The center worked for most of the decade on laser navigation devices, as well as on a helmet-mounted sight which allowed a helicopter pilot to define a target while still keeping his hands on the controls. Developed for the Army's Cheyenne helicopter project, the helmet sight linked a pilot's head movements with a camera outside the cockpit, allowing him to define a target simply by turning his head to it. This was, in effect, an early form of virtual reality, especially when the cameras were upgraded to infrared models allowing the pilot to "see" at night.

While Honeywell was helping the United States compete with the Soviet Union, a few salesmen were helping the Soviet Union in an unexpected, and illegal, way. During the 1970s industrial espionage was common with the Russians, said Roger Jensen, a lawyer with Honeywell since 1951. The Russians were eager to obtain specialized equipment in order to learn about American technology.

> "In 1975 we had one salesman on the inside and then there were four other people on the outside ordering expensive, sophisticated hardware to manufacture semi–conductors and importing them into Germany from the United States ostensibly to be used by Honeywell in Germany. But in fact it was never intended for Honeywell and this was all done in a way to obscure the transaction from Honeywell management.... Maybe a $100,000 machine would be the normal selling price but the Russians in those days were willing to pay one or two million dollars for the same machine.... Eventually all these people were arrested and it was sort of a James Bond type thing. ... At the time it was deemed very important... a few machines actually got to Germany and then were transported by truck to Zurich, Switzerland and then they travelled by air to Moscow. Fortunately, we caught it. There was a lot of other stuff in the order pipeline that hadn't gone all the way so we got it chopped off....Honeywell got a small fine but was praised for cooperating with the commerce department."[44]

Space

Many of Honeywell's technological resources were directed to the ultimate expression of the nation's scientific goals, the space program. This was a natural outgrowth of the company's flight control work, coupled with postwar Ordnance work on guided missiles. In fact, the company was a contractual participant in nearly every manned and unmanned U.S. space enterprise.

Begun as a response to the Cold War in general, and the Soviet *Sputnik* launch in particular, America's space program brought together its best scientists, engineers, technicians and planners. America was investing a tremendous amount of capital in companies like Honeywell with critical technological resources. The National Aeronautics and Space Administration (NASA) pointed out that this investment brought clear payoffs down to Earth as well, in the form of technological breakthroughs which

would have a profound impact on everyday life. Among these breakthroughs, NASA noted, were the rechargeable heart pacemaker, telecare emergency medical system, oxygen–hydrogen fuel cells, and computer image enhancement.

"The enormous technical and scientific advances needed to land men on the moon and return them safely to Earth," NASA stressed, "required the pioneering of new frontiers not only in the aerospace field but also in the wide variety of disciplines ranging from astronomy to zoology. It is generally agreed that this accelerated national effort compressed into roughly a decade the normal technological advances of several."[45]

Honeywell products helped guide spacecraft, missiles and satellites. "I believe I can say our

HONEYWELL

The "Integrated Helmet and Display Sighting System" carried virtual reality-type technologies into the 1980s by providing pilots with night imaging.

products are on probably just about every vehicle you can name, certainly in the United States and a lot of them outside the United States," said John Dewane, president of Honeywell's Space and Aviation Control business.[46] In the 60s, he worked in the Military Products Group in Texas when the Houston Space Center was being formed. "We had a lot of equipment on *Gemini*, on *Apollo*, a lot on Space Shuttles, a lot on the Space Station, so those are of interest to a lot of us in Honeywell, particularly in the early days of making launches."[47]

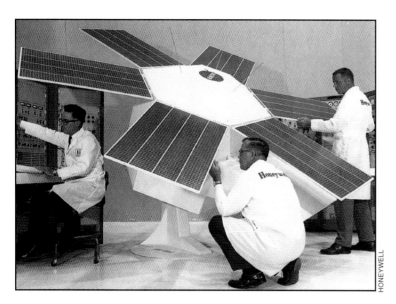

In 1966-1967, Honeywell developed its Orbital Scanner program for NASA's Langley Research Center. Here, Honeywell engineers work with a display mockup of the horizon-mapping vehicle.

"It was a time of tremendous energy and tremendous ideas. I remember talking to one of the guys in planning and he got to telling me about how you got a person to the moon, to land on the moon. One way you could do it, you'd put another little vehicle in the capsule, and then when the capsule was orbiting around the moon this little vehicle would come out and it would sprout legs and a couple of guys would go in it and they'd go land on the moon and they'd walk on the moon. ... I thought I had a loony on my hands. I thought the guy had one too many beers. Well, it turns out that's exactly what we did. But those were the days when people were coming up with ideas like you had never heard before." [48]

A number of projects helped pave the way to major contracts with NASA. The company had, in fact, been inching ever closer to space development. In 1958, Honeywell participated in Vanguard, "America's first earth satellite successfully launched."[49] In 1963, the company participated in an experiment called "APRE," which consisted of "a very large, high performance camera installed in a 3,000 lb. gondola and carried by a balloon to altitudes of 80,000 to 100,000 feet." The experiment was designed to "determine the effects of atmospheric turbulence on high altitude photography."[50] The company also developed a space cabin simulator for the U.S. Air Force School of Aviation Medicine, which could house two people for up to 30 days in a sealed environment.

In 1964 the newly formed Systems and Research Division won a contract to develop, design, and deliver a complete space vehicle. Called "Scanner," it was Honeywell's first prime contract for a space-related project. Willis Berry, an engineer in the Systems and Research Division, notes that the division was originally organized for the express purpose of pursuing Scanner and other space contract opportunities.

The Scanner project was a $2.8 million "spin–stabilized suborbital vehicle." Honeywell was responsible for all of the spacecraft systems, structures, guidance and control, telemetry, and power, which meant integrating all the system components of propulsion, payload instruments, booster, and launch complex. Scanner was designed to be launched at an 80–degree angle 400 kilometers into the stratosphere, and its payload of a star mapper and radiometer would scan the earth's atmosphere "to measure the natural radiation gradients which define earth's horizon." It was successfully launched twice in 1966 from Wallops Island off the coast of Virginia. Honeywell later developed a second Scanner project, Orbital Scanner, which was cancelled before it could be completed.

"We thought we were going to go into a lot of space work," said engineer Berry. "Honeywell Aero Division was making noises that they wanted

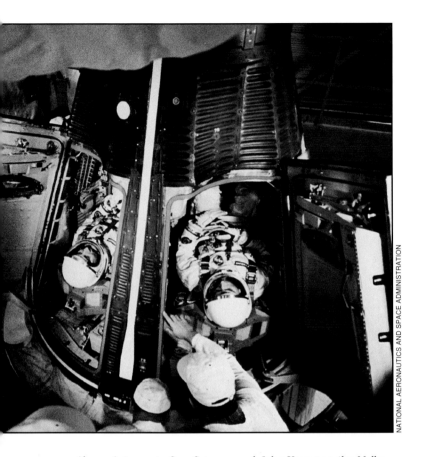

NATIONAL AERONAUTICS AND SPACE ADMINISTRATION

Above: Astronauts Gus Grissom and John Young on the *Molly Brown* before the first two-man mission into space in 1965. Honeywell technology and equipment were critical to the mission's success.

Left: Honeywell equipment was aboard the Vanguard, launched in 1958. The Vanguard was the nation's first successful earth satellite.

"May 17, 1965

Attention: Mr. W.T. Noll, Vice President and General Manager of Aeronautical Division

Dear Mr. Noll:

On the morning of March 23, 1965, a few minutes after 7 o'clock, we rode an elevator the 90 feet up the side of the Gemini-Titan II launch vehicle and entered our spacecraft "Molly Brown" for our first two-man mission into space. We had spent months of intensive training and a lot of people had spent years of hard work and extra effort to produce for us the best possible equipment. We were ready and so was GT-3.

It is difficult to single out one piece of hardware or one supplier to throw bouquets to, but one thing we know for sure; those critical items, some fifty-four of them, installed in the booster, performed flawlessly. Such performance is an absolute necessity for success.

We believe that the man–rating and Zero Defects programs, practiced by Martin Company and Honeywell Inc., as a critical part supplier, contributed immeasurably to our space venture. We also believe that all the "tender loving care" you put into the fabrication, assembly, and test of the GT-3 has culminated in a launch that was an unqualified success.

May we extend our sincere appreciation to you and to all your people for your extra efforts and outstanding contributions. We know you realize that you are a very important part of our team. We would also like to ask your continued dedication to the production of perfect equipment. We are just beginning. Let's have the same and more on GT-4.

Sincerely,

Gus Grissom
John Young

to get into the systems business. Now to them this meant becoming the prime contractor. So they pursued this era of spacecraft because it had a lot of attitude controls and things that they'd been working on for years and they thought they could use this background to expand into space systems."[51]

The next contract Honeywell sought after Scanner was "Earth Resources," intended to launch sophisticated sensing equipment into orbit. But Honeywell had to compete with General Electric to get the contract, and a successful bid would have necessitated a substantial cash outlay which company executives were unwilling to make. Instead, the company decided to forego prime contracts, and concentrate instead on sub-contract work. This strategy only enhanced its space technology reputation, as evidenced by a note of thanks from astronauts on the *Titan-Gemini* mission in 1965.

Other Gemini and Apollo programs followed in short order, with contracts for flight and stabilization controls, cockpit displays, and training and ground support. [52] *Jane's All the World's Aircraft* noted in 1969 that Honeywell "has contributed to more than 90 per cent of the U.S. space vehicles successfully orbited... and is currently involved in nearly every major civilian and military space effort, both manned and unmanned."[53] That same year, Honeywell teamed with McDonnell-Douglas to "provide attitude reference and control equipment" for Skylab. In fact, Honeywell has contributed to every manned space flight launched by the United States. Throughout the Seventies, the company helped develop digital flight controls and computer systems for the nation's first reusable, winged spacecraft, the Space Shuttle. In 1977, Honeywell systems performed flawlessly in Space Shuttle trial flights, and 1981 saw the first successful flight of *Columbia.* Honeywell digital flight control systems

Honeywell controls are used extensively throughout America's Space Shuttle program, including such precise control systems as the Manned Maneuvering Unit (MMU) shown in the cargo bay of a recent shuttle mission.

NATIONAL AERONAUTICS AND SPACE ADMINISTRATION

allowed manual and automatic control of the shuttle's flight, and the Honeywell main engine controller allowed full throttling control for the rocket engines during lift–off.[54]

Honeywell continued its participation in space programs throughout the 1970s. Scanning equipment for Skylab experiments was produced, as well as sun-sensing guidance devices for Pioneer 10, the 1973 probe which completed a successful fly-by of Jupiter. Honeywell guidance equipment also helped land the Viking spacecraft on the surface of Mars in 1976.[55]

Steve Keating remembers the space contracts with pride. "Our people could be proud. Back then, during Vietnam, it was hard to be really proud. Our employees were all loyal and dedicated and this was a time when we were all kind of heroes. We were doing something that everybody agreed was important."[56]

Honeywell In The Movies

Honeywell's reputation as a space age company had become such that management was approached by a young film maker named Stanley Kubrick in 1966. Kubrick was hoping to consult with company scientists and engineers on technical aspects of a new movie he was making entitled *2001: A Space Odyssey.* Honeywell responded by assigning four engineers to the project, and they spent several months researching and drafting fictional technologies like anti-gravity suits and

Above: The cockpit of every NASA Space Shuttle has been equipped with numerous Honeywell controls, including main engine and automatic flight controls.

Below: The Manned Mobile Unit (MMU) in action outside a Space Shuttle. Astronaut Bruce McCandless was able to maneuver as far as 90 meters away from the space craft with this Honeywell–controlled device.

NATIONAL AERONAUTICS AND SPACE ADMINISTRATION

The Space Shuttle *Endeavour* was launched January 13, 1993. Honeywell control systems have been used by NASA's shuttle program for more than 20 years.

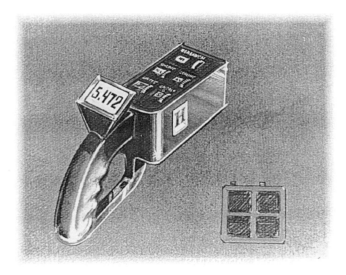 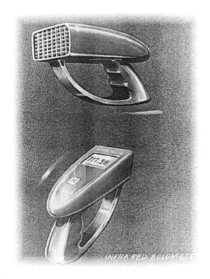

In 1966, Honeywell was asked to provide technical guidance for the movie *2001: A Space Odyssey*. Four engineers spent several months coming up with fictional technologies like the "Radiation Monitor" (Left) and "Infrared Bolometer".

radiation guns. Perhaps Honeywell's most important contribution, however, related to detailing characteristics of HAL, the computer which played a central role in the drama. When the engineering team had completed its work, lead engineer David Stubbs flew to London with a one–inch-thick notebook, which he turned over to Kubrick and screenplay writer Arthur C. Clarke during a consultation on the set.[57] The movie, of course, went on to become a screen classic, an enduring cinematic salute to high technology.

Honeywell computers were also featured in *Modesty Blaise,* a 1966 movie in which an H–200 selected clothes and accessories for a female spy. In 1967's *The Billion Dollar Brain,* an H–200 was portrayed as the heart of a vast computer complex.[58]

The Eighties: A Time of Growth

The company's defense and avionics concerns were riding the crest of a resurgence in military spending which would peak during the Reagan administration. In 1981, Aerospace and Defense Group revenues exceeded $1 billion for the first time. In 1983, President Reagan pledged to increase military spending with a five-year, $1.8 trillion expansion. Reagan's pledge came at a time when the job of one of every ten Americans was dependent on the defense industry. Defense accounted for 10 percent of U.S. manufacturing,

and employed more than 25 percent of the country's scientists and engineers, and the Pentagon was the single largest purchaser of goods and services in the nation.[59] Some analysts grew concerned that the U.S. economy was becoming too dependent on defense. This concern extended to a growing discomfort about the escalating arms race, the proliferation of nuclear weapons, and the spending of tax revenues for weapons of mass destruction. As defense spending increased, protests from concerned citizen's groups became more vocal. For the first time, Honeywell was called upon to answer critics who charged that the company was profiting from warfare. Starting in 1968, a group of protesters calling themselves "The Honeywell Project" regularly staged demonstrations at Honeywell World Headquarters in Minneapolis. The Honeywell Project consisted of several hundred anti–war activists from the Minneapolis-St. Paul area who regularly sponsored protests at the company's annual meetings, and on Honeywell property. Its purpose was to pressure Honeywell to stop research, development, and production of all weapons systems, though many observers believe the group simply wanted publicity. H.W. Sweatt's strongest fear, the "war monger" label," was coming back to haunt the company. (A full discussion of the Honeywell Project is contained in Chapter Nine.)

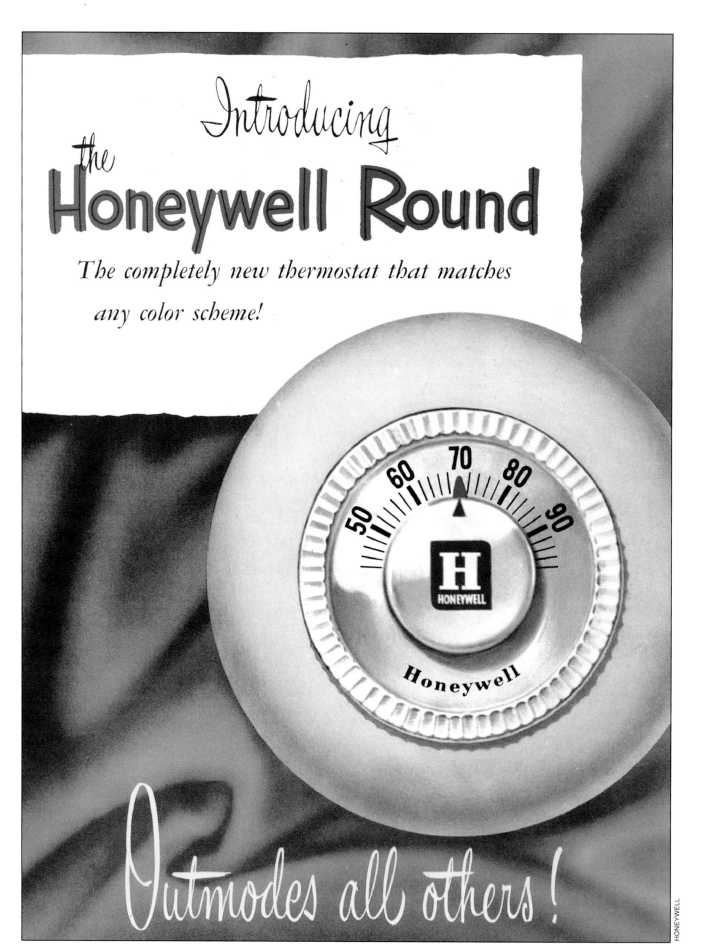

The Honeywell Round™ remains the most popular thermostat in the world. Introduced in 1953, it was a dramatic change from the boxy thermostats of the past.

CHAPTER SIX

THE RESTLESS SPIRIT

"Nobody has been able to copy it. They've come close and then it's gotten to the point that the good people who lasted in the business didn't really want to copy it because everybody said, 'well, it's just another copy. What about another real thing?'"

— former CEO Steve Keating, on the Honeywell Round

On rainy Saturday morning in the spring of 1954, H.W. Sweatt went to the offices of Minneapolis-Honeywell hoping to catch up on some work. Instead, he found himself meditating on his company, his role in it and its reasons for success. He also considered areas that could stand improvement. He developed his thoughts into a speech he delivered to Micro Switch Division executives and salespeople on April 13, 1954. It was a defining moment for both the company and the man.

"To me, one of our greatest weaknesses and one that I think is growing in this company is a failure to keep 'a spirit of restlessness' fully alive in our organization. Some of our people, as they have matured in age and responsibilities, tend to be content with things as they exist today. But in too many places they do not have the time or the mental energy to do the thinking, planning, and imagining that must be done to protect the future of the company – not next year, but in the decades that lie ahead. They tend to overlook that constant change is inherent in every business picture, and that an organization that can't change and lead the way to the new and improved can in the process of time only wither and die – no matter how efficient its present administration may be."

"As for me, while I always want to strive for perfection and never want to be satisfied with less, if I had to choose, I would prefer to settle for a little less perfection today and a little more imagining for tomorrow, recognizing that in this spirit of restlessness we are bound to make mistakes and sacrifice some immediate profits over what we could do if we just sit tight on what we have today."[1]

Sweat considered this spirit of restlessness, "one of our most priceless and fundamental possessions." Not only should the company constantly seek new product lines and markets, but all Honeywell employees should devote part of their daily effort to creative thinking about Honeywell's long-term future. Honeywell would guarantee continued success by making an investment in imagination.

Preparing for the End of War

Even before World War II ended, H.W. Sweatt was considering the company's future. In a speech to company foremen six months before V-E Day, he paused to assess the company's war record.

"I could stand here and list our war achievements one by one and praise many individuals in the organization for outstanding work. I could read letters of commendation that have been received from various generals, other officers, departments of our government and individuals, but I think the following quotation from a report sent in by one of the divisions of the war department sums up your record pretty well:

'The company has made an outstanding record both in pioneering and the production of fire control equipment. In the earlier period of armament expansion, when ordnance was urgently seeking facilities capable of producing highly complicated material, the company, because of the calibre of its engineering and production skill in other work, was asked to enter this new and strange field. Results, however, have proved the soundness of that selection, and the ability of Minneapolis–Honeywell, as a part of American industry, to meet extraordinary difficulties.'"[2]

H.W. quickly proceeded to the heart of his speech, the post–war activities of the company and the new markets he hoped to penetrate. In June 1945, Sweat appointed a "post war planning committee" headed by his brother C.B. and consisting of six top executives. This group was charged with surveying the company's major markets past and present, as well as evaluating its product lines and engineering directions. It was asked to detail two specific objectives for the post–war economy: increasing the company's business in fields already being served, and cultivating new markets. The goal was to install more and better home heating controls in homes from coast to coast.

The primary vehicle was to be the new Moduflow system, which had been so successful in its metamorphosis as the C-1 automatic pilot. By April 1945, the company had kicked off a nationwide ad campaign for Moduflow, generating more than 5,000 customer inquiries per week.[3] A handful of engineers had been kept busy throughout the war working on designs for post–war controls, and in 1947 they were ready to unveil a brand new Chronotherm. Designers were also returning to a program for a revolutionary new thermostat which had been shelved during the war. By 1953, the Honeywell Round would be ready to transform the post–war home.

In addition to an evolving line of home and commercial heating controls, Sweat was eager to explore new markets, particularly within the fastest-growing sector of the economy, transportation. He envisioned Minneapolis-Honeywell expanding into the new fields of automatic controls for heating and cooling of railroad refrigerator cars, passenger jets, and even automobiles. The company had already participated in a number of high-profile installations on luxury ocean-liners, as

C.B. Sweatt headed the executive committee, which was charged, in 1945, with charting Honeywell's course in the rapidly expanding post–war economy.

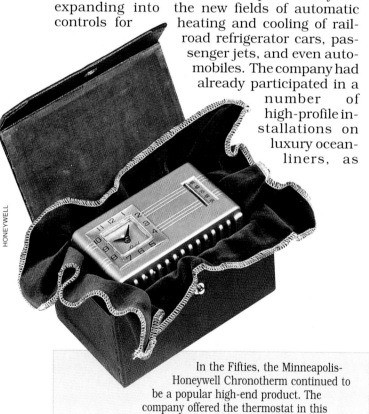

HONEYWELL

In the Fifties, the Minneapolis-Honeywell Chronotherm continued to be a popular high-end product. The company offered the thermostat in this sumptuous gift box lined with black velvet.

well as some sales to passenger airlines in the midst of the war.[4]

In the 1960s Charlie Sweat Jr. worked in the Apparatus Controls Division, which made products for industrial and agricultural markets. The products were designed to withstand the grueling conditions of factories and farms. Sweat would throw thermostats against walls to prove they would not break. He remembered how the small sales force kept the division profitable. "We were a bunch of mavericks," he said. "We never followed the rules at all. We would steal any sales we could get our hands on. We made sure that the telephone operators always had plenty of candy so that any phone call that didn't have a place, we got it." [5]

Post War Reality Check

H.W. Sweatt reminded employees that Honeywell had its origins in a peacetime economy, and to that economy it must eventually return. Just following V-E Day, he commented, "While we are geared for war and shall not let down for one minute until we have met every one of our obligations to the men in the Pacific... at the same time it is our responsibility to plan for peace."[6]   Sweat was anxious to return to the civilian market because he predicted a dramatic post-war expansion and spectacular growth in housing and transportation markets.[7]

Unfortunately, it was easier to recognize this pent up demand than to satisfy it, as the company would soon discover. The problem with conversion to a civilian economy was that critical raw materials were still withheld by a tremendous government bureaucracy. Despite the best efforts of its leadership, the company went through a painful period of readjustment, resulting in numerous layoffs and delayed contracts.

Executives did their best to paint an optimistic picture. Paul Wishart, who was being groomed by H.W. Sweatt to take his place at the helm of the company, reassured employees, saying "the company is moving as rapidly as possible into production of civilian goods and that by July 1 it is expected more M–H instruments will be scheduled than have been made since the beginning of 1945." Wishart was optimistic, saying that shortages of raw materials were eclipsed by a more serious shortage faced by all industry. American companies were suffering from a significant need for automatic controls—a need that would be satisfied by Minneapolis-Honeywell.[8]

> "Many industries and production programs are approaching bottlenecks today, because of the lack of automatic control instruments. Air conditioners, oil burners, stokers and gas burners are just a few of the industries and processes dependent upon automatic control, and therefore Honeywell, along with others in the industry, expects that the government will soon release the needed supplies of metals and other materials. Meanwhile, the layoffs are a necessary part of reconversion."[9]

A New President

In 1953, H.W. Sweatt left the presidency and became board chairman. Paul Wishart became the first president who was not a Sweat or Honeywell. Herb Bissell, retired marketing vice president, remembers that Wishart was "a somewhat surprising choice, coming out of production."[10] But, he added, "I thought Paul, during his tenure, did a workmanlike job"[11]

In 1972, when Bissell retired, H.W. wrote a letter ruminating on his own retirement.

> "It isn't an easy adjustment and it takes time. ...After 15 years I miss as much as ever the excitement of the daily grind at the office, as I now realize there was always something stirring there and something interesting going on."

> "For a long, long time I have had grave doubts about this 65 retirement rule. ...I suppose the main excuse for it is to make room for the people underneath so they don't become too impatient about their lack of moving forward. This is certainly something that has to be borne in mind. Sometimes I think this is vastly overrated, particularly in newer growth companies where natural increase in business and progress is always taking place. Look at Honeywell's growth from around [$]100 million a year in the late 40s or early 50s to approximately $2 billion and its relatively similar increase in employment."[12]

Growth In Every Direction

The lean times soon ended. In the decade following the war, the company's business expanded in every direction. A 1955 newspaper story commented, "In the past decade

Paul Wishart (standing) became the president of Honeywell in 1953. For the first time in the company's history, a Sweatt or a Honeywell was not in the president's seat. H.W., however, was a guiding presence on the board of directors for many years to come.

Ray Alvarez, vice president and group executive, Sensing and Control, which includes Micro Switch. "Micro Switch clearly has a tremendous future," he said.

high tech aeronautical devices. A decade later, it had entered the novel fields of computers, microelectronics, space exploration, atomic energy, submarine warfare and telemetry, and a growing list of other "space age" projects.

And it wasn't just new markets and products causing the expansion. Traditional product lines continued to grow as well. In the decade from 1945 to 1955, total employment rose from 8,628 to 25,000. The company invested $48 million in plants and equipment during the period, and sales nearly tripled, from $84 million to $244 million. Honeywell was hardly alone in this growth, as many American corporations were experiencing similar phenomena during this period. President Paul Wishart and Vice President Tom McDonald noted that General Motors had grown by five times, while GE had grown 3.2 times larger. 3M grew by a factor of 3.1, Westinghouse by 4.4, and RCA grew a whopping 6.3 times larger.[14]

Micro Switch

In 1950, the company purchased the Micro Switch Corporation of Freeport, Illinois. As its name implies, this company was engaged in manufacturing the "simplest form of control system," the switch.[15] The division manufactures switches, sensors, manual controls and fiber-optic products. These products detect presence, position, motion, color, shape, level, flow, pressure and temperature.

[Honeywell] has grown so fast, entered so many new fields and come up with so many new products that it can truly be said the company lives for the future."[13] At war's end, the company was just reverting production back to thermostats, limit controls, valves, pyrometers, and the like, complemented by a handful of

Honeywell purchased Micro Switch Corporation in 1950. The company, based in Freeport, Illinois, was once called a "gold mine" by H.W.

Also known as the T-86, the Honeywell Round™ redefined modern automatic control for the post-war home. Until the Round was introduced in 1953, thermostats tended to be coffin-shaped. In its advertising, Honeywell took advantage of the featured removable exterior ring, which could be painted to match any decor.

In 1994, Micro Switch served more than 300,000 customers around the world with products found everywhere from the home to the Space Shuttle. Micro Switch products are used on automobiles, airplanes, appliances, photocopy machines, facsimile machines, vending machines, hospital equipment, air conditioning systems and more. The switches can handle extreme temperatures and harsh environments. "Our specialty is harsh environments like factory floors where you've got bits of metal flying at you all day long," said Ray Alvarez, who heads the division, which is part of Industrial Control. "Or an aircraft that's sitting on the ground in Phoenix at 130 degrees, and gets up in minutes to minus 70 degrees."[16]

Many Micro Switch products are sold directly to manufacturers. The division makes trackballs for computer mice, motion sensors, fiber optic components, pressure sensors, and more. It produces and ships about 165 million switches a year, about 10 percent of which are sold to other Honeywell divisions. "One of the missions of Micro Switch is to supply other divisions of Honeywell with switches and sensors," Alvarez said. Worldwide, Micro Switch has about 12 percent of the switch market. "We have a very strong position in the United States," he said.[17] "Micro Switch clearly has a tremendous future. We're going into the 21st Century in a very robust way." [18]

The Round

Another product emerging in the Fifties had been in progress before the war. In 1953, the company introduced the world to the T-86 "Round" thermostat, which replaced chunky, rectangular models. It was an immediate success, and has remained in production ever since, with roughly a million sold every year. The T-86 became synony-

Carl Kronmiller (left) was the man responsible for the development of the Honeywell T-86 "Round" thermostat. Begun in 1943, the Round was shelved for the war effort. It was revived in 1953, when it went into production and met with spectacular success.

The world famous Honeywell T-86 Round in production in 1970.

mous with Honeywell, and can still be found on more household walls than any other thermostat worldwide. Considered industrial art, the Honeywell Round is scheduled to go on display in 1997 at the Cooper-Hewitt National Design Museum, Smithsonian Institution. Russell Flinchum, guest curator at the museum, said the exhibit will honor the work of renowned industrial designer Henry Dreyfuss, who holds the design patent for the Round. The unique thermostat, one of the most recognizable designs in the world, is critical to the exhibit, Flinchum said.

Inventor Carl Kronmiller first saw a round thermostat in the 1920s when he was chief design engineer for Time–O–Stat controls, which manufactured a round thermostat in 1928. When Minneapolis-Honeywell bought the company in 1931, the model was dropped. Kronmiller, who moved to Minneapolis with the acquisition, started working on a new round thermostat in 1940.[19] According to Charles Hoyt, a personnel employee who retired in 1964, Kronmiller was angry that Dreyfuss, a consultant on the project, got the design patent for the Round.

"[Kronmiller] told me quite frankly that H.W. came to his area one day in 1940, sat down on his desk, and they talked about products. Carl told H.W., 'We need a radically new thermostat. Why can't we make something a lot different from our competitors' models?' As they talked, H.W. picked

up a piece of paper and started drawing circles on it. He handed the paper to Carl and said, 'Here. Go ahead and make something of it.'"[20]

The project was interrupted by World War II, but resumed in 1946. After a series of starts and stops the design almost languished on an engineering shelf, said Herb Bissell, Honeywell's marketing vice president until 1972. He described how he resurrected the project in a 1993 letter to the Smithsonian. He wrote that when he was hired in 1950,

> *"There was nothing to promote to consumers other than the current wall thermostat. It was a plain–Jane rectangular box with no distinctiveness from the competition. It was tough, if not impossible, to merchandise. One day I learned there was an old clay model of round design gathering dust on a shelf in the Engineering department. I went to see Charles B. Sweat, brother of Harold and Executive Vice President, and explaining our marketing dilemma, asked for permission to see what we could do with the round model.*
> *The lead Heating Controls engineers was Carl Kronmiller. He welcomed my visit while claiming the round design was really his idea rather than that of Henry. In any event, Henry Dreyfuss and his people cooperated to improve and simplify the clay model, eliminating the slot feature of the original."[21]*

Dean Randall, who retired in 1985 as vice president of communications, supports Bissell's story. "Herb Bissell took this original design ... and saw in it a device to move us one giant step forward," he said.[22]

Minneapolis-Honeywell's Wabash, Indiana plant in about 1945. After the company merger in 1927, Wabash became headquarters for oil burner controls and research. Mark Honeywell retained his office in Wabash as the company's president until 1934, when H.W. Sweatt took over.

In 1965, Honeywell created the H.W. Sweatt Award to recognize its top scientists and engineers. This award was designed to encourage technical creativity.

Kronmiller and Dreyfuss share credit for T–86. The mechanical patent in Kronmiller's name was granted on January 3, 1956 and the design patent in Dreyfuss' name was granted January 17, 1956. Kronmiller was named "Inventor of the Year" in 1987 by the "Minnesota Intellectual Property Association." Dreyfuss, Bissell wrote, "suggested we tell the consumer to paint the removable exterior ring to match the decor of their walls. The idea represented an exciting visual opportunity for the use of color in our advertising and gave us a marketing feature not possessed by our competition."[23]

Executives went to the trouble to trademark the thermostat's distinctive shape, as well as the word "Round," always written with a capital R. "We stopped companies from making a round thermostat until the patent expired," said Clyde Blinn, who was in charge of patents. "And then we filed an application for the trademark—just for the looks of it. ...We went to about five cities and showed the Round thermostat with no marking and asked people on the street if they knew what it was. Then we went into heating dealers and said, 'Do you know what this is?' And I think we had about 99 and nine–tenths success on their knowing."[24] In 1987, a trademark was granted for the word "Round" and in 1990 a trademark was granted for the shape.[25]

Former CEO Steve Keating described the Round's introduction as a highlight in Honeywell

HONEYWELL

Honeywell places a great deal of importance on research and development of technologies. This is a clean room at Honeywell's ultra-modern Solid State Electronics Center in 1985.

history. "I always felt it was the symbolism that helped us take off in the home control business. Nobody has been able to copy it. They've come close and then it's gotten to the point that the good people who lasted in the business didn't really want to copy it because everybody said, 'Well, it's just another copy. What about another real thing?'"[26]

Kronmiller also invented a safety device that made it easier to light pilots in automatic gas systems. The safety pilot made it possible to avoid opening the main valve until the pilot was lit. "Probably, there's no home in the United States that doesn't have one or the other of his inventions," Blinn said.[27]

A Tradition of Inquiry

Technology depends upon the continuous advancement of scientific research, for the technologies of today are quickly supplanted by those of tomorrow. The company dependent upon high tech sophistication must resolve to make a serious investment in its scientific and engineering resources. It is an investment whose dividends, when paid at all, are often paid very far down the road. Honeywell has always viewed technological achievement as the lifeblood of the company, and such advancement depends upon the resourcefulness of people at research and development desks in every division. Jim Renier, Honeywell CEO from 1988 to 1993, commented that this commitment must thoroughly suffuse Honeywell management if the company hopes to continue its formidable tradition of growth and success. "We are a very high tech company," Renier said, "And we will become more so, not less. We're going to need a significant number of highly knowledgeable executives in [the year] 2000 to understand the explosion of technology that will be happening."[28]

Honeywell has enjoyed a long tradition of inquiry. When Minneapolis Heat Regulator merged with Honeywell Heating Specialties in 1927, company directors had established the Wabash, Indiana facility as a research division reporting directly to Mark Honeywell, himself the inventor of mercury valve technology. The Wabash center was disbanded during World War II, when the main plant focused on the production of optical instruments for the armed forces. In 1939, the famous "brain trusters" were convened, including Willis Gille, Russ Whempner, Gil Taylor, Bob Kutzler, and Hub Sparrow, and together they developed the technologies for the C-1 autopilot. Immediately after the war, an *ad hoc* research department was established under the directorship of Waldo Kliever, who had been involved in the early stages of the autopilot project and was the company's first Ph.D. Two groups of researchers eventually evolved, one in Aero, and the other a general Research Center, established in 1954. Honeywell research would go through many organizational changes over the years, and by the Eighties, each division would have its own research section. Whatever their organizational structure, research and development continued to remain a focal point of the company's future plans. As early as 1953, the company boasted that one of every ten Honeywell employees was a scientist or engineer directly involved with research.[29]

Bill McGoldrick, head of engineering during the middle years of the century, fit this mold perfectly. "He had all kinds of interests among which was developing talented inventors," recalled Jim Binger, CEO between 1964 and 1974. "He had a stable of them and he kept them in a back room where nobody could see them. But a number of us learned to appreciate what he had there, and he was inventive... I don't think he could screw in a light bulb himself, but he was very good in working with people who had bright ideas." [30]

In 1965, the company instituted the H.W. Sweatt Award, to recognize its top scientists and engineers for outstanding contributions to technological advancement. Award literature noted that "Honeywell was founded and shaped by inventive technical people... the H.W. Sweatt Awards for outstanding engineering and scientific achievement are designed to encourage this vital technical creativity."[31]

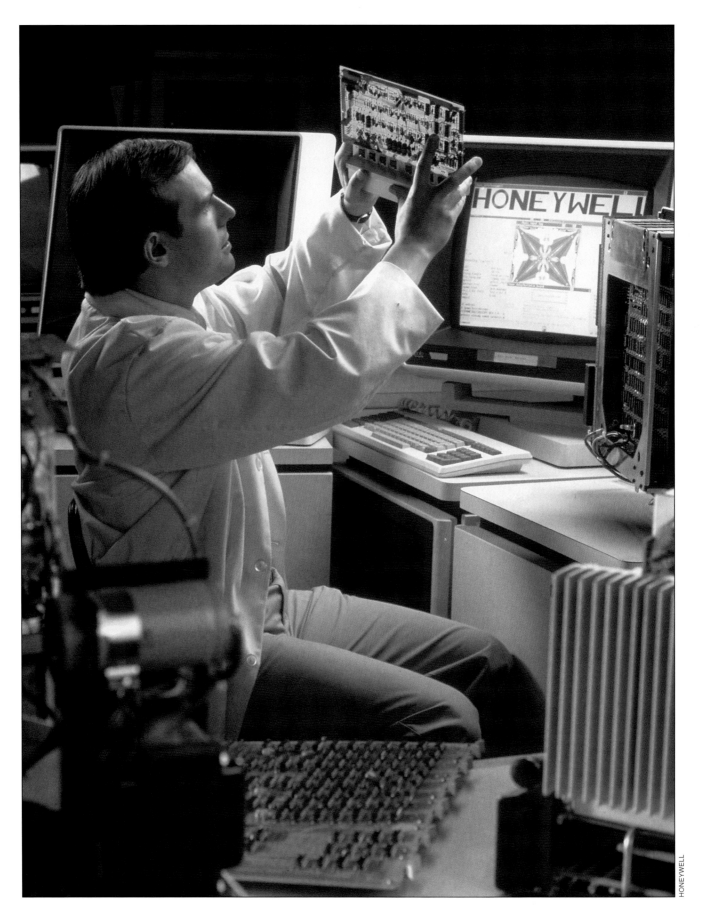

HONEYWELL

Despite many successes and innovations, Honeywell never found the right niche in the highly competitive computer market.
Eventually, the company realized that, as with space contracts, it was better to supply other manufacturers than compete with them.

CHAPTER SEVEN

THE NEW DIGITAL REALITY

"It was a field of technological application that could have an impact even greater than atomic energy as far as the business was concerned. In other words it was a field of great growth... We found that digital computers were a must in our future in many areas."

— Al Wilson, Aeronautical Division

omputers and fax machines, voice–mail and cellular phones, satellite dishes and CD players — today we rely on these innovations both at home and in the office. When digital computation became possible in the 1940s, a global revolution began changing the way we work and play. Honeywell played a major role in this revolution, with its pioneering work on computers and the new digital reality. Once Honeywell had re–established production for the civilian heating and air conditioning controls marketplace following World War II, H.W. Sweatt and his management team examined the potential of the emerging computer market.

An important technology born during the war was the electronic digital computer. Honeywell executives were curious about the invention's impact on the company's own markets and operations. What, exactly, could computers do? What could they do for engineering and business? And did they hold promise for a controls company like Honeywell?

Early Computers

Computers, if defined as mechanical devices for counting, have been around for thousands of years. The abacus, still used in parts of Asia, is a mathematically sophisticated computer (with a simple design) which has been in use for 4,000 years. In the West, the first mechanical devices for computation were developed by French inventor and philosopher Blaise Pascal in the 17th Century. Pascal designed and built a gear-driven adding machine which could add as many as eight columns. The German philosopher Gottfried Leibnitz improved upon Pascal's machine by designing one which could subtract, multiply, divide, and even extract square roots.

In the Nineteenth Century, Englishman Charles Babbage made his own contributions to the science of computers. To correct what he considered shoddy math in the Royal Society's astronomical and mathematical tables, he designed a "Difference Engine" and an "Analytical Engine." His "Analytical Engine," had it been produced, would have added, subtracted, multiplied, and divided. It would have been able to perform a series of operations in a predetermined sequence, as well as retain results for subsequent calculation. Incredibly, Babbage's mechanical computer had a memory of one thousand 50-digit numbers, as well as a printer. But like Da Vinci's flying machines, Babbage's machines never made it off the sketch pad. They were so far ahead of their time that they couldn't be built. Their constituent components did not exist, and manufacturing them from scratch would have been too costly.

What has come to be called the modern mechanical method of computation really has its origins at the Massachusetts Institute of Technology, where, in 1925, Dr. Vannevar Bush developed the first electric analog computer. An analog computer directly measures a variable such as speed or temperature, and continuously records changes through a mechanical or electrical analogy, like a speedometer or thermometer. Most analog computers are specific to a particular task. More general applications of computing machines required the development of techniques and machines dealing strictly in discrete numbers and values. In other words, digital technology would have to be developed before a general computer with variable applications could be invented.

In 1938, M.I.T. scientist Claude Shannon wrote a ground–breaking paper that paved the way to digital technology. "A Symbolic Analysis of Relay and Switching Circuits" described what Shannon saw as the fundamental compatibility of symbolic logic, positive and negative symbolic statements, with modern electrical network theory. This was the insight that hastened the dawn of the digital age, for it argued that electricity and electronics could be made to behave in logical ways, and that logical statements could be transmitted electronically.

In October of 1939, a mathematics professor at Iowa State College, John Vincent Atanasoff, along with graduate student Clifford Berry, developed a working bench model of a digital computer. The ABC (Atanasoff Berry Computer) was designed and built simply to make life a little easier for Atanasoff's math students. Yet it came to be known as the first electronic digital computer. During the late Thirties, Atanasoff was in contact with a University of Pennsylvania scientist named John Mauchly, who was fascinated with the possibility of digital computation. Four years after the ABC was born, Mauchly, with the help of J. Presper Eckert, built the first fully operational electronic digital computer. The Electronic Numerical Integrator and Computer (ENIAC) put Claude Shannon's ideas directly to work by using vacuum tubes that switched on and off, translating a binary numeric system into an electronic impulse. Developed to help with the arduous calculations of the Armed Forces' ballistic tables, it was partially funded by the government. The finished machine weighed 30 tons, contained 18,000 vacuum tubes, and cost $400,000.[1] ENIAC could perform 5,000 additions or subtractions a minute. In one hour, it could equal two months of production by 100 mathematicians using desk calculators. After the success of ENIAC, Mauchly and Eckert formed a computer company of their own, which was eventually bought by Sperry Rand.

Like the ABC, the Bush Difference Analyzer, and ENIAC, most early computers were designed for scientific research, while later machines extended the applications to other uses. UNIVAC, built in 1951 by Sperry Rand, was sold to the U.S. Census Bureau. It gained national attention when, on network television, it predicted the outcome of the 1952 presidential election between Eisenhower and Stevenson. The first fully operational systems like ENIAC and UNIVAC used vacuum tube technology and required huge power supplies and extensive cooling because of their high output of heat. But, amazingly, it would be only a matter of months before the next generation of digital computing machines ren-

dered the first generation obsolete. This was a period of dizzying technological change, when designs often became obsolete overnight, before they even made it off the drafting board.

Early Honeywell Computers

From one perspective, Honeywell's very first product, the Butz damper-flapper, was an analog computer. It transferred information from thermostat to furnace, dealing directly in the variable of room temperature. The Norden bombsight was a rather sophisticated analog computer that determined the time of bomb release according to the interaction of variables such as wind speed and direction. It processed the information, producing a useful, discrete result in much the same way a slide rule works. The Honeywell C-1 autopilot, of course, helped to make the Norden computer more accurate by eliminating human pilot error. Minneapolis-Honeywell developed a computer similar to the Norden bombsight in 1947, calling it the B-D computer. Developed by Hugo Schuck and Waldo Kliever, the B-D was designed to determine airline schedules by factoring wind speed, visibility, and other changing conditions of flight. It took its name from two of these variables— Bearing and Direction.

John Mauchly, the scientist who developed ENIAC with J. Presper Eckert, referred to electronic computers as control devices, because they controlled information, as early as 1941.[2] Apparently, H.W. Sweatt foresaw a close relationship between information management and environmental or industrial control.[3] Sweatt understood digital technology as the pure reduction of physical principles and processes to electronic binary numeric information. Just about anything could be distilled into "yes" or "no" logical statements and run through a vacuum tube. There appeared to be great opportunity for Minneapolis-Honeywell in this emerging field.

"It was probably around 1955 or '56 that the long-term significance of the computer business began to elevate itself in the minds of businessmen," Herb Bissell said. "They didn't know the first damn thing about computers, but there was this suspicion that a new world was lying out there."[4]

Back in 1950, the company's products employed electrical, pneumatic, and electronic systems for the automatic control of temperature, industrial processes, aircraft flight, and many other functions. Honeywell management saw that these early examples of automation were related to the use of the new digital technology to process and control the flow of information. And it was convinced that this technology would become vital in Honeywell's principle markets.[5]

H.W. Sweatt talked to University of Minnesota professor Athelstan Spilhaus, who informed him that "computers were the coming science—one that Honeywell should be in." Spilhaus and Honeywell executive Al Wilson were sent to Stanford University to consult with experts there. The Stanford group recommended entry into the computer market, with the caveat that Honeywell should be prepared to make a substantial long-term investment without expecting any significant immediate returns. Spilhaus and Wilson reported their findings to Honeywell's board of directors in December of 1954.[6] Al Wilson explained the company's interest as a natural evolution of its normal activities and product lines.

"For the last two decades," he noted in a 1961 memo, "electronics has been all important in our business. Electronic Data Processing, which uses electronics in an advanced form, is a most natural evolution for the talents of a large number of our 40,000 employees."[7] Though digital computers were a logical step in the process of improving automatic controls, it was a step that required a substantial investment. Computers require a high degree of skill in electronics. They require service, a commitment to developing software for computing, and educational activities to train customers and installers. Management reasoned that the investment was great enough to guarantee there wouldn't be a lot of competition.

"But over and above all these factors," said Wilson, "we saw that [Electronic Data Processing] held the promise of an extraordinary revolution in the paperwork area of business and in the scientific aspects of business. It was a field of technological application that could have an impact even greater than atomic energy as far as the business was concerned. In other words it was a field of great growth... We found that digital computers were a must in our future in many areas— our complex military systems for planes, missiles and satellites

were carrying us rapidly into airborne digital computers. Our industrial control systems for refineries and chemical companies were carrying us into digital process controls."[8]

By the mid Sixties, Honeywell's early faith in the importance of computers was born out with astonishing clarity. The computer industry grew at an annual rate of 36 percent between 1958 and 1965,[9] and *Forbes* called it "the most spectacular new business to appear since World War II."

Sweatt's vision was "that our business was sooner or later going to be computer driven, and he was right," said Dean Randall, former vice president of communications.[10]

Datamatic Corporation

As the result of its feasibility studies, Minneapolis-Honeywell formed a joint venture with the

John Vincent Atanasoff invented the first digital-electronic computer at Iowa State College in 1939. He was not generally credited until a lawsuit between Sperry and Honeywell updated the history of the modern computer.

Raytheon Corporation to develop and manufacture a digital computer for general business and scientific use. Headquartered in an old leather tannery building in Newton, Massachusetts, the new business was named Datamatic Corporation. Honeywell retained majority stock in a 60-

Thousands of blueprints were needed for the design and construction of Honeywell's first computer system, the D-1000. The finished product weighed 25 tons and took up 6,000 square feet.

40 ownership stake. The papers were signed on April 12, 1955 by Honeywell President Paul Wishart and Raytheon President Charles Adams. Honeywell executive John Wilson was named president of Datamatic, though he retired one year later. He was succeeded by Vice President and General Manager Walter Finke.

Honeywell soon found itself with majority interest in a company with no products and no customers. Raytheon, though, had considerable experience in computers. By tapping Honeywell's marketing and research expertise, the new venture proposed to use designs already developed by Raytheon for a "special purpose government computer" and adapt them for general purpose business applications.[11] This early machine, called the Raytheon Digital Automatic Computer (RAYDAC), had been developed under a contract with the U.S. Navy.

In addition to RAYDAC, Raytheon had made progress on a contract for the National Security Agency involving an advanced system for the storage of information on magnetic tape. The contract had been canceled, but Raytheon's development of the product continued. This cancellation in the midst of important breakthroughs was what prompted Raytheon to seek investors like Honeywell.[12]

Datamatic Corporation started business with about 200 employees, mostly engineers and mathematicians hired by Raytheon for government projects. This was a distinguished group of Harvard, M.I.T., and Aberdeen Proving Ground people. They were involved in the earliest breakthroughs in digital computing, including Harvard's Mark I, II, and III analog computers, ENIAC, EDVAC, and ORDVAC.[13]

Despite Honeywell's conclusions that high investment stakes would keep many companies out of the market, by 1960 a number of North America's largest corporations were jumping in, including General Electric, Westinghouse, Bendix, Burroughs, NCR, and RCA. Many companies were springboarding off the office machine market, giving them an advantage over Honeywell, which had no customer base in that line. "Honeywell provided a systems approach to problem solving, a tradition of customer service, a strong R&D orientation, and an imaginative, entrepreneurial management style. But it provided absolutely no existing base of office equipment customers."[14] Of course, this disadvantage became clear only later, when International Business Machines maintained a death grip on most of the market.

From the earliest days of its computer business, Honeywell approached the marketplace aggressively. Even before Datamatic's first computer was completed, Honeywell bought out Raytheon's interest. Raytheon had decided to "concentrate its resources on other areas of military-industrial activities."[15] The joint venture then became Datamatic Division of Minneapolis-Honeywell, and in 1960, the name was changed to Electronic Data Processing (EDP).

The Datamatic 1000

Datamatic's first computer was the D-1000, developed from 1955 to 1957. Scientists and engineers worked long hours preparing the first customer tests in October 1957, prompting Walter Finke to refer to Datamatic employees as "Sleepless Knights of the D-1000." The computer got its name when Finke told H.W. Sweatt that "it sounds bigger than 700," [IBM's most advanced product at the time].[16] The Datamatic D-1000 was a vacuum tube system costing $1.5 million, first sold and installed in 1957. It weighed 25 tons, and took up 6,000 square feet.

Though it was comparable to many other first generation vacuum tube computers, it did embody several technical innovations. The most important was the 3-inch magnetic tape storage system that Raytheon had been developing. The D-1000 used an air suction system which made magnetic tape storage much more reliable for digital computers. It was a relatively fast computer, with a 10 micro-second logical access time. It performed 4,000 11-digit additions per second, handled 10 tapes simultaneously, and boasted a printer which could print 900 characters per minute, and a punched card reader which could read 900 cards per minute.

Of course, the first complete D-1000 had a number of bugs which were worked out with time. Irma Wyman, a longtime Honeywell computer systems executive and Honeywell's first woman vice president, was one of the first console operators of Datamatic's flagship machine. "The D-1000 had an interesting characteristic," she recalled. "No matter what type or length of malfunction, as soon as the customer staffs walked in, the problems would disappear. The machine would work until they walked out, then it would promptly go down again! As console operator, I used to practice looking at the console typewriter in a calm manner nodding sagely, no matter what queer things came out."[17]

This first D-1000 was sold to Michigan Hospital Service (MHS) in Detroit in 1957. With 1.4 million subscribers, MHS was the second–largest Blue Cross organization in the country, conducting 25,000 transactions per day. The D-1000 was a welcome tool in the management of such a huge corporation. In 1958, installations were made for First National Bank of Boston, Baltimore and Ohio Railroad, County of Los Angeles, and the U.S. Treasury, along with two machines sold "in house" to Honeywell's home offices and to Datamatic itself. Michigan Hospital Service's D-1000 operated for the next seven years, until it was replaced by a later Honeywell model. The fact that Honeywell sold only seven D-1000's wasn't troubling. Company officials had anticipated that the first systems would be a hard sell, given Honeywell's limited experience as a computer manufacturer. Irma Wyman recalled, "We had to do a lot of selling just to get in the door. People thought of Honeywell as a thermostat company. We had to provide customers with very detailed explanations because, in most cases, we were proposing data processing concepts that had never been attempted before."[18]

Marketing vice president Herb Bissell said selling those early computers was a difficult task. "Getting a second or third line company into a million–dollar expenditure or greater was a tough selling task and there was a lot of courage shown,"

The first generation Honeywell computer, the Datamatic D–1000, was introduced in 1955. It came equipped with a powerful air conditioner, needed to keep the computer and surrounding area from overheating.

he recalled. The problem was intensified by personality conflicts within the sales department. Inexperienced with computers, Honeywell hired sales staff from outside the company. "They got the cast–offs from Sperry Rand, from IBM. They lived in a different world than this great mass of Honeywell salesmen and marketing people, working stiffs who were out selling pneumatic and electric and electronic controls and industrial instruments. Here was this flamboyant bunch coming in, taking over lovely suites in downtown office buildings, and it was a great conflict."[19]

Communications executive Dean Randall remembered "We were the mavericks in the computer business. We had some pretty aggressive hotshots. They were on commission. And this was entirely different from the old–fashioned, stodgy Honeywell engineer salesman. At that point there were two companies that were entirely different. One was old–fashioned Honeywell, the other was a new go–go world of computers." [20]

The first of Honeywell's second-generation transistor computers, the H-800, was installed at Associated Hospital Service of New York in 1959.

By the Sixties it was clear that the computer market was going to outpace even the most optimistic projections. At the time of ENIAC, experts had felt that the country wouldn't need more than five or six of the huge "electronic brains." But it was becoming apparent that the market was potentially enormous, with hundreds of applications in business and engineering. Expansion, however, would be dependent upon reducing both the size and cost of the product. After all, only the largest blue–chip corporations could afford a $2 million system that required nearly half an acre of office space.

The Second Generation:
The Transistorized H–800

The emergence of new technologies culminated in the 1959 announcement of a new system incorporating so many advances that it became known as "second generation." The most obvious advance was the replacement of large, heat–generating vacuum tubes with transistors. Honeywell announced its H-800 computer just as the last D-1000 was shipped and installed. The 800 could run up to eight programs simultaneously, and was much faster than its predecessor. Each second, it could handle 1.67 million characters, 40,000 additions or subtractions, and 6,200 multiplications.

Honeywell dedicated itself to every aspect of the computer business. Facilities were expanded at Wellesley, Massachusetts for increased marketing and education, and branch sales offices were established in New York, Chicago, Los Angeles, Boston, and Washington. In 1960, the company delivered its first H-800's to Associated Hospital Service of New York, American Mutual Life Insurance Company, the Army Map Service, and the Army Finance Service. The price tag on the new computer was about $1 million, but this high price could be offset by a rental system developed by EDP in which a customer could lease an H-800 for a base price of $15,000 per month.

Compared to the D-1000, initial sales and interest in the 800 were very encouraging. Thirteen H-800's were installed in the first quarter of 1961, and several companies in Australia purchased the system.

In 1962, the H–800 demonstrated an exciting new facet of digital technology. It became the first computer to successfully transmit data by satellite, sending information from Honeywell to Bell Laboratories via the Telstar satellite.[21] Honeywell, repeating UNIVAC's 1952 performance, used the H–800 to predict the

The Honeywell H-800 was much faster than its predecessor. Each second, it could handle 1.67 million characters, 40,000 additions or subtractions, and 6,200 multiplications.

outcome of the national elections on ABC television. Viewers were periodically updated on the election, as well as the performance of Honeywell's computer. In tandem with a later model, the H-400, the H–800 gathered reports from 16 sources in 12 states transmitting updates by teletype directly to ABC. These teletypes were received on punched paper tape which was fed directly into the computer.[22]

Even with such widespread popular exposure, sales continued to lag behind those of IBM. The public still thought of Honeywell as a controls company, not a computer company. At one point, executives wondered if they had made a mistake. "They questioned whether staying in the computer business was the right thing to do and concluded that it was," Bissell recalled. "They *didn't* do the right thing in my view. I think it was an initial mistake, but that's very, very easy to criticize because I can understand they didn't fully understand the financial dimensions of the situation or the marketing problems. It changed Honeywell's reputation, from a highly conservative, very profitable business, to one that had its decorations lowered."[23] In 1963, the company had made 150 computer installations. Three years later, the number was over 1,000. In 1967, EDP division made a profit for the first time.

In 1964, Honeywell launched its most aggressive campaign against IBM.

The Third Generation: The Liberator

Honeywell's base of computer customers grew slowly until 1964. Then came EDP's finest hour. The company announced the release of its H-200 system, incorporating integrated circuit (third generation) technology. Also called the "Liberator," the H-200 was specifically designed to "liberate" IBM 1401 users, by offering better performance at 5.5 times the speed and 25 percent cheaper. The announcement was made in December 1963. Within two weeks Electronic Data Processing division had received 200 orders amounting to $50 million.[24] The H-200 helped Honeywell capture 5 percent of the worldwide computer market by 1970.

Despite its success, a *Business Week* article suggested that "the Honeywell 200 brought some hard lessons. It proved that getting a narrow market share away from the competition was simply too expensive."[25] The success of the H-200 actually proved unfortunate in the long–term, as it helped seal Honeywell's commitment to a market that never blossomed. But the H–200 proved that technological insight coupled with strong marketing could compete successfully, even against a long–term monopoly like IBM. It was an intoxicating triumph for a company that had never before been recognized as a serious competitor outside of its traditional line of controls.

The Honeywell H-400 computer system was introduced in 1960. It was the company's first entry into the medium-scale market. The system could process 6,000 additions or subtractions per second.

1968–1969: The Other Computer Company

The success of H–200 enhanced the company's reputation as a scrappy and often irreverent competitor in the computer business. Unaccustomed to challenger status, Honeywellers actually seemed to savor their outsider image in this new industry. By 1969, EDP carried a comprehensive line of 2,000 computer products, and more than 5,000 computer systems had been installed. In 1968, Honeywell adopted the corporate slogan "The Other Computer Company." Chairman Jim Binger told a reporter, "Maybe it is a smart–aleck phrase but we're getting our message across. There's a new willingness on the part of the customer to look at alternatives."[26]

President Steve Keating pointed out that Honeywell (with only 5 percent market share) was now "exceeded only by the giant of the industry," and that "we now have the broadest product line and the largest marketing organization in the industry."[27] Keating also noted that Honeywell's hopes were pinned partly on contin-

ued market growth. "The computer business has grown almost independently of the forces of the economy," he said. "We expect that growth rate to continue at an undiminished rate for the foreseeable future. We plan to keep pace and gradually improve our market share."[28]

Time Sharing

In the late Sixties, government agencies began using computers to create a nationwide communications network that could be used in a national emergency. These early efforts would ultimately lead to the Internet, a loose association of colleges, universities, corporations, institutions, and individuals. In the Nineties, millions of users log on to the Internet every day. The Internet is actually an association of several computer networks, including ARPANET, one of the pioneer networks developed by the Department of Defense in 1968. Honeywell hardware was used in the creation of ARPANET because its developers "concluded that the most efficient and reliable interface between a large number of dissimilar computers and the network itself was a specially modified Honeywell Model 516 mini."[29]

An earlier development had helped to accommodate the establishment of networks like ARPANET. General Electric had pioneered time-sharing, a method by which many different users could use the same computer at the same time for different purposes. GE conducted timesharing experiments in Phoenix in 1964, and installed an experimental system of the same type at Dartmouth College that same year.

As early as 1960, Walter Finke, then president of the Datamatic Division, was predicting the development of a system like the Internet. He referred to the possibility of expanding the communications capability of digital technologies in order to "give electronic computation a sort of geographical omnipresence."[30]

The Big Push: Merger With GE

The year 1970 marked "Honeywell's single biggest and most challenging undertaking in the computer business."[31] Honeywell merged computer operations with General Electric's information systems in a concerted effort to catch IBM, or at least gain a more profitable market share. The merger doubled the size of Honeywell's computer interests, and the resulting entity was the second–largest computer company in the world.

GE had been in the computer business since 1956, when the company had won a $60 million contract with the Bank of America. Like Honeywell, GE's computer section dreamed of capturing "the title of ranking contender" against IBM. Hilliard Paige, GE's vice president of information systems, "decided that a bold stroke was the only way to avoid further years of meandering on the same business plateau." In 1969, Paige called a gathering of top management and engineering staff, code–named Shangri-La. Sixty participants checked into a Florida hotel for three months. They analyzed the markets, speculated on future technologies, and planned an advanced product line. Every effort was directed toward snaring some of IBM's huge market share. Shangri-La resulted in eight new computers, from a terminal to a super–computer, designed to challenge IBM from top to bottom. There was only one problem. Estimated pre–production cost was between $450 and $500 million. Paige believed that General Electric simply wasn't in a position to make that kind of investment. So, as Raytheon had approached Honeywell in 1955, GE contacted Honeywell in February 1970.

In 1964, Dick Douglas (Left) and Joe Keady sold one of Honeywell's first Model 200 computers to Northwestern Bell in Omaha. During a demonstration at the telephone company, it was pointed out that Honeywell had misspelled its own name on the nameplate affixed to the control unit door. Douglas and Keady were later presented with a plaque bearing the incorrect panel.

Honeywell management evaluated the plan carefully, and accepted in principle the proposal of merging EDP with General Electric information systems. After a series of complex negotiations between two very large companies, a "partial purchase, partial pooling" approach was approved, in which a third company, called "Honeywell Information Systems" would be formed. Honeywell would own 81.5 percent of the company's stock, and GE would control 18.5 percent. Honeywell paid General Electric 1.5 million shares of stock and $100 million in notes. Public announcement of the planned merger was made in May 1970.[32]

President Steve Keating explained the merger to *Business Week*, saying that when it came to computers, the company had a choice between getting bigger or getting out. "We were into computers so far," Keating said, "that we never thought of selling out, and we couldn't abandon it." Though company sales were increasing every year, Honeywell was

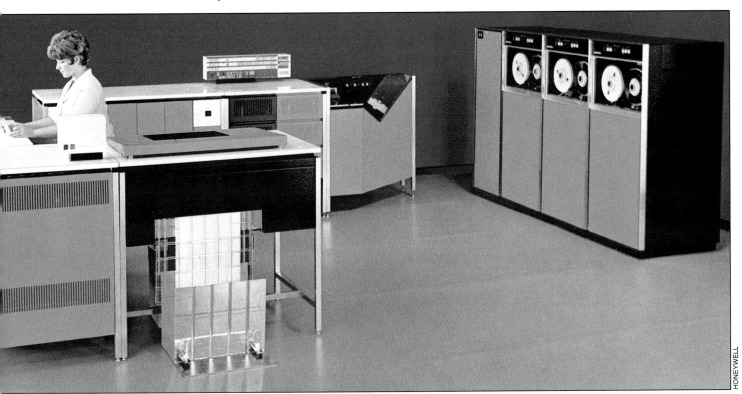

Honeywell's Model 200 "Liberator," introduced in 1963, made quite a splash in the computer industry, offering software bridges to IBM's 1401 system. This allowed Honeywell to "liberate" customers from IBM's monopoly.

Two weeks after the H-200 "Liberator" was introduced, orders exceeded $50 million. Walter Finke (left) and Claude Smith, president and vice president of Honeywell's Electronic Data Processing division at the time, enjoyed a moment of pride during this high point in Honeywell's computer business. The "Liberator," a direct challenge to IBM's 1401, was 25 percent cheaper and 5.5 times faster than the IBM model.

not gaining market share. When GE elected to get out of the business, Honeywell officials felt they were being handed a golden opportunity. "We faced ourselves," Keating concluded, "realized we had to be bigger, and made the biggest decision since the company decided to go into heating control."[33]

"I had a little concern," recalled Stan Nelson, who was head of the Commercial Division. "I always had a lot of respect for GE. Very sharp guys. And I thought, "Geeze, if they're getting out of this business, I wonder. On the other hand, what they've got certainly will complement what we've got."[34] The resulting company won Honeywell 10 percent of the worldwide computer market.

"On paper, it was a perfect marriage," said Mannie Jackson, director of human resources in the computer division at the time. Working on the transition team bringing the GE interests on board was, he said, "quite a task."[35]

"General Electric had more of an engineering, scientific and manufacturing culture. We had more of a marketing and distribution culture. All the business units were competing for investment. When you've got one that's growing really fast and chewing up a lot of resources, you have tension in the organization."[36]

Ed Spencer, then an executive vice president who would become CEO in 1974, said there "was a difference in culture between the two businesses, one of which was kind of go-go and let the figures fall out where they may, and the other one that had been built over a hundred years very cautiously and carefully." But the companies also had a lot in common, he said. "The people who came from GE were very much like Honeywell people. They were steely-eyed, conservative business managers."[37]

One important spin-off of the merger was that it added more opportunities for Honeywell's global computer marketing. GE affiliates in France and Italy were included in the deal, to form Compagnie Honeywell Bull and Honeywell Information Systems Italia. These firms complemented Honeywell's EDP efforts in the United Kingdom, Canada, Japan, and Australia. Honeywell acquired majority ownership of Bull, but according to Spencer, who headed international operations at the time, there were problems.

Spencer explained that differences between American and European systems of computing debt and equity made Bull a drain on Honeywell's financial picture. "Honeywell ended up with a balance sheet with a lot of debt on it, much of which was Bull's. It was easy to say that it was Bull's debt, but with Honeywell owning two thirds of it, the banks and rating agencies looked on it ultimately as Honeywell's liability."[38]

The company merged in 1976 with a French computer concern, Compagnie Internationale pour l'Informatique, also known as Cii. The merge created Cii Honeywell Bull, owned 47 percent by Honeywell. CEO Michael Bonsignore explained how it happened.

"The French government believed it needed a national computer industry. So they set up a rival company, Cii, which had grown substantially and had lot of government business. Honeywell Bull acquired that French company and its market share, employees, designs, products and so on. In return we reduced our ownership from 66 percent to 47 percent and improved the Honeywell Inc. balance sheet substantially."[39]

In the years after the General Electric merger, Honeywell Information Systems maintained offices in 66 countries, with manufacturing facilities in four.

Continuing Malaise

Throughout the 1970s, the general perception was that Honeywell was mired within a market in which it couldn't compete. Typical was a 1974 *Business Week* article asserting that the company was "in the worldwide data processing arena with no possibility of a graceful escape. From now on, Honeywell's future will depend on how aggressively the company can scratch in across-the-board competition with IBM and the others in the industry."[40] In the mid-1970s, "the others" were Burroughs, NCR, Sperry Rand, Control Data, and Xerox, each with extensive experience in the office equipment market. Although its computer revenues grew to $2.5 billion in 1974, Honeywell's profits were well below the average set by the company's non–computer businesses.

Forbes in 1975 also speculated about Honeywell's future in the industry.

> *"The rumor is going around that Honeywell Inc., the world's second-biggest computer company in terms of installed base value, is about to drop out of the business. The rumor is not surprising. Such giants as RCA, Xerox, and General Electric, after first saying they would stay the course against*

In 1978, Honeywell made an effort to capitalize on its 16-bit technology with the Model 23 minicomputer. The 16-bit architecture became industry standard, but Honeywell fumbled by trying to develop 32-bit mini systems.

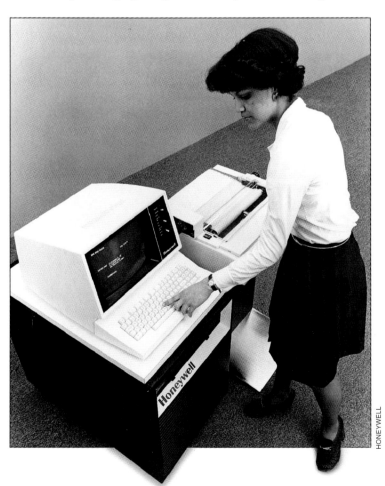

Honeywell's Model 23 minicomputer, introduced in 1978, was smaller, faster and cheaper than its predecessors.

> *IBM, ended by throwing in the towel. And the game is getting no gentler. Honeywell has only 10 percent of the world market vs. IBM's 69 percent."*[41]

By the time the article appeared in 1975, Spencer had taken over the helm of the company. Spencer, who was hired in 1954, would be CEO from 1974 to 1987.

Reflecting on Honeywell's bumpy history in the computer business, Spencer said, "We got into it in 1955 and it wasn't until 1967 that we made our first profit," he said. "Is that a good return for the shareholders? There was always a conflict for resources in the early days. When computers were very small it didn't make much difference, but as they became big, particularly after buying General Electric, there was a lot of competition for resources from 1970 on."[42]

Forbes noted: "Honeywell is in too deep and has made too much progress to follow RCA and General Electric out of the business. It has little choice but to stay the course."[43] Nothing the company did seemed to affect its dismal market share.

"We did not know the computer business and not only that we didn't know the marketing of computers," Herb Bissell recalled. "I can remember meetings in the boardroom year after year when Walter Finke and his financial guy Dan O'Brien would project next year's earnings, saying we would either break even or make a little money. And then at the end of the year we'd lost anywhere from $12 to $15 million. And that was the way that thing went for years."

Minicomputers

Analysts throughout the Sixties and Seventies asserted that Honeywell could not survive in the computer industry without finding some sort of niche. As one writer noted in 1976, "Survival against International Business Machines in the computer race has meant finding a niche: Burroughs in banking; Control Data in giant scientific computers and time-sharing; Sperry Rand in real-time applications. Only Minneapolis's Honeywell Inc. lacks such a niche—and that, in the long run, could prove its downfall."[44]

An opportunity of this kind had fallen into Honeywell's lap in 1966, when the company became "the first general purpose or 'mainframe' computer maker to enter the minicomputer business" through its acquisition of Computer Control Company (CCC).[45] By the mid–Sixties, minicomputers were already being used for such important applications as missile guidance and industrial process control.

Honeywell might easily have cultivated the minicomputer niche with its acquisition of CCC, based in Framingham, Massachusetts. For a brief time, Honeywell carried a CCC minicomputer, designated the 516. The mini was an innovative 16-bit system designed by Gardner Hendrie. "With CCC, Honeywell had it all: the most advanced mini technology, products, and markets. It lacked only vision."[46] Competitors, like Digital Equipment Corporation (DEC) picked up the 16-bit technology and ran with it, but Honeywell discontinued this approach. One commentator noted, "When you are trying to compete with IBM you can't afford any mistakes. In losing out in minicomputers, Honeywell bosses made a whopper."[47]

When Honeywell merged with GE, the resulting company, Honeywell Information Systems, gravitated toward the larger systems both companies had spent time and money developing. Instead of working on a new generation of 16-bit machines, Honeywell "diverted resources into producing a 32-bit machine. The new machine never caught on and Honeywell dropped it." The company also allowed Hendrie to be lured away.[48] Binger, who was CEO at the time, said Honeywell made the same mistake that IBM was making. "We thought the major thrust of that business was going to be in big mainframes. It has gone in quite a different direction."[49] Stan Nelson said, "Instead of really pushing the opportunity in minis, our management just wanted to sell a big mainframe."[50]

Spencer said "we made a mistake in saying we cannot afford to have two sales forces calling on the same customers. We folded the CCC sales force into our business computer sales force, which was much bigger. In effect it swallowed what could have been a very, very strong minicomputer business. Instead, it became sort of an adjunct to business computer sales.... We might have had ten years of super prosperity if we had managed it differently.... We didn't do as well with it as we might have."[51]

In any case, the "potential inherent in the CCC acquisition was soon dwarfed by the challenge of the GE-Honeywell merger...[and both companies] had a focus in large systems."[52]

In 1969, the development of the micro computer sparked yet another industry-wide revolution. With the micro computer, digital

The TDC 2000 central operator station allowed for the total management of an industrial process from a single point of access. TDC 2000 evolved to the TDC 3000 in the 1980s, a system with complete integration of process and management control.

In 1975, Honeywell celebrated its 20th year in the computer business with this company publication. The "cake" is a magnetic tape reel.

technologies could be applied to any electronic operation. The tiny "computer-on-a-chip" was a complex of circuits on a miniature silicon chip the size of a thumbnail. These Lilliputian computers had twenty times the power of ENIAC, the first digital computer, and cost about $10.[53] Microcomputers could be tucked in a calculator, wristwatch, or a typewriter, or perhaps even a thermostat. They would make possible an almost complete digitalization of electronic products by the Nineties. The microcomputer began replacing mechanical and electromechanical parts of all kinds by the mid Seventies, and would have a profound effect on Honeywell's controls and computer businesses.

1965–1970: The Prospect of Integration

One niche the company did develop quite naturally was that of digital computers for its traditional fields of automatic controls. When Honeywell entered the computer business in the

Sixties, it made sense for the company to begin using digital computers for its traditional fields of automatic control. Even before then, H.W. Sweatt and Al Wilson both recognized that the computer was in fact a fundamental kind of automatic control. They could foresee a time when digital computers would be at the heart of automatic controls of any kind, acting to integrate vast arrays of sensors and activators.

As early as 1961, Honeywell's Industrial Products Group had applied a 290 computer to "automatically control an entire industrial process, or even an entire plant." Philadelphia Electric was just such an application, where the computer components of the system were designed and manufactured by EDP but installed by Special Systems division.[54]

Honeywell also signed a contract with Sara Lee Bakeries of Deerfield, Illinois, for a $22 million computerized process control system that allowed the same number of bakers to produce twice as many cakes. Sara Lee claimed the quality of its

Honeywell developed a reputation as a scrappy underdog fighting giant IBM. This ad campaign featured whimsical animals created from computer components like transistors and diodes.

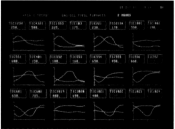
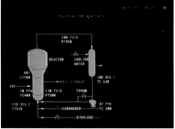

HONEYWELL

In 1983, Honeywell announced its TDC 3000 system for total process and information control. It provided better computing capability than the TDC 2000 and featured touch-sensitive color screens.

product improved with the Honeywell system. Each morning, a Honeywell computer oversaw the bakery's operations, which included the mixing of 36,000 pounds of milk, 90,000 pounds of butter, and 60,000 pounds of eggs. The computer at the heart of the process control system issued 180,000 commands every 15 seconds.[55]

Through the Sixties, similar systems were sold to Monsanto, Celanese, and the U.S. Navy. The early success of the Philadelphia Electric and Sara Lee systems prompted CEO Jim Binger to say in 1964, "We don't want to just sell hardware. We want to sell a complete system to do an entire job." Observers who could see beyond the fierce battle for market share in general-use computers noticed that "Honeywell has carefully built both the computer and controls capabilities [to] do the entire job."[56]

The market for computerized process control was growing so fast that Special Systems division needed a better computer. Not finding one forthcoming from Honeywell, it started using an SDS Corporation 610 (SDS was later acquired by Xerox). Special Systems sold about 100 process control systems with SDS computers from 1962 to 1965, generating enough business to invest in the devel-

opment of its own computer system and software, designed specifically for industrial process control. The result of Special Systems' research and development was the Honeywell H20/21. Technically it proved an outstanding machine, but it was abandoned by Honeywell headquarters with the acquisition of CCC in 1966. In another misstep, Honeywell headquarters replaced the process control-specific H20/21 with the 516. The 516 was an excellent minicomputer, but it had no applicable software for process control. The end result was considerable attrition at Special Systems, and many talented engineers, scientists, and salesmen left the company to pursue perceived greater opportunities.[57]

There was a wealth of opportunity in the growing field of digital process control, however. Throughout the Sixties, Honeywell pursued these markets through acquisition and diversification. Medical electronics were developed through Heiland Division, a Denver-based technology firm acquired in 1954. "Watchdog" systems were developed in the late Sixties with the acquisition of Security Burglar Alarm Company, making use of a central computer center to process information from a wide variety of sensors. And many

In the early Eighties, Honeywell continued to manufacture and ship large computer systems, such as this DPS 8/20 which was sold to Eddie Bauer, Inc. in 1980. The "Distributed Processing System" was gradually made obsolete by networked personal computer systems.

Aerospace and Defense contracts involved the application of digital computer technology. Anti Submarine Rocket, or ASROC, one of Honeywell's first and most important missile contracts, was a ship–launched, anti–submarine weapon that was computer controlled.[58] By 1970, it could accurately be said that "digital products and solid state technology underlie Honeywell systems for industrial process control, traffic control, energy management, building security, and aerospace applications."[59]

Successful Integration in the Seventies and Eighties

When the old Special Systems division was disbanded after the lost opportunity of the H20/21, some of that group's process control specialists moved to the company's Morton Grove, Illinois development facilities for the Commercial division. In Morton Grove, the first major achievement in commercial building automation came with the design of a "digital data highway," a coaxial cable which "could link

various elements of a building control system and, using digital technology, bring sensor data to a central control location." In 1974, Honeywell acquired GE's process control business, which infused some 600 employees into the business of process automation. As a consequence of the company's research, development and acquisitions, Process Controls division introduced the TDC (Total Distributed Control) 2000 for automating industrial processes. The TDC system used a series of microcomputers to integrate sensors and activators which could be adapted to nearly any industrial process, from petroleum refining to paper making. The system was an immediate success, and it would evolve into the TDC 3000. Introduced in 1983, the TDC 3000 represented three years of development and $80 million of investment. It was the grand integration of every aspect of process control for industry. The "process management system" fully synthesized plant operations, production, planning, and data processing for quality and efficiency management. A central digital computer station gave managers "single point access" to a plant's complete operations.

The Delta system, an application of digital technology to automatic control of buildings, was developed in 1970. Through integrated sensors and activators, Delta governed a building's heating, air conditioning, fire alarms, and security. The earliest generation of Delta management systems used digital technology, but without computer integration. In 1971, the Delta 2500, complete with computer, was introduced. Honeywell developed the Delta 1000 five years later, a machine that could collect, display, and control information provided by a network of sensors throughout a facility. In the 1980s,

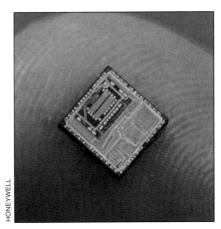

Tiny "computers-on-a-chip" were integrated into many Honeywell products by 1985, including this one for use in Honeywell Protection Services security systems.

the Delta family evolved into DeltaNet, a system which provided for "intelligent" buildings with "continuous data exchange between computers for environmental control, energy management, fire protection and security, telecommunications, and office automation."[60] This full integration depended upon the convergence of computer, control, and communications technologies.

Honeywell developed its DeltaNet fire management system for institutions in 1985. The system incorporates numerous sensors and processors to provide accurate information at a moment's notice.

Honeywell entered the field of communications control through acquisitions and joint ventures beginning in 1981, when the purchase of Telamerica Inc. heralded the formation of the Communications Services Division. Action Communications Systems Inc., a Dallas voice and data networking company, was also purchased. A 1983 joint venture with L.M. Ericsson in Sweden further consolidated Honeywell's development of technologies for communication. Honeywell's expansion into the field of communications boosted its related commercial services such as central station security protection. The acquisition in 1969 of Security Burglar Alarm Co. of Oklahoma City propelled the company into the field of building security, and in 1973, this business became the Protection Services Division.

"It was complementary to our commercial building controls business," said Ray Alvarez, now vice president and group executive of Sensing and Control. Alvarez worked as controller of the Commercial Division during this active period. "We made about 44 acquisitions in a five or six year period. Some were a couple of hundred thousand dollars, some were ten million. We were buying the central alarms in cities like Tampa or Baltimore to align these small companies into a national operation that could compete with the likes of ADT."[61] The division provided for the integration of digital

and communication technologies by installing sensors in a home or building that were networked to a central computer station. The growth of Protection Services through the Eighties and Nineties was visible in many North American cities, where red and black "Protected By Honeywell" window stickers and placards became nearly as ubiquitous as the T-86 Round thermostat.

Another field in which Honeywell integrated computer and communications technology for environmental control was in its BOSS services. By contract, a central Honeywell BOSS station could monitor and manage the environment of small businesses through leased telephone lines. BOSS services were established in many American, Canadian, Australian, and European cities throughout the 1970s and 1980s.

The Eighties

Despite the company's achievements in integrating digital computer technologies in its traditional control markets, it continued to suffer from its small market share in general–use computers. By 1984, Honeywell's market share had dwindled from a high point of 10 percent to 2 percent. Honeywell Information Systems maintained about 10,000 customers who made up, in respect to overall computer revenues, a negligible handful of loyalists. The *Wall Street Journal* put it mildly in 1984 when it stated, "computers have brought the company more grief than profit. Torn by internal conflicts and sagging morale,

The DeltaNet micro control system manages all aspects of medium and small institutional environments.

Honeywell's Information Systems Division has been outflanked in hardware by IBM and in software by nearly everyone."[62] Strained by the constant effort to increase profits, the division was forced to constantly cut back costs, often through layoffs. By the time Jim Renier took over as head of Honeywell's computer operations in 1983, his predecessor had laid off 1200. Renier followed with layoffs of his own totaling 2,300, "It was a very painful decision, but we simply did what we felt we had to do." [63]

Renier, said Spencer, "has about as deep an understanding of technology and where it could take a business as anybody I've run across. In the early Eighties, as personal computers (PCs) began to appear on the market, he was saying, 'PCs are going to take over a lot of the work that's now done on big mainframes. They are going to get more and more powerful as circuits become cheaper and faster.' That was really the time when in my own mind it seemed that we might be at a dead end. We were heavily dependent on the large mainframe business, and that was a red flag. He wasn't saying, 'let's get out of the business' but rather, 'we better watch what's going to happen to PCs.' He was dead right."[64]

Like his predecessors, Renier was simply trying to surmount the insurmountable. Honeywell's problems in general-use computers worsened in the early Eighties, when HIS computers consistently ranked poorly in terms of performance and in competitive software.

New Direction and Old Markets

As the Eighties progressed, Honeywell's traditional ambivalence toward its computer operations began to change. Gradually, management began to put more emphasis on the company's successful integration of digital computing technologies into the broader field of traditional automatic controls. The *Wall Street Journal* reported in 1984 that "The company hopes for big profits by tying together general data processing functions with the controls that regulate operations such as heating and cooling systems and manufacturing processes. Technologies for doing this are just developing but they hold the key to Honeywell's future."[65] The more CEO Ed Spencer and his management group considered the situation, the more they became convinced of the truth of the *Journal*'s conclusions. Finally, in 1986, Spencer made the painful but inevitable decision to discontinue Honeywell's computer business. Ironically, the company had entered the computer business to guarantee its future. Now it had to abandon it for precisely the same reason.

A Honeywell vehicle in Moscow. With the decline of Communism, Honeywell is poised to benefit from experience in the former Soviet Union that dates back to the 1930s.

CHAPTER EIGHT

A WORLD OF OPPORTUNITY

"We have exported our instruments and controls to every far-flung country. We have built a strong foundation, and on that firm base we propose to build an even greater export trade... Our company's growth demands a territory larger than the United States. We need the world, and the world needs our controls."

— Cran Sharp, 1945

By the end of World War II, Minneapolis-Honeywell had made an international name for itself. The war had presented extraordinary opportunities to prove its mettle in research, engineering and manufacturing, and to showcase its products and services throughout the world. Scientists, engineers, managers, and workers had proven that Honeywell was a company capable of applying its resources to an ever-widening circle of automation. Hardly any home heating controls had been sold in the civilian market during the war years because Honeywell had devoted virtually all its creative resources to military production.

Early International Experience

With its long heating season, Canada was a natural first target for Minneapolis Heat Regulator's first efforts to penetrate international markets. The company's home state of Minnesota borders on Ontario and Manitoba, and branch offices in Buffalo, Chicago and Boston were relatively close to the border. Though the company did not sell its products directly to Canadian customers, they arrived in Canada as standard equipment on furnaces and boilers exported there.

There is some indication that Minneapolis Heat Regulator products were sold through distributors in Canada in the years 1900-1920, though there are no precise records for the period and these sales may not have been recorded as exports. The first year that company ledgers specifically identified international sales was 1920 – when "Unsolicited, Incidental" sales for export amounted to $90. As modest as these figures were, Sales Manager C.B. Sweatt apparently saw potential in them, and he placed a young Charlie Hoyt in charge of expanding the company's export markets. Hoyt did his job well, for in just one year he increased export sales 400 per cent— to a grand total of $350.

From 1920 to 1935, the company handled exports through its New York office.[1] There was no division devoted to international sales—simply a desk. Mark Watkins, a native Russian, managed the office and was able to provide an entree into the Soviet Union during the 1930s. Business there became so brisk that plans were made to bring several Russian nationals to Philadelphia, and train them to manufacture Minneapolis-Honeywell's Brown potentiometers. However, World War II intervened, followed by the Cold War. The budding trade relationships between Russian companies and their U.S. counterparts would not flower for many decades.

Neighbors To the North

Large American concerns were already exporting heating plants across the Canadian border in the nineteenth century, and furnaces, boilers, burners and controls were in high demand. As alternative fuels and automatic controls became standard in the United States, Minneapolis-Honeywell controls became standard equipment on many of the plants that arrived in Canada. In 1930, the company established a wholly–owned subsidiary in Toronto, incorporated as the "Minneapolis-Honeywell Regulator Company Limited." Soon after, Minneapolis-Honeywell purchased the Time-O-Stat company of Elkhart, Indiana, which manufactured competitive controls. Time–O–Stat products were also distributed in Canada by the McDonald Company, a distributor also based in Toronto. Time–O–Stat employed an engineer named Carl

Left: Thomas McDonald was a longtime director of Honeywell. He was originally hired as the manager of Honeywell's first international subsidiary in Toronto, following the acquisition of Time-O-Stat Instruments in 1931. A man famous for his idiosyncrasies, McDonald once took off a pair of new shoes and ordered an employee to wear them for the rest of the day, to break them in.

Right: Jan Amand established a Honeywell subsidiary in Belgium following World War II. He and Tas Taselaar held the Amsterdam office together during the Nazi occupation.

Kronmiller, who would later develop the famous Honeywell Round thermostat.

The McDonald Company was owned and run by a charismatic young Canadian named Thomas McDonald. After six months of operations, McDonald was hired as general manager of Minneapolis-Honeywell's Canadian subsidiary.[2] He would eventually become integral to Honeywell's success during and after the second World War, at one point overseeing the Aero Division, and later becoming executive vice president and a member of the board of directors.

The Canadian market proved strong, and it soon became clear that a manufacturing facility in Canada was warranted. This would make it possible to ship components from Minneapolis to Toronto, where they could be assembled. Eventually, the individual parts could be completely manufactured by the subsidiary. By 1936, the Canadian subsidiary began assembling Minneapolis-Honeywell products in its own factory.[1]

Across the Atlantic

After several years of success in Canada, the company began investigating the European market. Some trade relationships already existed with European concerns. And Honeywell already had a presence there with furnaces, boilers, and burners exported from the U.S. and fitted with Honeywell controls. Expansion of these lines seemed natural, and after 1935 the company's line of Brown indus-

trial instruments were also considered potential best-sellers in Europe.

Amsterdam was selected as the ideal window into Europe, and "N.V. Nederlandsche Minneapolis-Honeywell" was established in 1934. Holland's stable currency and liberal commercial policies provided for free port facilities, which meant that equipment could be stored in bonded warehouses, from which shipments abroad could be made without payment of duty.[2]

The increased popularity of automatic fuels in Europe, especially oil, led to increased orders by European oil burner manufacturers. In 1984, the Dutch subsidiary marked its 50th anniversary with this explanation of its origins. "In countries such as England, France, Germany, Italy, and Yugoslavia, there were agents and manufacturers of oil burners that ordered controls directly from Minneapolis. The constant growth of this business led to a need for a European coordination point: Amsterdam."[3] The first employees of the Amsterdam subsidiary were an American manager named Herman Wex and a Dutchman named Jan Amand.[4] When Minneapolis-Honeywell acquired Brown Instruments in 1935, two technical people, A.S. Taselaar and M.H. Theo Hollema, were added to the Amsterdam staff. Taselaar was selected because he had recently earned a degree in electrical engineering. Hollema, who had sales experience, was told his job was a "lifetime position."[5] Leaving Taselaar in charge, Amand eventually went to Belgium to work on opening that market in the years leading up to the war.[6] At its prewar peak, the Amsterdam office employed 15, all Dutch or German.

International Growth, 1934–1942

In 1934, Minneapolis-Honeywell posted international sales of $286,000, with an operating profit of $50,000. Three years later, sales had increased to $710,000, with an operating profit of $57,000. Honeywell executives determined that business was suffering in England because of unsatisfactory distribution arrangements. So they sent Tom McDonald to establish a wholly–owned subsidiary, and Honeywell-Brown, Ltd. was incorporated in 1936. This office was to become a vital European outpost during the war, serving as a distribution center for Honeywell's defense-related products for the Allies.[7]

Not all subsidiaries were established through such careful business planning. A Scandinavian subsidiary, for example, was the direct result of a vacation. Jack Nelson, a Honeywell employee of Norwegian descent, vacationed in Oslo in 1937. While there, he saw great potential for Honeywell products in Scandinavia. The following year, he was sent to Stockholm to establish a Swedish subsidiary. Although he returned to the United States during World War II, Nelson remained active in the Swedish operation for 25 years. Like the Amsterdam subsidiary, the Swedish office managed to stay open through much of the war, "rendering service and maintaining contacts" despite the fact that they received no shipments and no direct contact from Minneapolis management. "In some cases they're even manufacturing some controls from parts and equipment left over from prewar shipments," noted a report in a 1943 edition of the company newspaper.[8]

Distributorships were also being arranged all over the world. By 1941, Minneapolis-Honeywell had sales arrangements with distributors in Chile, Panama, Trinidad, New Zealand, Argentina, and South Africa. The product line had grown to include extensive industrial instrumentation from the Brown division, as well as items like hot water controls.

An important international relationship grew out of the acquisition of Brown Instruments itself in 1935. Back in 1920, Brown had executed contracts with a Japanese distributor called Yamatake Shokai to manufacture Brown instruments in its own factory. This relationship with Yamatake would grow to be one of the most important in Honeywell history.

By 1939, Tom McDonald could tell Minneapolis bankers that company exports constituted a small but "desirable" percentage of total sales. McDonald even asserted that, given "normal world conditions," exports were the most promising division of the business, since expansion into world markets helped stabilize seasonal and regional trends, giving the company a "balanced demand" for its products.

"Our instruments are sold throughout the entire world. They are used extensively in Japan and France where we have manufacturing arrangements. Hundreds of thousands of dollars worth of our controls manufactured in the United States are installed in Russia. They are used in South America in brick, glass, and mining plants. Australia sends to us for instruments for her steel plants, and many controls are installed in the tea drying plants of India. The sugar refineries in Cuba, the oil refineries in South America, the air conditioned plants in Egypt, and bombproof shelters in China have our equipment."[9]

In 1942, with war raging, the company established an Export Department, quickly dubbed the "Cloak and Dagger Division," to formalize expansion into overseas markets. Export personnel like Cran Sharp and Sherwood Berryann became experts on establishing distributorships and subsidiaries just about anywhere in the world.[10]

In 1934, Amsterdam became the site of Honeywell's first European office. The country was chosen for its free port facilities and stable currency. This photo depicts shipping activities in about 1950.

Honeywell's first England office, established in 1936, was in a London pub that was converted to office use.

The War Years In Amsterdam

When war erupted in Europe, the Dutch operation was considered an American company and enjoyed diplomatic protection from the U.S. embassy. Even so, headquarters sent "not a single screw" to its Amsterdam office, fearing company assets would be seized. [11] Jan Amand, returning from his organizing efforts in Belgium, was forced to release the entire Amsterdam staff except for Taselaar. Theo Hollema moved to northern Holland where he started his own company.

Still, Nederlandsche Honeywell-Brown N.V. survived. The day after Pearl Harbor, a Nazi administrator announced that he had come to "take over" the company. He was enthusiastic at first, but lost interest when he saw that the business was in shambles, Taselaar recalled. In truth, the business was not as bad off as it seemed. Taselaar and Amand had carefully staged the appearance of disrepair. They managed to hide the company's entire stock by "selling" it to Taselaar's father. The elder Taselaar was a farmer, and the entire inventory of controls, valves, and other equipment could be hidden in his barns. When they needed something, they would simply buy it back at cost.

Despite the fact that most of Amsterdam's stock was either obsolete or incompatible with existing systems, Amand and Taselaar were able to keep the business running well enough to pay their modest salaries. They even hired a few technicians to rewind motors and disassemble components, selling unusable parts for scrap.

These technicians were occasionally Jews in hiding, so Amand and Taselaar developed a ruse in case Nazi officials came into the office unannounced. They kept an empty parcel on a desk near the door which could be picked up and carried out on a moment's notice, giving the impression that the illegal worker was just a delivery person. [12]

Against all odds, Amand and Taselaar were able to keep the subsidiary running. But by the winter of 1945, business had all but stopped, and they had to burn old records for heat. [13]

Amsterdam After the War

Shortly after V-E Day, Taselaar notified Minneapolis that the Dutch subsidiary had miraculously held together through the war. Their files recorded the endless hardships they

In 1950, Honeywell international managers convened a meeting at Minneapolis headquarters. Present were Jack Nelson, Vic MacLachlan, Charlie Meech, Jim Fraser, Pat Sullivan, Tas Taselaar and Jan Amand. Bill Westphal and Cran Sharp look on.

had suffered to keep the office running—and to stay alive. In characteristically understated Dutch fashion, the files concluded "We believe that we have summarized everything that might be of interest to you, except the fact that we have taken the liberty to divide amongst our small staff part of the timber of our old stockroom to make firewood."[14] The company, deeply impressed with Taselaar and Amand's efforts, considered the team essential in re–establishing a European presence. Taselaar was put in charge of managing the Dutch operations, and Amand resumed his work in Belgium. Hollema, with his "lifetime position," returned as sales manager in Amsterdam.

Post–War Strategies Abroad

World War II effectively grounded Minneapolis-Honeywell's international business just as it was starting to take off. Even so, the company moved its international office from New York to Washington, D.C. during the war years, in order "to handle the priority orders of the lend-lease program." During this period, the company continued to supply the Soviet Union with substantial orders, many of which remain unpaid because of their official lend–lease status.

It was said that Paul "Cran" Sharp could start an office abroad with $10,000 and the articles of incorporation. In the post-war period, he played a large role in developing Honeywell's international subsidiaries.

On V-J Day, August 15, 1945, H.W. Sweatt convened a meeting to discuss post–war strategies. Cran Sharp, Brown Division's export manager in Philadelphia, wrote in 1945: "We have exported our instruments and controls to every far–flung country. We have built a strong foundation, and on that firm base we propose to build an even greater export trade... Our company's growth demands a territory larger than the United States. We need the world, and the world needs our controls."[15]

Sharp was responsible for the lion's share of the legwork involved in surveying a new market and establishing a distributor or a subsidiary. Another longtime Honeywell International employee, Sherwood Berryann, worked alongside, and commented at Sharp's retirement that "many people in foreign lands never heard of 'Honeywell,' but mention the name 'Cran Sharp' and their eyes light up."[16] Sharp was also instrumental in developing the relationship with the Japanese firm of Yamatake, both before and after the war. That company's longtime director, Toshihiko Yamaguchi, credited the success

HONEYWELL

Charlie Meech was commonly known as "Mr. International" at Honeywell. Meech was a much-admired Honeyweller who spent his most productive years in Europe and Asia developing Honeywell's international subsidiaries through the 1950s and 1960s. Meech spoke French, German, Japanese, Latin, Italian and Spanish.

of the Tokyo firm in part to Cran Sharp's accurate knowledge of Japan and Japanese customs.[17] After the war, Sharp and others flew all over the world setting up distributorships and subsidiaries. Sharp often left the United States in January, and didn't return until June.

International Operations Flourish

In the autumn of 1945, international operations were moved to Minneapolis from Washington D.C., and Honeywell began the process of renewing contacts with European subsidiaries. The Amsterdam and Stockholm offices were reopened, and the London operation quickly converted from materiel distribution to the company's traditional peacetime lines. Jan Amand was sent to establish a Brussels subsidiary in November of 1946, and other subsidiaries were set up in Mexico

and Switzerland. By the end of 1945, the company had renamed its U.S. exports department, calling it the International Trade Division. Bill Westphal and Cran Sharp were given the responsibility of managing the Minneapolis office,[18] and Westphal, H.W. Sweatt, and Tom McDonald embarked on a long European trip to survey markets there. But Europe was just the first overseas objective.

"How to pronounce Honeywell in Hindustani is no problem," noted a 1946 *Circulator* article. "It isn't a problem in Egyptian either. Or in Turkish, Russian, Dutch, Siamese, or Hodmezovasarhelian. No matter what their accent, customers say 'Honeywell' and distributors in 27 countries of the world know what they mean."[19]

Jack Nelson, returning to Stockholm after weathering the war in Washington, said, "Our company's contribution toward winning the war, and with it, the peace, has definitely furthered our international acceptance, to the point where I feel that our export business will be a very important post-war factor. The credit for our foreign acceptance and success goes without a question to the ingenuity of our engineering department, and the

HONEYWELL

Amsterdam's A.P. Taselaar (Right) with Jim Binger in 1967.

high standard of workmanship and the support from the sales department in getting our equipment accepted as standard on the multitude of products which find their way to foreign shores."[20]

Another Mr. International

Before 1948, management of the European sales region came all the way from Minneapolis. But that year, Minneapolis-Honeywell established the International Division in Switzerland. Charlie Meech was appointed the new division's first director. Meech is a legendary Honeywell character who spoke French, German, Japanese, Latin, Italian, and Spanish. He had served in the Pacific during the war before joining Honeywell. Having travelled all over the world to establish a Honeywell presence, Meech has been referred to as a "Johnny Appleseed of international operations, traveling the world to plant the seeds of distributorships and subsidiaries."[21] The first International Division meeting was held in Amsterdam in 1947. In attendance were Meech, Amand and Taselaar from the Dutch office, and Jack Nelson from Stockholm. A year later, several members came over from the British offices, and H.W. Sweatt, Tom McDonald, and Bill Westphal made the trip across the Atlantic. The major outcome of the 1948 meeting was a decision allowing the subsidiaries to purchase a company car—"preferably used," urged the conservative Sweatt.[22]

Honeywell posted 1949 international sales of $6,507,000, and profits of $1,248,000. The cost of doing business internationally remained relatively high, but the company continued to expand this business by consistently reinvesting its modest profits.

Two years after the establishment of the international office, International was moved to Amsterdam and placed under the direction of Taselaar, with Hollema succeeding him as manager of the Dutch organization.[23] Charlie Meech was heading for South America and the Far East.

Manufacturing Abroad

A distributorship was the most conservative entry into a new market. If it was successful, the company would move toward a wholly-owned subsidiary, or perhaps cultivate a relationship with a distributor which could evolve into a joint venture. Once the subsidiary was established, the next step was to provide for local manufacturing by building a plant and hiring a crew. At first the facility might simply assemble parts shipped from Minneapolis or some other production site. The ultimate goal, however, was to operate an independent production plant.

Jack Nelson (Left) and Tom Olafson met in Honeywell's Stockholm facilities in 1953. Nelson established Honeywell's Swedish subsidiary just before World War II. Olafson was a Swedish emigrant who worked for many years in the company's Minneapolis manufacturing plant. Both worked together on the production floor in the 1920s.

This plant would eventually establish its own research, design, and engineering facilities.

In 1936, Honeywell founded its first foreign assembly facility in the company's oldest subsidiary in Canada. Nine years later, the first full-scale factory began operation outside Toronto. In 1948 a Honeywell factory opened in Blantyre, Scotland, and five years later Amsterdam established a Dutch manufacturing facility. Typical of Honeywell's initial small-scale international manufacturing, Amsterdam produced a limited line of oil burner relays, boiler thermostats, and room thermostats.[24] Through the Fifties, Honeywell expanded international manufacturing in Scotland at Newhouse Industrial Park, and in Doernigheim, Germany.

Continued Growth: the 1950s and 1960s

Throughout the 1950s, the company forged ahead in establishing distributorships and subsidiaries around the world. Typical was the

1912-1927

1936-1946

1909-1927

1946

1927-1936

The Evolution
of a Logo

1950

As Honeywell evolved, so did its logo. Before 1927, Minneapolis Heat Regulator's logo featured the name of the company in forward-leaning print. After the 1927 merger of Minneapolis Heat Regulator and Honeywell Heating Specialties, the new company adapted Honeywell Heating Specialties' brazier design, incorporating the new intitials "MHR." This design was used throughout the 1930s, until the stylized "MH" appeared in 1936. This later logo was the company trademark through the war years. In 1946, the "pillow" design appeared, first as a background for the 1940s MH design, later as a placard for an increasing emphasis on the Honeywell half of the company's name. By 1950, "Minneapolis" had all but disappeared from the trademark, replaced by a single boldfaced "H" on a red pillow.

establishment of a subsidiary in Cuba in 1951. Cran Sharp travelled to Havana to assess the political, cultural, and economic situation under Fulgencio Batista. Sharp believed it sufficiently stable, and proceeded to establish an office there. Whatever risks there were, he believed, would be outweighed by the substantial business to be gained from Cuba's extensive sugar refining industries. Sharp anticipated $150,000 in gross sales in the Cuban operation's first year, with eventual annual sales of $200,000-$300,000.[25] His financial report on Cuba was accurate enough, but he couldn't foresee the revolution in the making there. Ten years after the subsidiary was established, it was seized by the Castro government.

Honeywell continued its European expansion in 1956, adding subsidiaries in Denmark, Germany, France, and Austria. International sales reached $32,649,000 that year, with profits passing the $5 million mark, and employment outside the U.S. topping 3,000. In 1962, Honeywell purchased its longtime Australian distributor, Liddle and Epstein of Sydney. In the mid–Sixties, with international sales approaching $175 million, subsidiaries were established in Italy, Venezuela, Brazil, Argentina, Spain, and Taiwan. While the company was aggressive about adding subsidiaries, the process of actually starting one was more cautious. Gone were the days

when someone like Cran Sharp could start an office abroad with "just $10,000 and the articles of incorporation."

Honeywell Inc.

In 1963 the company changed its name to "Honeywell Inc." from Minneapolis–Honeywell. The change was hardly unexpected, since it had been casually referred to as Honeywell ever since the merger of 1927. Corporate logos and letterheads had increasingly identified with the Honeywell portion of the name.

In the Forties, the corporate logo evolved from the elongated, perfectly proportionate "MH" to the prominent red "pillow" with the large white "H." From the earliest days of the merger, employees referred to themselves as "Honeywellers." Actually, the parent company was the last to change its name, as most foreign subsidiaries had already dropped the reference to Minneapolis.

International Express

In 1965 Honeywell sent its entire board of directors on a tour of the European facilities. The fourteen directors held their regular quarterly meeting on a moving train, where they elected Jim Binger as chairman and Steve Keating

The directors' meeting aboard a train travelling from Frankfurt to Amsterdam in 1965. Holding the meeting in Europe emphasized the company's committment to international commerce.

Australian operations were centered in this Sydney office building in 1960.

president. A writer for London's *Financial Times* remarked on the significance of the directors' tour and the now-famous meeting on rails:

> *"It is becoming fashionable for American companies to prove that their heart is also with their European subsidiaries by sending their entire boards across the Atlantic. Ford made a monster descent on this country not long ago. Now Honeywell, that dynamic company, has gone one better. On Wednesday, it held its board meeting on a train en route from Frankfort to Amsterdam, getting two countries for the price of one, and elected a new, young chairman while they were at it."[26]*

Business Week commented that the meeting "was a session possibly unique in American corporate history."[27]

Jim Binger, a graduate of University of Minnesota Law School, was 48 when he took the helm of Honeywell. He had been president since 1961, and had worked in International for three years beginning in 1952. "I got into that [International] because of H.W.'s influence but also mainly because of Tom McDonald's bent toward the international business," Binger recalled. "He always took a major interest, as Harold Sweatt did, in the international side. They gave me an opportunity early in my career to see something of Honeywell overseas."[28]

When Binger was promoted to CEO, Steve Keating became president. '"We ran the company together for a long, long period of time," Keating recalled.[29] When Binger retired in 1974, Keating ascended to the CEO spot.

The two men had an interesting history. They had gone to law school together and had risen together through the ranks of Honeywell. "We were young, Binger and I," commented Keating. "We were fortunate in the sense that there was a senior group that grew up around H.W. who were largely men of his age, and then there was us."[30]

Binger had been the one who convinced Keating to take a job at Honeywell in 1948, Keating said. "Binger, who was here and was an old friend, knew that they had contacted me. When I expressed no interest, Binger called me and said, 'gee, I think you're making a mistake.'"[31] In 1960, both were named directors. Keating worked in the Aero Division, and Binger headed International.

The newly–elected Binger capitalized on this international background at a London press conference. He announced that "the company expects its international operations to account for 25 percent of the company's sales by 1968."[32] This was reinforced by the news that Honeywell was adding 100 new positions at its Newhouse factory to complement the 800 which had recently been added.[33] Keating, who

Honeywell's first factory in Germany. This Dornigheim facility produced valves beginning in 1956.

had just been appointed president, told *Business Week*, "We are an international company now, with an international viewpoint."[34]

Between 1960 and 1970 his point was proven with solid growth. From 1961 to 1970, international sales rose 175 percent. The expansion was similar to the company's evolution in the 1930s. But the growth of the Thirties was due to domestic acquisitions and diversification of the product lines, whereas the growth of the Fifties and Sixties was fueled by international expansion.

Golden Opportunities: 1970–1980

In 1970, Honeywell celebrated its golden anniversary in international sales, which began with Yamatake's distribution arrangements with Brown Instrument Company in 1920. That was the year C.B. Sweatt noted a total of $90 in incidental export sales. Fifty years later, Honeywell sales outside the United States amounted to $662 million, or 34 percent of the company's overall sales.

Also in 1970, the company restructured its European organization. The thirteen European subsidiaries had previously been coordinated from Minneapolis, with regional administration channeled through the large subsidiaries in Great Britain and Germany.[35] Honeywell then adopted a continent-wide approach based in Brussels, with Tom Reed in charge. The new strategy was partially designed to accommodate the ongoing development of the European marketplace. The reorganization was an evolution to a more centralized organization which could "coordinate product development, manufacturing, and marketing strategies."[36]

In fact, Honeywell Europe would come to be seen as a training ground for the company's CEOs in the 1980s and 1990s, according to CEO Michael Bonsignore, who was president of Honeywell Europe for five years starting in 1982.

"Europe is really a miniature of Honeywell. While I was in there, Honeywell was having to make a psychological shift in its evolution from a primarily domestic company with some foreign operations to a company with global potential. I think that without my European experience, it would have been very difficult for me to capture the essence of Honeywell's opportunity to move up to the next run on the global leadership ladder."[37]

Charlie Sweatt Jr. said Honeywell developed its international markets earlier than other companies. "It's something that most corporations ignored in the Fifties and Sixties. More than others, Honeywell had its feet in international markets early."[38] This international outlook was a source of pride.

"Harold Sweatt was the one who envisioned going international," Steve Keating said. "We have been international for a long, long time. Fortunately through all the generations of management we stuck to it. We are very proud that all the people who have been at the top of the company have been, in a sense, internationalists. Now in Mike [Bonsignore] you have a real internationalist who was president of [Honeywell] Europe."[39]

By 1972, company predictions that international business would comprise one quarter of total operations had been far surpassed. International sales accounted for 39 percent of Honeywell's $2.1 billion in overall sales that year, and of the company's 97,000 employees,

A Honeywell 125 computer rides through the fabled harbour of Venice on a gondola in 1960.

39 percent worked outside the U.S. Design and manufacturing operations were carried out in 26 factories in 14 countries. By 1972, Honeywell boasted 25 wholly-owned subsidiaries, 142 branch offices, and joint ventures in five countries.

In a speech in Paris, Chairman Jim Binger delineated the company's formula for international success:

> *"First, when we go into a foreign market, we go in for keeps. We reinvest a major part of our profits in the countries where they are earned. We are extremely careful in respecting the customs, traditions, and sensitivities of the people and governments in the countries where we do business. Second, we believe in staffing and managing our international companies with nationals of the areas and countries in which we operate. We treat our employees the same way we do in the parent company. Third, we believe in giving the market the product it wants, not the product we want it to have. We plan our new products on a world–wide basis, with the design and development done where we have the most pertinent engineering capability, irrespective of borders. We travel extensively so that our marketing people are intimately familiar with our customers' needs. We place maintenance and service ahead of sales. We stress quality in all our engineering and manufacturing departments."[40]*

In 1995, Chairman Michael Bonsignore still agrees. "We consider our global presence to be one of our strongest competitive differentiators today," he said. "That's because, increasingly, our customers are global companies. They tell us that no other company is as well positioned to be where they are and to do what we can do for them."[41]

Much of Honeywell's spectacular growth between 1960 and 1980 was directly related to the maturation of developing economies. In addition to its traditional line of domestic heating and air conditioning controls, Honeywell also dealt in thousands of systems for the control of industrial processes, ranging from tiny assembly line operations in Singapore to mammoth petroleum refinery operations in Saudi Arabia. The company eventually provided products and related services for petroleum, chemical, paper, and utility plants in every corner of the globe. In 1980 industrial control projects numbered over 12,000, with 96 jobs in the Middle East, 3,600 in the Far East, 140 in Australia, 50 in South Africa, and 200 in Latin America.

Honeywell's experience in the Middle East, not surprisingly, has been fraught with drama. Giannantonio Ferrari, president of Honeywell

Europe since 1992, was hired in 1965, and has been "moving around to different countries, different jobs," all at the management level, since then. He was general manager in Iran for a few years in the Seventies.[42]

> *"The experience was good in one way and very bad in another. I say good because we were able to expand the business significantly in that country, enjoying quite a good profitability, and there are still some very loyal customers. But it was very, very sad because I had to close down the company and lay off everybody. About three weeks before the Ayatollah Khomeini went back to Iran [in January 1979], we returned to Europe. It was a company decision in the sense that it was really impossible for me to maintain a decent level of operations. Several times I had my car splashed with spray paint. We were really feeling very uncomfortable. So I decided to close down."[43]*

Fred Kaiser opened Honeywell's first office in Buffalo, New York in 1935. A 1938 sales contest pitted salesmen against one another—"You started with shorts and additional clothing was allotted as you made your quota," said Kaiser, the nearly naked man in the center of the group.

Honeywell also suffered during the Gulf War in 1992, Ferrari said.

> *"We were in the very late stage of completing the largest TDC 3000 order that Honeywell ever received, which was for an oil refinery in Kuwait. It cost around $30 million. It was the second part of July, so we put it in an air conditioned warehouse to be ready. Later on, the TDC disappeared. We never found out what happened to it.*
> *We were the first company to go back into Kuwait [after the war]. We were the first company to get our operation up and running. Ten days after arriving, we already had 12 people, then we went up to 24. Now there are 80. We didn't ship another*

TDC 3000 because the oil refinery was damaged. Now we are waiting for another order. Sooner or later, that refinery will start production again."[44]

By 1979, international sales surpassed $1 billion, comprised a quarter of total sales, and represented efforts in 80 countries. Honeywell's 28 manufacturing operations in 14 countries meant that one–third of Honeywell's factories were located outside the U.S.

Process control systems had been an outgrowth of the Brown division's business since the 1930s. New technologies to centralize the management of industrial processes had been developing rapidly over the previous forty years, along with the management of security and environment in large commercial buildings. The TDC 2000 central control room was in wide use at petroleum refineries in Germany and France during the late Seventies.

The family of Honeywell Delta systems, for climate and security control in large commercial and institutional buildings, was also popular abroad. In 1978, nearly half of all Delta installations were outside the U.S. The attraction was clear: one Delta 1000 installed at Rank Xerox, in Mitcheldean, England, controlled environment, fire detection and security, while delivering a remarkable 25 percent savings in energy consumption. A similar system in Pau, France, allowed for the centralized management of 50

Yamatake-Honeywell's Fujisawa, Japan manufacturing facility.

public buildings – some built in the 11th Century. The larger Delta 2500 computerized building management system was installed in 1978 in the International Congress Center in Berlin; this sophisticated system automatically monitored 4,000 points in the center's temperature, lighting, elevator, and fire alarm systems. Another controls system that found popularity abroad was the BOSS system, providing centralized

Yamatake-Honeywell commercial engineers discuss plans in Osaka in 1970.

building control for smaller businesses. Through leased phone lines, a BOSS center could manage temperature and security systems at a number of small business locations. In 1978, international BOSS centers were established in Sydney, London, Montreal, and Toronto.

New Markets and Old Strategies

In the 1970s and 1980s, the Middle East and Far East were targeted as regions of strong growth and Honeywell began studying the potential of China. The best way to get to the mainland, company executives believed, was through Japan and the longstanding Yamatake-Honeywell relationship. By 1987, international business accounted for 25 percent of the company's total profit and volume. While over $1 billion of international sales was based in Europe, $700 million resulted solely from the Yamatake partnership.[45]

Ed Spencer, CEO from 1974 to 1987, was hired in 1954 for the Aeronautical Division and moved to International after one year. He became Far East regional manager in 1959, a post that included responsibility for Yamatake. He remained in Japan until 1964, when he returned to Minneapolis as director of exports. In 1965, he was elected corporate vice president, with responsibility for all international operations. In 1980, Spencer reaffirmed Honeywell's position of respect for the politics and customs of host countries. He also emphasized that each subsidiary should develop its own national identity. "For example," said Spencer, "we want our German subsidiary to be regarded as a German company—not a German branch of an American company. We encourage our subsidiaries to become self-sufficient so that they may design, manufacture, and export."[46] Geri Joseph, a member of Honeywell's board and the U.S. Ambassador

Honeywell established a subsidiary in Brazil in 1965.

to the Netherlands during the Carter administration, said Honeywell "tried to understand the culture in which they were operating. It is one reason they are a successful company. You just can't throw your weight around in these countries. You've got to work within their cultures."[47]

One of the ways Honeywell provided this encouragement was its policy of staffing foreign offices with citizens of the host country. Out of 23,000 people employed by Honeywell outside the U.S. in 1980, only 100 were Americans. Longtime Honeywell internationalist Tom Donahue called this a "classic example of how to make your company grow on a sound and lasting

Built in 1956, Honeywell's plant in Amiens, France, manufactures industrial controls.

basis."[48] In 1982, a Honeywell executive described the company's long tradition of respecting other cultures.

"Our corporation has been working on the problems and challenges of cultural diversity for nearly fifty years. We view these cultural differences as a key strength of the corporation, and a source of vitality. Our strategy is, rather than try to force our foreign managers into an American mold, we attempt to draw upon the unique characteristics of managers in different parts of the world to strengthen our market position and our worldwide organization."[49]

Experience – A Valuable Commodity

With the formation of Honeywell High Tech Trading on January 1, 1984, the company began leasing its considerable overseas marketing and distribution experience to other corporations, through offices in Brussels, Milan, Athens, Singapore, Vienna, and Minneapolis.

HHTT's first goal was to give Honeywell a presence where it had no affiliate, by making contacts and distribution arrangements that could lead to the formation of subsidiaries. The second goal was to identify U.S. and foreign companies seeking to trade internationally, but lacking the experience and size to do so. HHTT could provide international distribution appropriate to the product in question. Frequently, companies and products handled by HHTT would complement Honeywell products already trading in the international market. The third goal was to act as an agent for countertrade, a modern form of bartering in which a nation or corporation would demand to make payment for imports with products of its own. Primarily involving countries with weak or convertible currencies, countertrade was "an imaginative way of adapting to the changing environment of international trade," said Biorn Biornstad, HHTT president and general manager at its inception. "Some countries insist on countertrade as a means of marketing their products."[50]

The key to making countertrade work for Honeywell was to ensure that the company could resell the products it received in exchange. Honeywell usually made sure the bartered products were sold before the deal even went through. This could be a complicated but attractive transaction where Honeywell would distribute, say, a shipment of West German instruments to India, and receive as payment medical supplies needed in Venezuela. Honeywell High Tech Trading would act as the international courier in such a deal. The HHTT organization was also important

Honeywell expanded into the Middle East around 1970. But the company was forced to shut its Iranian office in 1978, just weeks before the Ayatollah Khomeini returned, forcing the Shah of Iran to leave the country he had ruled for 37 years.

through the Eighties as a contact for Central and Eastern European markets still under the Soviet sphere of influence.[51]

South Africa

The troublesome history of race relations in South Africa made Honeywell's offices there a crucible for the company's policy of respecting the cultures of its host countries. By Honeywell standards, the political practice of apartheid could not in good conscience be condoned or defended.

The South Africa subsidiary, established in 1969, experienced spectacular growth between 1970 and 1982, as employment rose from 61 to 188. Much of the company's success was due to the huge Sasol oil operations, for which the company had constructed the largest TDC 2000 industrial control complex ever undertaken. But by 1980, media and public pressure came to bear on South Africa because of apartheid, and some of this pressure spilled over to U.S. companies operating in South Africa. Companies were under pressure to divest their interests there. Yet, perhaps because of Honeywell's pledge never to abandon a chosen market, the company was reluctant to leave. So Honeywell, like many other U.S. and international concerns, proposed to help change South Africa. In 1982, Honeywell South Africa instituted an aggressive affirmative action program. Unfortunately, it was hard to find qualified applicants because apartheid had kept black

South Africans from the training and education needed for even semi-skilled jobs. Even with this dearth, the subsidiary did hire several black students in 1982. At the same time, Honeywell contributed to a wide variety of programs to improve the welfare of black South Africans. In a 1982 report, subsidiary director R.E. Maroukian said the outlook remained hopeful:

> *"South Africa is a country in transition. The interaction between internal and external pressures for change has resulted in a process of institutional and social reform that is gathering momentum. In this dynamic environment a major challenge to Honeywell South Africa is to develop an organization of people who have the flexibility, expertise, and creativity to cope. Essential to our coping strategy will be access to and continued usage of the accumulated knowledge and expertise in the worldwide Honeywell organization."[52]*

Unfortunately, the situation did not improve measurably, and in 1986 Honeywell elected to sell the South African subsidiary. Seven years later, the company became one of the first American companies to reinvest in South Africa, after Nelson Mandela was released from prison and the process of dismantling apartheid had begun in earnest. Ferrari, current president of Honeywell Europe, said the company's return to South Africa is going well.

> *"We bought back the company about one year ago. We are very, very pleased. Number one, because we made the decision to reinvest, and number two, because our customers are glad that Honeywell is back. We are*

Honeywell Austria's offices were built after the company established its subsidiary there in 1956. Austria performed double duty as a corridor for trade with Eastern Bloc countries including the Soviet Union until the establishment of Honeywell High Tech Trading in 1984.

getting a lot of encouragement through solid orders, which is important."[53]

China

A 1979 *Honeywell World* article identified a promising market: "The world's largest single untapped market, without doubt, lies behind just one border – that of the People's Republic of China. Honeywell has already begun an aggressive pursuit of this business, primarily through Yamatake-Honeywell but also through a recently-established subsidiary in Hong Kong."[54] China was indeed an attractive market, and some of the bonds of state control seemed to be loosening. In January, 1979, the United States had established diplomatic relations with China after nearly three decades of estrangement.

In 1976, former CEO Jim Binger had headed a Honeywell trade mission to Peking, now Beijing. Efforts were stepped up to approach China through Charlie Meech and the Yamatake organization, by way of the trade show circuit active within Japan.[55] These efforts paid off in the early 1980s, when a contract for a "technical export license" was signed by Haruo Okinobu, president of Yamatake-Honeywell, and the director of China's Technical Import Corporation. The contract called for Yamatake-Honeywell to supply engineering support to China for the production of a control valve. China's largest control valve factory started production in April 1981. This was not the first such arrangement for Yamatake-Honeywell, for in 1973 the company had executed a similar agree-ment with an Indian government corporation known as Instrumentation Limited.[56]

Jim Renier, then Honeywell's vice chairman, visited China in 1984. Following his tour he explained, "China is an almost unbelievably difficult place to do business." Honeywell had encountered challenges at almost every turn. Security approval from the governments of both China and the U.S. confounded problems of language, distance, and transportation. "But," added Renier, "business conditions are improving so rapidly that China is becoming a real opportunity for us." The main reason for his optimism was the fact that China was trying desperately to catch up with Western technology. Chinese universities were key to this effort, with 14 state-administered institutions seeking contracts for Honeywell computer systems by the close of 1984.[57] "China is a nation of some 800 million," the *Honeywell World* reported, "with most of the basic resources they need and a commitment to rapidly modernize an economy that, in some respects, is like that of the U.S. 20 or 30 years ago." In other words, the market in China was something like that of America in about 1950—a period during which Honeywell experienced unprecedented growth and incredible success.[58]

Renier, who has a Ph.D. in physical chemistry, was hired as a senior research scientist in 1956. He held a variety of management positions within Honeywell's research and defense–oriented operations before joining the computer side of the company

HONEYWELL

Honeywell's Paris facility in 1975. The company had been in France since 1950. During Honeywell's years in the computer business, the company's French connection expanded through the acquisition of Bull.

in 1970 as vice president. He was chairman and CEO from 1988 to 1993.

The Soviet Union

One of the company's earliest international ventures was with the Soviet Union during the 1930s. When Russian–born Mark Watkins managed the New York office, through which all exports were handled until World War II, contacts were made with Soviet purchasing agencies. He dealt primarily with a Russian purchasing company known as the Antory Organization, and at one point, plans were made to dispatch a Honeywell team to Moscow and return a Russian team to Honeywell's Industrial Division. Russians were to learn how to manufacture the company's instruments, and to lay out a suitable manufacturing plant. The plan was abandoned with the onset of World War II.[59] When the war began, both the Russian purchasing agency and the Minneapolis-Honeywell export desk moved to Washington, D.C. Cran Sharp, stationed at the Washington desk, had many dealings with the Soviets through the war, and in 1941, he oversaw the printing of a company catalog in Russian.[60]

Twenty–five years later, Sharp participated in a trade mission endorsed by the Minneapolis Area Chamber of Commerce. The first program of its kind, the mission was designed to foster business between Minnesota, the

Soviet Union, Yugoslavia, Poland, and Romania. Jim Binger, then CEO, eventually travelled to Moscow to establish a one–person office there in 1974. In 1976, Honeywell signed a "cooperation agreement" with PRVA/ISKRA of Belgrade, allowing the Yugoslavian company to manufacture Honeywell industrial valves and actuators. Honeywell agreed to provide the "fabrication know–how for these products and support the production startup in Yugoslavia."[61] Contacts between Honeywell and the Soviet Union and Eastern Bloc countries were coordinated mostly through the Austrian subsidiary, until the incorporation of Honeywell High Tech Trading in 1984.

Australia and New Zealand

In the Southwest Pacific, Honeywell's largest operation is Honeywell Limited of Australia, with 15 branch offices, plus technical and software centers. Honeywell Limited got its start in 1962, moving up, like many Honeywell subsidiaries, from distributor status. The affiliate's workforce has grown from 100 at its inception to a current total of more than 1300, and much of this growth came during Australia's boom years of the late 1970s. Phil Myles, who headed the Australian company during this period, reported 25 percent sales growth for each of the last three years of the Seventies. Then, as now, Honeywell was the primary provider of industrial and building con-

HONEYWELL

Honeywell's Brussels, Belgium office in 1970.

Honeywell's presence in Krakow, Poland is indicative of a growing concern in formerly communist countries to control emmisions and other environmental pollutants.

trols to Australia's dominant mining, petrochemical and agricultural industries.

Honeywell has been a presence in New Zealand since 1931 when Paykel Brothers Ltd. became distributors for Brown Instruments Company, part of Honeywell. The New Zealand company became a 50–50 joint venture in 1972. That operation, known as Paykel–Honeywell Limited, changed its name to MSI Honeywell Limited in 1977 before becoming a wholly–owned affiliate, Honeywell Limited, in 1981.

John Emery became head of the operation in 1960 and recorded substantial sales growth in 19 of his first 20 years at the helm. By the early Eighties, Honeywell New Zealand's workforce had reached the same level it maintains today, and Honeywell continues to be the dominant force in both the industrial and building controls marketplace in New Zealand.

Honeywell New Zealand has only 120 people, said John Wadsworth, current managing director. "But we seem to tackle everything Honeywell throws at us. We're very proud of being small but innovative. We can bring things to fruition very quickly."[62]

In 1995, Honeywell New Zealand is enthusiastic about two key projects. One is with the country's only oil refinery; the other is supplying automation and controls for the Sky City Casino in Auckland, New Zealand. Home and Building Control has received a $3.6 million contract, its largest ever, for the design and installation of various systems including building management,

environmental control, fire alarms, security and power control and monitoring. The casino is expected to open in January 1996.

Japan

Perhaps the single most important international relationship developed by Honeywell was the one with the Yamatake organization in Japan. The relationship began in 1920, when company founder Takehiko Yamaguchi signed agreements to import Brown instruments into Japan, and continued when Honeywell acquired Brown in 1935. By then, Yamatake was already assembling Brown instruments in Japan from imported parts.

World War II cut off all relations between Honeywell and Yamatake.[65] But after the war, Yamaguchi's son Toshihiko "quietly appeared at Honeywell offices in Minneapolis and gave an accounting of business during the war years with ledgers documenting revenues, expenses and profits and showing in detail how much he owed the company. But with much of his factory space damaged or destroyed by bombs, he said, there was no way he could readily pay the debt." [66] Yamatake had manufactured Brown technologies through the war and had sold Brown instruments to the Japanese navy. But the company kept track of royalties due Honeywell because Yamaguchi felt 'there was never a war between our two partner companies'. After looking into the situation, Cran Sharp told Honeywell executives

Honeywell's Golden Valley, Minnesota facility is a strategic manufacturing site for Home and Building Control products shipped worldwide.

that Yamatake "owed us a huge amount in depreciated Japanese yen, and that they were clearly bankrupt."[67]

Jim Binger recalled meeting with the Yamatake executives to figure out how to collect the debt. "After talking to them and looking at the balance sheet, I remember saying, 'they have got a huge obligation and acknowledge difficulties getting the money. Tom [McDonald] said to me, 'well why don't you just take $12 and call it even. I said, 'why don't we take 50 percent of the company?' I proposed that and the next day they said 'OK.'"[68] A joint venture was formed, one that eventually became a model for U.S.–Japanese business relations.

In 1956, Yamaguchi's company took the name of Yamatake-Honeywell, and began a long period of prosperity. Yamatake's employment in 1952 was 200; by 1970 it had risen to nearly 3,000,[69] and Yamatake-Honeywell even exported various products to the United States.

In 1959, the Japanese camera maker Asahi provided Asahi Pentax cameras to North American markets, where they were sold as the Honeywell Pentax and distributed by Honeywell. In connection with the camera

The Global Presence

Honeywell worldwide locations. By 1993, the company served customers in 95 countries on six continents. Since foreign sales are growing faster than U.S. sales, by the end of the century non-U.S. sales are expected to approach 50 percent of total business.

Honeywell began distributing, designing, and producing photographic products in the late 1950s, when the company acquired the Heiland Research Company in Denver. Heiland had developed the "Strobonar" flash unit pictured at right.

Honeywell distributed Asahi-Pentax cameras from 1959 until 1974, when the company began to divest its photographic product intrests.

business, Honeywell acquired from Heiland a strobe flash unit, developed a slide projector, and later, automatic focus technology.

Chuck Ungemach, a Honeywell patent attorney, said Honeywell profited greatly from its auto focus technology. "We had patents in Japan and many other countries. We successfully sued Minolta for patent infringement and then licensed 15 other companies, including Canon and Kodak. By the time it was over [in the 1990s], we collected $400 million in settlements and royalties." [70]

Dean Randall, former vice president of communications, said Honeywell "also obtained a line of recording measurement devices from the Heiland acquisition." That line evolved into the Visicorder, "a tremendously sensitive recording device." Success of the Viscorder and related instrumentation gave rise to the Test Instruments Division, an organization that flourished well into the Eighties.

With its auto–focus technology, and the Pentax camera, Honeywell took on the Japanese camera industry, Randall said. "And we did fairly well. I don't think we lost any money at it. But it wasn't a growth business. Sooner or later, we got tired of it."[71]

In 1974, the company stopped distributing Asahi Pentax, and eventually got out of the photographic equipment business. "[Asahi Pentax] decided they wanted to distribute them-

Honeywell's international presence is typified by its Amsterdam business. Over 70 percent of Dutch homes are fitted with Honeywell Controls.

selves just as they have with everything else," Steve Keating, CEO at the time, recalled. "It was never a really big money maker. But it probably enhanced our image to some extent because we weren't really a consumer company." [72]

The Yamatake-Honeywell partnership was a successful merging of Eastern and Western corporate styles. In the Japanese corporation, for example, employment security is central to any successful organization. Workers are rarely dismissed, and many work their entire lives for the same firm. Literacy skills are very high, and Japanese workers tend to identify more closely with their employer than do their American counterparts. Japanese workers typically receive a substantial package of fringe benefits, and many of their social activities are linked to the company. Japanese employees are also more inclined than Americans to identify themselves as part of a group. Sales competitions at Yamatake-Honeywell, for example, are won by groups rather than individuals.[73]

Charlie Meech, one-time head of Honeywell Far East operations, asserted that the success of the Yamatake–Honeywell partnership was a direct result of a symbiotic relationship, based upon "deep understanding and close personal relationships at many levels" between the two companies.[74] Yamatake-Honeywell was "one of the largest, fastest-growing and most profitable arms of Honeywell's increasingly international business organization."[75]

"The relationship with Yamatake goes back into the 1920s," said CEO Bonsignore. "Our relationship survived World War II. In 1953 we created a jointly–owned company with Yamatake.... I put myself back in that year and ask what would I have done differently with the Yamatake–Honeywell relationship? It would have been to try and look out 10 years, 20 years and say, 'What do we want this relationship to be in 1973, in 1983?' as opposed to, 'What do we want it to be next month or next year.'" [76]

Trade Tensions

By the 1980s, Honeywell was ensnared by increasing tensions between the U.S. and Japan, the result of continuing trade imbalances between the two nations. Chairman and CEO Ed Spencer played a key role in defusing anti-Japanese sentiment in the United States by arguing that trade protectionism must be avoided at all costs. Spencer downplayed Japanese-American competition as a cause of the general malaise in the international market in an April 1984 address to the U.S. House Ways and Means Committee's Subcommittee on Trade.

"The very size, complexity, and interdependence of economic and political relationships between the U.S. and Japan," Spencer said, "are inevitably going to lead to friction between us. We will continue to be major customers of each other, and at the same time, keen competitors... to cast Japan as a principal cause of our domestic and international trading problems is to do ourselves and Japan a disservice."[77]

Spencer's answer to resolving the imbalance was to work at reducing the old protectionist mechanisms still in place from the period following World War II. He asserted that the U.S. had to increase its own competitiveness, and prevent growth of new restraints, rather than block other countries from trading in America. Trade restrictions, he emphasized, would likely lead to trade wars.

"The best industrial policy for our country avoids import quotas and restrictions and lets the market decide which industries expand and which contract. The lead in competitive improvement must come from individual companies, not from government actions. We should start with the proposition that exporting is not only important, but essential to the economic health of our nation."[78]

Honeywell enjoys a long tradition of volunteer work in the communities in which the company operates, like the Special Olympics held in the Twin Cities.

CHAPTER NINE
A TRADITION OF CARING

"Let us not confuse business motivation with social goals. Let us not confuse the profit motivation of business with the goals of society. But let us recognize that in many instances they are parallel."

—CEO Steve Keating, 1968.

Companies have a way of reflecting the personalities of the people who run them. Honeywell still reflects the personality of the man who first opened its doors, W.R. Sweatt.

W.R. never lost sight of the fact that *people* make a company, and *people* are the customer base. The proof is in Honeywell's history of charitable social activities and extensive efforts to improve the conditions of employees. The company also boasts a unique and enviable record of concern with improving society as a whole.

W.R. Sweatt

The man who took over the Electric Heat Regulator Company at the turn of the century could safely be described as cantankerous. But W.R. Sweatt's brash manner could not hide a deep humanitarian streak. Though he died nearly sixty years ago, stories about his loyalty to his employees survive still.

A good example is the story of Bill Harrison. Harrison was a service and installation employee who bought a new Ford after getting married in 1924. Four months later, the new Mrs. Harrison became ill. In order to pay her steep hospital bill, Harrison needed to sell his new car. When W.R. heard of Harrison's predicament, he summoned Harrison to his office, and reportedly stormed, "Damn it, why don't you come up and tell me these things? We'll help you out."

Harrison answered, "Why should I bother you with all my troubles? You've got enough to think about with things around here."

W.R. retorted, "You're working for me, and your problems are just as much mine as they are yours. You're not going to sell that Ford."

He led Harrison out to the cashier's desk and demanded, "You give this man whatever money he needs, and let him sign a note for it. He'll pay it back whenever he can." Sweatt walked briskly away. Halfway back to his office he turned and shouted with the loud voice of a practiced curmudgeon, "Make damn sure you don't charge him any interest on that!"[1] Sweatt authorized similar interest-free loans to employees making down payments on new homes.[2]

In the 1970s and 1980s, it became fashionable to speak of corporate ethics and social responsibility in terms of "enlightened self-interest." W.R. Sweatt pioneered in this area in the first decade of this century. In the years before 1912, when Electric Heat Regulator Company began to grow in the sale of damper-flapper systems, the company was having difficulty finding enough employees to fill production lines. Many people were hired from outlying areas some distance from the Minneapolis factory. Dayton, Minnesota was one of these places, a sleepy country town with working–class folks. The eighteen Dayton employees liked to let loose on the weekend. They held Saturday and Sunday night dances that sometimes lasted until 5 a.m. Every Monday, the Dayton crew staggered in around noon, hung over and somewhat ornery. Naturally, Monday's production schedule lagged. W.R. took matters into his own hands. He traveled to Dayton and spoke to the local priest, taking with him a gift of two bottles of wine, a box of cigars, and money for charity.

W.R. didn't waste words: "We're a small company and we just can't afford the loss of time from the eighteen people we have working here from your community. Please accept this small token of our appreciation and do your best to

HONEYWELL

Mark Honeywell oversaw the planning and construction of the Honeywell Community Center in Wabash, Indiana. Built in 1939, the Center was a model facility for Honeywell's hometown community.

stop the Sunday night dances at midnight or earlier."[3] Legend has it there was never a problem on Monday mornings again.

A Legacy of Giving

By the 1920s, Honeywell Heating Specialties was challenging the Minneapolis Heat Regulator Co.'s monopoly on home heating controls. The companies resolved their bitter competition by merging in 1927, and Mark Honeywell became president of the newly formed company. Honeywell was nearing retirement age at the time of the merger, and in 1934, he turned the presidency over to young H.W. Sweatt. For the next thirty years Honeywell devoted himself to philanthropic activities. In 1939, he designed and donated a state-of-the-art community building in his hometown of Wabash. The Honeywell Memorial Community Center was a 1,000,000 square-foot public facility built in honor of his wife, Eugenia Hubbard, and her parents. In 1941, Honeywell incorporated the Honeywell Foundation, a non-profit company chartered to support worthy community programs in Wabash. In the 1960s, he built a community swimming pool and donated an 80-acre park planted with 1,000 roses. Eugenia Hubbard Honeywell was also an active philanthropist, and in 1971 she was awarded the first Eisenhower Distinguished American Award, for her work in establishing a scholarship at Butler University.[4]

A New Commitment To Giving

In 1931, the board of directors agreed that philanthropy was as rewarding for the company as for as the communities in which it operated. Willard Huff, Mark Honeywell's longtime assistant, recommended that donations to charitable causes should be a continuing effort in all communities in which Minneapolis-Honeywell did business:

"Mr. Huff pointed out to the meeting that a distinct benefit accrued to the company from its contributions to Community Funds, not only in Minneapolis but also at all of the points where such contributions were being made. It was emphasized particularly that at least a portion of these funds was in many cases used specifically for the protection and care of some of the company's own employees. It was also pointed out that in all of these communities where the company was called upon to make these contributions, that the company and its interests would be in disrepute on failure to make such contributions. After discussion, the following resolution was therefore unanimously adopted: RESOLVED: That in keeping with its former practice, the company should make reason-

able donations to Community Fund Drives, not only in Minneapolis, but at the other points where offices are maintained. It was further resolved that this expense was considered as an essential part of the company's operations."[5]

H.W. appreciated the civic works of his employees. "I think he had a very soft heart," recalled Herb Bissell, who was marketing vice president during Sweatt's later years with the company. "I remember particularly him speaking to me on several occasions when I had accomplished something in the community or was recognized on the radio. And when I was general chairman of the United Way, he went out of his way to be very, very nice to me."[6]

A Helping Hand in the Depression

Independent of the company, a Minneapolis-Honeywell employees' group called the Minnregs (after MINNeapolis REGulator) donated thousands of dollars to needy employees during the Great Depression. At the prompting of W.R. Sweatt in 1925, the Minnregs had been established as a kind of company fraternity for veteran employees.[7] Members paid dues, attended regular meetings, and helped out with programs and events. Originally chartered to encourage fellowship, the Minnregs' activities expanded to include a broad field of athletic leagues and social events. But when the Depression hit, the organization spent thousands of dollars to purchase food, coal, clothing, and medicines for employees who were recently released or had their hours reduced. This relief program, formalized in 1932, provided volunteers and funds "to take care of the ever-increasing numbers of employees needing help due to reduced work hours and wages caused by the Depression." Relief work, in fact, was the "main endeavor" of the Minnregs during the Depression.[8] By 1950, the Minnregs had a budget of $28,000, a substantial portion of which was dedicated to charities and Honeywellers in need.[9]

A parallel social and service organization for women, the Honeybelles, was formed in 1955 for female employees in Minneapolis. Like the Minnregs, this organization developed a tradition of special–event fundraising. In its 40 years, the club has raised an estimated $800,000 for good causes, and has volunteered thousands of hours for community service.

Community Chest Drives

Honeywell encouraged local agencies to make annual appeals to company employees, and these

Starting before the days of the 1927 merger, Minneapolis-Honeywell's employees group—the Minnregs—sponsored athletics teams. In addition to the pictured hockey team, a baseball team and band were also formed.

drives usually met with great success. On "Red Feather Days," for example, employees were asked to donate up to six hours' pay to the Minneapolis Community Chest; in 1948, Honeywellers gave over $20,000 to this charity alone. That same year, 92.5 percent of all employees pledged an average of $5.20 to the Chest.[10] The money was distributed to 60 Twin Cities relief agencies, from job training for the handicapped to food programs for orphanages. Honeywellers also responded impressively to *ad hoc* relief efforts. In 1946, when the company received word of the terrible conditions in Holland from its Dutch officers, it sent 1800 pounds of clothing to Holland for general distribution from the Amsterdam offices.[11] After World War II, Red Cross launched several appeals at company headquarters, and employees responded with $10,000 in donations. These drives were so successful that in 1950 the many appeals were combined into one United Appeal.[12]

The Sixties

The 1960s were a time of great social upheaval in the United States. The country was split over the conflict in Vietnam, as well as new attitudes toward race, sex and politics. Like the government itself, large American companies were often seen as "the establishment." Corporate directors and executives had to fight public criticism of their companies' policies and products. Honeywell's fans and foes alike would agree that the company was fortunate to have Jim Binger and Steve Keating in charge during such difficult times.

HONEYWELL

Jim Binger (left) and Steve Keating led Honeywell through the turbulent but productive years between 1965 and 1974.

Early in the 1960s, Honeywell joined other progressive companies in a plan aimed at reversing the unwritten code of discrimination against minorities and women in the workplace. In 1961, Vice President Lyndon Johnson initiated a national Plan for Progress which evolved into Equal Employment Opportunity legislation. Honeywell participated in a 1961 White House signing ceremony at which the company affirmed its own commitment to the Kennedy administration's social and civil rights agenda. The company adopted an Equal Employment Opportunity policy statement, pledging itself to proactive hiring practices: "It is the policy of the Minneapolis-Honeywell Regulator Company that all employees be recruited, hired, trained, assigned and promoted without discrimination because of race, color, creed, or national origin." Today, the policy sounds rather common, but at the time it was a bold and progressive initiative.

There were several reasons for adopting the Plan for Progress. First was the important goal of improving society. In 1964, Honeywell Vice President Gerry Morse commented to an Equal Employment Opportunity Seminar at the University of Pennsylvania, "The chance to make a good living is of paramount importance to any lasting correction for the disadvantaged. As business leaders we cannot turn away from our direct involvement in this problem.'"[13]

Another reason why Equal Opportunity was an important business initiative was that it made financial sense. Disadvantaged people were an untapped market for producers. As consumers, they could strengthen the economy. Morse noted that the Plan for Progress was useful even to companies that did not discriminate. An explicit commitment to the tenets of equal opportunity would encourage other companies to make the same pledge.

"Our country cannot afford to waste its man-power talents and resources. Our chances for success are increased in proportion as we can locate, develop, and use the talents of all our people cost-effectively. Over the years we felt that our non-discriminatory employment practices did work and that we were providing Negroes and members of other minority groups with equal employment opportunity. However, the record has proven that we were wrong. We have made more progress in finding, hiring, and promoting quality minority group individuals after signing [The Plan for Progress] 2-years ago than we had in all the previous 75 years."[14]

Of course, the success of such a plan depended on management's commitment to it. "To us," Morse said, "these commitments are just as much a part of running our business as sales or production commitments." And the numbers bore his statement out: In 1961, the year before company officials signed the Plan for Progress, minority employment was 1 percent of total employment. In 1963, total Honeywell employment was up 10 percent, while minority employment increased 42 percent.[15] This trend continued, apparently independent of the company's general fortunes. In 1964, total employment increased just 1.1 percent, while non-white employment increased by 38 percent. That same year, minorities made up 2.7 percent of Honeywell's total payroll, up from 2 percent in 1963.

Honeywell's policy had always been "to hire employees on the basis of qualifications without regard to race." The limitations of this policy were apparent. As late as 1966, Fred Laing, of Honeywell's corporate employee relations department, said, "I think that qualified women and members of minority groups often have not sought employment because they were afraid of being turned down or felt the company might not be sincere in its equal opportunity policy."[16] Honeywell's problem was *finding* qualified minorities and women—few had gained access to the education, training, and experience that would qualify them for a position at the company. The Plan for Progress seemed to demand more, and Honeywell responded by supporting education programs for minority youth, and hosting them on "career day programs."

In the second half of the 1960s, this approach evolved into programs specifically designed to qualify minorities and women for jobs at Honeywell. Fred Laing told a group of insurance companies in 1967 that *legal* equality was no guarantee of *real* equality.

> "I think we all recognize that change is essential, not because of new laws or executive orders, but because it is time to change. And further because it is right to change. The easy assumption that since the Negro has achieved legal equality, he can now achieve economic equality has limited, if any, validity." [17]

> "It is not enough for us to beat the bushes for engineers, trained managers, qualified stenographers, or electronic technicians who happen to be Negro. Employment trends being what they are, it is not surprising that the majority of Negroes available for work and pressing for jobs are simply not qualified for these jobs. We in business and industry must take our place in the effort to see that Negroes become qualified." [18]

The Honeywell Project Protests

A loosely affiliated group of political and social activists, eventually known as the Honeywell Project, began protesting Honeywell's defense production in the late 1960s. The company responded in a most unusual manner—by granting permission to the demonstrators to peaceably assemble on Honeywell property. It even allowed protestors to use company restrooms and telephones. Many executives were personally acquainted with protestors. Founding project member Marvin Davidov was on speaking terms with then-chairman Jim Binger, and would usually phone Binger's office to let him know when demonstrations were planned. When Honeywell Project protestors planned to show up at Binger's suburban church with parts from a Honeywell-manufactured anti-tank shell, Davidov phoned Binger in advance. Binger told him, "You have every right to do this. And you are *certainly* doing it." [19]

Protests took place at company headquarters, said Warde Wheaton, then vice president of Aerospace and Defense. "They would almost never come out to the manufacturing plant because they would have been met, I think, with some emotional

resistance on the part of our employees who were proud of their work." [20] In 1970, protesters broke door and window glass at Honeywell's corporate headquarters, causing company officers to adjourn the annual shareholder's meeting. Binger had told Davidov that a spokesman could address the meeting as long as he kept the protesters under control. "The meeting was on the company pre-

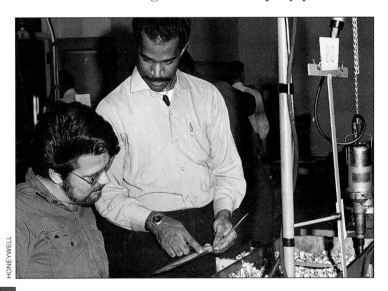

Above: Honeywell's 1965 Plan For Progress program included a preliminary training session called "Passport," in which disadvantaged recruits were given paid training in production positions.

Left: After a training period, "Passport" recruits were given an opportunity to work without supervision in a simulated factory situation.

Below: As part of Honeywell's evolving commitment to social concerns during the Plan For Progress, the company established secretarial training centers in inner-city communities to give disadvantaged citizens basic training in office procedures.

In 1982 and 1983, the Honeywell Project escalated its protests outside company headquarters in Minneapolis. From the earliest demonstrations at Honeywell in the 1960s the company maintained an open, conciliatory attitude toward protestors, even allowing them to use restrooms and telephones inside corporate offices. The company withdrew the privilege of demonstrating on company property in 1983, when demonstrators interfered with Honeywell employees trying to get into the building to work.

mises," Binger said. "We shouldn't have done it, but we did. Some of their people tried to force their way into our building and it was quite obvious that it was getting out of hand. We went to Plan B and adjourned the meeting. ... I talked to Davidov after that and said, 'You promised me that you would keep this thing under control, why didn't you do that?' He said, 'Well, I've been in a lot of protests in my life but I've never led one before and it just got out of hand.'"[21]

Jim Renier, CEO from 1988 to 1993, said he felt no moral qualms about Honeywell's defense operations. "These people objected to the company's being in the defense business. My view was, as long as there have been history and civilizations there have been wars, and people have had to defend themselves. I felt that supporting the defense was simply doing our patriotic duty." [22]

Steve Keating, chairman from 1974 to 1978, voiced similar sentiments. "I had lots of good friends who felt strongly that all of us had measles or something because they didn't believe in the Vietnam War. But we were non-political. We felt that we were supplying equipment that was being used by our military forces. But I was unhappy. You didn't like having people calling you names and writing nasty stories and parading in the streets and picketing at annual meetings. It was an unhappy time."[23]

By the 1980s, the Honeywell Project had achieved a high profile nationally, and its well-organized office then had an answering service and two full-time staff members. But even with the increasing publicity given their demonstrations, the Project continued to elicit only conciliatory comments from Karen Bachman, manager of corporate public relations at the time.

"Clearly the Honeywell Project, a small core of very dedicated people, picked Honeywell as the symbolic target for their social, political and ecomomic agenda. They chose us because they knew we were a decent company that would be 'thoughtful' about the issue. I guess that's a compliment."[24]

In a recent interview, Bachman, who has been vice president of communications since 1990, said she was opposed to United States involvement in Vietnam, but she did not think protesters should have targeted Honeywell. "I always felt that the proper focus for protest was the U.S. government and its policy. Food companies were providing rations to the military, clothing companies were providing uniforms... How far was it going to go?"[25]

"We did take the Honeywell Project very seriously in terms of listening," she said. "While we certainly didn't agree with their position, I think we became a model for how a company can handle a protest like that. ... On the day of the protest, we would all get here at five in the morning so that we were assured of being able to get in. We would always advise employees, 'You don't have to defend the company,' and, 'The last thing we want is a confrontation.'"[26]

Honeywell was also singled out for protests because it was the largest company in the Minneapolis area involved with defense contracts. By 1983, Honeywell was a $5.75 billion corporation employing 93,500 worldwide, with 16,500 employees in the Minneapolis area. And it was the sixteenth–largest defense contractor in America, with a quarter of its business derived from defense–related activity.[27]

But relations became increasingly strained between the Project and the company in April 1983, when demonstrators began blocking sidewalks and entrances of Honeywell facilities and interfering with employees as they tried to enter the building. Honeywell president Ed Spencer circulated a memo which clearly elucidated his and his company's position with regard to the protests:

> "We know that many people who engage in these protests are sincere in their concern about U.S. defense policies and expenditures. We also understand that they protest at Honeywell as a way to increase public awareness of these concerns, many of which we share. Despite the sincerity of their beliefs, however, we think that they have abused their use of our property, and therefore we will no longer permit them to demonstrate on our premises.
>
> "We understand that the country's defense efforts are expensive and compete with funding with the other needs of society. However, we believe that Honeywell cannot take positions for or against specific defense programs or budgets, because we don't think corporations should be making national defense policy. That is the task of the President and Congress, whom we all elect to office. Every election gives us the opportunity to send them packing for home if enough voters disagree with their political views.
>
> "We believe, just as sincerely, that our position on our defense business is reasonable and responsible. We decided long ago to respond to the country's defense needs. As long as the nation needs defense products, and as long as we have the needed technologies and are a cost-effective supplier, we will provide these products – and we are proud of being able to do so.
>
> "We know that, like the American public, our employees hold a wide range of views on what constitutes an adequate defense and what is required to maintain peace. We respect your rights to your own opinion, and we urge you to let your representatives know what they are." [28]

Spencer struck a convincing balance between empathy for the demonstrators' cause and realism about Honeywell's commitments to the U.S. government and military. And yet, the Honeywell Project continued its demonstrations, becoming "the largest act of civil disobedience in Minnesota history."[29] Honeywell finally felt com-

pelled to respond. At a cost of $10,000, the company commissioned a poll of Twin Cities residents as to their impressions of the Honeywell Project's concerns. The results were published in a full-page advertisement in a local newspaper, finding that "32 percent of the public say they agree with the point the demonstrators are trying to make." The obvious implication was that 68 per cent did not agree – though this wasn't precisely the case. What the poll did find was that many Minnesotans were comfortable with Honeywell's defense contracting, and that most appreciated the fact that Honeywell Inc. was one of the area's largest employers.

Even so, Ed Spencer made it clear that the Honeywell Project demonstrators and their sympathizers held no monopoly on concern over the escalating arms race. Despite the fact that his own company was profiting from the buildup, Spencer publicly stated his own personal desire to see some sort of arms control in place. In an editorial in the *Minneapolis Star and Tribune*, he outlined his own "Tactical Zero" plan for putting a brake on the arms race. This radical proposal urged U.S. legislators to eliminate all short–range nuclear weap-

In 1983, the Honeywell Project organized several large protests at Honeywell World Headquarters in Minneapolis. The protests were generally peaceful but often resulted in numerous arrests when protesters blocked entrances and prevented employees from going to work. Protests sometimes included huge puppets created by a local theater company to draw attention to the controversy.

ons from Europe as a sign of goodwill, hopefully encouraging the same of the Soviet Union. Spencer asserted that excessive arms stockpiling was aggravating the international situation such that the world was in greater danger of war than when Hitler had marched across the Rhineland. But, wrote Spencer, Honeywell's defense business had no direct role to play in these affairs other than to respond to government contracts, for better or worse. "There is no question that we are proud to supply the means for a strong defense as determined by our democratically-elected government," he wrote. "And we will continue to do so. But that does not prevent us, at the same time, from hoping as ardently as any nuclear-freeze proponent that the United States and the Soviet Union will find a way to wind down the arms race..."[30]

"Privately, Spencer was a little uneasy about our defense activity," recalled Warde Wheaton. "But his public demeanor was that he stood behind the operations and presented the company's views effectively."[31] Wheaton was marketing director in Honeywell's Aerospace and Defense Operation in the Sixties, becoming general manager on the Industrial Control side of the business in the early Seventies and general manager of Defense Systems Division from 1975 to 1977. He was president of the Aerospace and Defense from 1978 to 1988.

The demonstrations never really achieved concrete results; defense contracts actually increased during the most active period of demonstrations. Still, Marvin Davidov said The Project "has succeeded in making it known that Honeywell makes more than thermostats."[32] In April 1983, Honeywell organized and sponsored a public forum entitled "Prospects for Peacemaking: Rethinking National Security and Arms Control." At a cost of $150,000, Honeywell funded the University of Minnesota's Humphrey Institute of Public Affairs, which conducted the conference. The company was applauded for supporting the conference without setting the agenda or controlling the speakers. The Honeywell Project refused to participate. Though some presenters at the conference were openly critical of the company and its defense business, others praised it for being "willing to hazard the results" of such a public forum.[33] The conference helped establish that Honeywell was very much interested in cultivating a constructive public dialogue about defense and security issues.

Dean Randall, then Honeywell's vice president of communications, realized that the pro-

MINNEAPOLIS STAR TRIBUNE/STAFF PHOTO RITA REED

Melissa Bruninga is frisked while being arrested at the 20th annual Honeywell Project Protest in 1988. About 400 demonstrators marched, and while police reported the demonstration to be peaceful, 82 people were arrested.

In October 1983, the Honeywell Project made national head-lines when Erica Bouza, the wife of Minneapolis Police Chief Tony Bouza, was arrested and charged with trespassing. She served ten days in jail. Hundreds of other protesters were arrested the same day for blocking the entrances to Honeywell.

testers only wanted attention. "There was all kinds of television coverage, and that's what they wanted," he said. "I don't think in their wildest dreams they thought they could shut us down. I don't think they cared." [34]

Part of the Honeywell Project's goal was to convince employees to consider their own roles at Honeywell, and the moral issues of their employer's defense contracting. A very few employees actually did quit, joining the ranks of the Project and protesting the business of their former employer. Mark Paquette, for example, was a design engineer who had worked on nuclear weapons systems. He left Honeywell to join The Project, saying with invective hyperbole, "What I was doing was nothing less, and probably more, than the people who designed the gas chambers and were later convicted at the Nuremburg trials. I felt it my duty to stop making weapons of mass destruction." Statements like his were powerful and, of course, potentially damaging to Honeywell. Dick Boyle, a group vice president for Defense and Marine Systems during this period, was quick to agree that the Project helped employees more closely consider their roles in

the company. But, he said, this almost always caused them to "reaffirm their patriotism and dedication to doing good work..." He echoed many Honeywell employees' sentiments when he said, "I happen to believe that a strong defense contributes to peace. I feel that what I'm doing is right for me, right for the company and right for our country."[35] In a speech to the Minnesota League of Women Voters in 1984, Boyle attempted to reconcile the conflicting emotions which surfaced during the protests.

"We all seek peace, freedom and security. The conflict arises when we attempt to tie means to those ends. How much defense is enough? How many weapons equal how much freedom? We don't have an adequate moral calculus to compute those kinds of relationships, and so there will be differences of opinion, different comfort zones, different fears. Corporate responsibility in this context doesn't mean withdrawing from the debate or seeking to preempt it. It means participating. It means listening. To academics, to average citizens, to government experts, to government protestors, to Honeywell employees. And, yes, to Honeywell protestors...

"In the middle of the night, we ask ourselves the deepest questions. ...What is the balance point between preserving peace and encouraging war? What acts move the fulcrum away from security and closer to chaos? We wrestle with the contradictions. We wonder about the extent of our personal responsibilities. We worry about our children. We all have these questions in common. We all want to find the answers. We hope for the best, yet because we fear the worst, we disagree how to achieve the peace and freedom we all desire... And the irony of our quest for peace is that we may never know when we are right. But we will all know for certain if events prove us wrong."[36]

Two months after Boyle's speech, the Project staged yet another sizeable demonstration. Two hundred and fifty–six protestors were arrested in what was described as a "generally orderly" demonstration. Dean Randall, vice president of communications, commented at the time, "They use a lot of energy on this... It's a tremendous waste of political energy and effort."[37]

Steve Keating and the Minneapolis Urban Coalition

Honeywell president Steve Keating played an important role in the Greater Minneapolis and national communities during the late Sixties. After the urban riots of the summer of 1967,

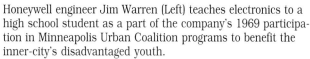

Honeywell engineer Jim Warren (Left) teaches electronics to a high school student as a part of the company's 1969 participation in Minneapolis Urban Coalition programs to benefit the inner-city's disadvantaged youth.

Steve Keating (Right) hosts Clinton School principal Bob Christman and students in a 1969 Urban Coalition function.

fourteen Minneapolis businesses (including Honeywell) donated $1,000 each to fund a study on the formation of a coalition to address race and poverty problems in the Twin Cities. [38] Keating was named president of the Minneapolis Urban Coalition in January of 1968. The coalition sought him out partly because of a speech he gave in Boston, where he discussed the need for "bridging the cultural and geographic gap between suburban plants, which have labor shortages, and jobless tenement areas in the core cities."

"I believe all levels of government might work together," Keating said, "to make the center city inviting to industry again."[39]

The spring of 1968 would prove a trial by fire for Keating and the coalition. In April, after Dr. Martin Luther King was assassinated, the coalition sent telegrams urging the government "to go beyond the apprehension of Dr. King's killer and to the root of the problem of racism in this country."

Keating immediately went on the record speaking for the coalition. "Racism killed Dr. King," he said. "In recognition that such racism exists here in Minneapolis, though hopefully in less virulent form, the Urban Coalition will organize immediately an anti-racism program to deal in our area with the basic root of tragic violence in America."[40]

"I have nothing to gain," Keating once said of his involvement, "but real personal satisfaction."[41]

Doing Its Part

Honeywell became a proving ground for progressive programs aimed at ending discrimination in the workplace, and Keating saw to it that the company actively trained and hired the disadvantaged. Honeywell developed a number of programs to help the unemployed and underemployed, working in association with the 1968 National Association of Businessmen's plan to train and employ 100,000 "hard-core" unemployed nationwide by June of 1969. Keating and Chairman Jim Binger pledged 629 permanent jobs, which involved recruiting and training the long-term chronically unemployed in the city's urban centers. "If they can't write, we'll fill out [the application] for them," said Keating.[42]

The *Minneapolis Tribune* profiled Honeywell's efforts in a 1968 article entitled "Search and Employ."

"We knew our recruiting methods would have to be aggressive to meet this goal, and it didn't take long to find this out," Keating said. "Conventional recruiting techniques, such as classified ads in the newspapers, did not produce as satisfactory a response as we had hoped."[43] Van Cooley, an African–American who had worked at Honeywell for seven years, was hired as a special recruiter. He drove through the low-income districts and inner city problem areas of Minneapolis and St. Paul, seeking the underemployed and unemployed. His van was a sort of mobile personnel office in which he conducted interviews and signed people up for the program. Because of his own minority status, he was able to talk to many people who otherwise would not have considered employment at Honeywell. Sometimes Cooley worked with a second recruiter, Native American Dennis Banks. The two interviewed 15 to 25 people a day. They would sign interested people up for a physical examination, and if they passed the exam, they were usually hired on the spot; the applicant's job history didn't matter, and neither did a police record. If they were illiterate, they would get a position that didn't require reading or writing. Once applicants were accepted, they were enrolled in an orientation program that acquainted them with business practices and expectations, job skills, and basic personal management. Most of the orientation period was devoted to training in job skills such as welding or drill pressing. The new employee was paid regular wages while being introduced to the job. Honeywell even provided counseling when necessary, recognizing that many disadvantaged and the "hard-core" unemployed suffered from extensive personal problems. The company developed a system of follow-through for Cooley and his colleagues, to help employees keep their new jobs. Cooley often acted as a problem-solver for program participants, providing transportation to and from work, testifying in court appearances, and in one case, buying an alarm clock for a man who had trouble making it to work on time.[44] Honeywell also started "sensitivity" seminars for supervisors and managers of the new employees.

Charles W. "Chuck" Johnson was hired as a research engineer scientist in 1956, and rose through divisional research and management ranks to become Honeywell's first African-American corporate officer in 1984. He retired in 1989 as vice president and group executive of the Industrial Systems Group.

Other aspects of Honeywell's Plan for Progress program through the late Sixties included a summer hiring agenda for 500 youths. Money and equipment were donated to Bryant Junior High School in Minneapolis. Students there were also given the opportunity to "see the world of work," by visiting Honeywell and meeting its employees. The Bryant program was the "first large-scale involvement of private industry with public education in the nation."[45]

The company extended its educational programs to its own employees, as well. For example, voluntary courses on African-American history were offered through a local institution to any interested Honeywellers.

A late-Sixties statement by management was quite clear: "Honeywell believes that it is vital to the successful conduct of business and to long-range national welfare to promote economic, social, and educational equity for all citizens."

Enlightened Self-Interest

To some degree, corporate America's good deeds in the Sixties were motivated by self-interest. There was an immediate payback in the form of good public relations for the company. And there was a long-term payback in the form of new markets for company products. Honeywell believed that a socially aware corporation would attract quality employees. "A business has an identity," Keating said. "What our individual people are will depend on the total stance of the corporation—and we can't get good people unless we are conscious of the world around us."[46]

In a 1968 speech to University of Minnesota business students, Keating presented his own platform for enlightened self-interest in the corporate world:

"I do not want to sound unnecessarily harsh but businessmen must be concerned with their markets. And businessmen recognize with increasing respect the potential that lies in our under-consuming poor."

"Let us not confuse business motivation with social goals. Let us not confuse the profit motivation of business with the goals of society. But let us recognize that in many instances they are parallel."[47]

Charles W. "Chuck" Johnson was hired as a research engineer/scientist in 1956 and rose through research and management ranks to become Honeywell's first African-American corporate officer in 1984. He retired in 1989 as vice president and group executive of the Industrial Systems Group.

After one year, Keating stepped down as president of the Minneapolis Urban Coalition, drawing high praise for his work.

"He is entitled to a round of applause from the community," the Minneapolis Star said. "The coalition is designed to gather all of the forces of the community—business, labor, the minorities, churches, social and political agencies—to attack the problems of race and poverty in the city. It is uncharted territory, and in some cases tough going. Coalition meetings on occasion have become vitriolic and Keating has taken his lumps along with the others. Through it all, however, he has kept his cool and the organization's eyes on the goals, and, if those goals have not been achieved, there has been progress at least toward more jobs for the hardcore unemployed and putting minority people into their own businesses and their own homes. In its short life, the Minneapolis Urban Coalition has gained national recognition; some of the credit must go to Keating."[48]

Carrying On the Tradition

In 1974, Edson Spencer became president and CEO. He became chairman of the board and CEO in 1978, running the company in those capacities until 1987, when he stepped down from the CEO seat. He remained chairman of the board until 1988. Spencer inherited the Equal Employment Opportunity program, and he began to look for ways to increase minority presence in the company's engineering ranks. He noted with concern that 15 years after the Plan for Progress and the establishment of a proactive EEO statement, the number of minority and women engineers in the nation had not really changed:

"In a democratic society," Spencer said, "in a nation committed to the moral cause of equal opportunity, we have far too few minority engineers. Less than 3 percent of our 1.2-plus million engineers come from minority groups that account for almost 18 percent of the population. Yet the importance of increasing minority participation in engineering isn't simply an ethical responsibility. It happens to be smart bottom-line business too."

Spencer foresaw a critical shortage of engineers in American industry: "The tragedy is that one of the few large talent pools immediately available to us has not been properly utilized. The gift exists among minorities in the same ratio it does among any other group. Ability knows no color line, intelligence is not fixed by race. An aptitude for engineering, like any other discipline, is determined by something other than racial background. These are not platitudes. They are facts."[49]

Spencer felt that the way to increase the number of minority and women engineers was to encourage education programs which would begin at elementary school. "Too many minority youngsters with a genuine aptitude for engineering never even see the inside of a college classroom."[50]

He also felt strongly about encouraging volunteerism among Honeywell employees. In 1974, when he became CEO, and again in 1984, he articulated the "Honeywell Principles." In both documents, Spencer asserted that "everyone benefits when the company supports employee involvement in community and national

The "assembling department" in 1923 was supervised by Daisy Arnold (seated at desk on left), the first woman supervisor at Honeywell. Women were frequently employed in this department because their smaller fingers were believed to be more adroit for most assembly procedures.

affairs."[51] Spencer was concerned with the social ramifications of the arms race, having published a widely-read plan for a "Tactical Zero" disarmament in 1984, and, as an expert on international trade issues, he testified before Congress on several occasions.

The Women of Honeywell

The first known female employee of Electric Heat Regulator Co. was Mary Hawkins. The minutes of a 23 February 1898 stockholders' meeting indicate that Electric Heat directors approved a $50 payment to Ms. Hawkins, "with the thanks of the company," apparently for work she had performed.[52] Jessie Wilson Sweatt, wife of W.R. and mother of Harold and Charles, was a member of the board from 1902 to 1916, and a stockholder from 1891. In 1912, four of the nine people staffing the Minneapolis office were women. And in the same year in Wabash, Indiana, Marvel Walrod was hired as Mark Honeywell's secretary. She rose through the ranks to become treasurer following the merger of Honeywell Heating Specialties and Minneapolis Heat Regulator in 1927.

In the 1920s, stenographers and secretaries in Minneapolis were typically paid 25 cents an hour. For the first time, though, women were also hired for factory positions, because it was determined that men's larger fingers were not suited to some of the more exacting assemblies. In 1923, Daisy Arnold became the first female supervisor, a position known as "forelady," and was in charge of the Assembling Department.

In the 1930s, women were paid $10 a week in production jobs, while men were generally paid $15. At one point, employee income was based on the number of pieces they assembled. A woman named Geneva Markstrom earned up to $16 a week by the piecework arrangement, but her foreman thought her salary was too high for a woman, and her pay was reduced to $10 per week.[53] Another woman, Helen Haertzen, working on the thermostat assembly line in 1943, overheard a manager announcing to visitors that this type of work

As early as 1930, Minneapolis-Honeywell supported female employees in informal clubs and organizations. This photo of the "Girl's Bowling League" from 1947 shows the Methods department in a tournament with the Valve division.

was "ideally suited for women because they could stand the monotony."[54]

Despite a general business culture that was not conducive to true equality as it is understood today, the company stood behind its female employees. In 1930, it sponsored a women's softball team. Women were encouraged to be active in the Union. After receiving its charter in 1939, Local 1145 officers included at least one woman every year from 1939 to 1965.[55]

The war years propelled women into the workforce *en masse*. Honeywell women were called upon to take positions traditionally held by men, and part of the credit for the company's 16 Army-Navy "E" Awards for war production goes to them. At Aero division, which produced the C-1 autopilot and turbo regulators that made Honeywell a name recognized around the world, women were essential to war production.

"There's a job to be done and women are stepping in and doing it. The women who have entered the war plant have gladly given up their glamour and the brass buttons of the regimented women to step into men's jobs."[56] (Women Honeywellers also joined the armed services during the war, taking volunteer positions with the WACs and WAVEs.)

One of Honeywell's divisional newspapers published a feature in 1944 on female war workers operating drill presses, riveters, hydraulic lifts, and welders:

"No small share of the credit for our success on the production front must surely go to the girls and women who have stepped into the toughest kinds of jobs to keep the wheels of industry turning while our boys are away at camps and on the battle-fronts. Who would have dared to predict just a few short years ago, that members of the "gentler sex" could step into jobs like those shown on these pages! Even those who had faith in the girls' willingness to tackle the assignment could not anticipate the splendid job they would do in filling the gaps left in our industrial picture by military manpower requirements. Women war workers have proved to skeptics that they can keep production up, stay on the job, and play a big part in beating the Axis. Of all the different kinds of work that go to make up war production, more than 30 percent is now performed by women. It's certain that

Karen Bachman is vice president of communications for Honeywell. She started with the company in 1964 in a clerical position and eventually became the first woman to serve on Honeywell's Policy Committee.

Geri Joseph was the first woman on the Board of Directors in modern times. "On some issues, I think women do bring a somewhat different perspective," she said.

Dana Badgerow, first and only female general manager at Honeywell, heads up the Skinner Valve division in New Britain, Ct. Purchased by Honeywell in 1979, the division makes valves with many applications.

without the help of the girl war workers, industry could never have performed its tremendous wartime assignment. The women war workers of America deserve the salute and thanks of the nation."[57]

Women remained in many of these positions after the war. By the late forties, they were joined by women entering the ranks of Honeywell as skilled specialists. In 1948, Marjorie Brimi was hired as an engineer. She applied for the job, and like any other perspective engineer, was given a battery of tests to assess her abilities. When she passed these, she was asked if she could type. Brimi lied and replied "yes." She was hired officially as an engineer but the company really wanted her to do secretarial work in the Chemical/Metallurgical lab. Her supervisor soon noticed she couldn't type, so he put her to work as a full-time engineer. After a number of years at Honeywell, Brimi noticed she was the only engineer who still punched in. She asked the male personnel manager about it, and was told that all female workers were paid on an hourly basis. Brimi thought a moment and then posed a suggestion: "Okay, here's what we'll do: The minute you want to use me as a female, I will punch in, and when you have wrought your will upon me, I will punch out and be an engineer." There was a shocked silence. Brimi never punched the clock again.[58]

In 1950, Honeywell acknowledged the need for special services for its female employees by providing career counseling services, the first program of its kind in the Midwest.[59] In 1962, as part of a Plan for Progress, the company initiated a free retraining program for women and minority women. This program, which provided office-skills training to inner city women, was funded by Honeywell, the Minneapolis Urban League, and Augsburg College. In its first year, the program trained 21 women.

In 1978, Honeywell's Community Relations Equal Opportunity Committee formed a subcommittee on women's issues, which evolved into the Honeywell Women's Council. The HWC was the first Honeywell "special interest to develop goals, programs, and activities to address perceived needs." The Women's Council sought in its charter,

"To build Honeywell's image as a concerned employer and a good place for women to work. To facilitate moral and legal compliance with Equal Employment Opportunity legislation. To educate and support Honeywell women seeking career mobility. To foster employee participation in decisions which affect them. To identify, study, and make recommendations on issues affecting all Honeywell women."

Seminars, conferences, and networking were sponsored by the HWC on topics such as personal safety, child care, job mobility, and health and wellness. The Women's Council became the "Focal point of women's issues in the company."[60] In November 1985, Honeywell's women's group was mentioned prominently in *Working Woman* magazine. Its success led to the formation of similar groups for Black and Hispanic employees, handicapped employees and Vietnam veterans.

But these programs could not take the place of enlightened management that recognized the value of female employees. Karen Bachman, vice president of communications, was among a small group of women who rose rapidly within the company. She credits her success to supervisors who recognized her abilities. "Within six years of walking in here not knowing which end was up, I was a manager," she said. "It really did impress me."[61]

Bachman applied to Honeywell in August 1964. She had recently graduated from the University of Minnesota and married. "Unlike today's young women graduates, I was quite unfocused about my career. Actually it was the failure of my apartment air conditioner during a very hot August that spurred me to find a cool place to spend my days. So I applied at Honeywell and, per standard procedure in those days, was interviewed for a clerical job. When I failed the typing test, I was offered a "market research"position—which turned out to be a non-typing clerical job in the inquiry-handling department.

"I quickly saw there were a lot of people—men—doing jobs that I could certainly do. That was when I realized that I had entered a world where the capability of women was yet to be acknowledged or appreciated."

Bachman said Dean Randall and Herb Bissell, executives in the marketing department, "were very, very open to having a bright woman around with some unusual ideas. And so they watched for opportunities for me or made them happen. I will say that I worked hard and brought some skill and ability to the job, but there's no question in my mind that it would have been a lot harder and maybe wouldn't have happened at all if not for Herb Bissell and Dean Randall."[62]

In two years, Bachman became a supervisor in the graphic arts department, and she became a manager of the department in 1970. In 1990, she became vice president of communications. [63]

Dean Randall (Left), and Herb Bissell, are considered pioneers at Honeywell, both for their creativity in the marketing field and their dedication to equal opportunity for women.

Honeywell has other high ranking women. In 1981, Geri Joseph became a member of the board of directors. Joseph was a journalist in Minneapolis for 15 years, and was elected chairwoman of the state's Democratic party. Her background includes a three year appointment as Ambassador to the Netherlands under President Carter. Despite these credentials, she felt uncomfortable as the first woman in modern times on Honeywell's board of directors.

"I don't think it is ever a comfortable feeling for a woman. Particularly since this is a company very much into technology and my background was bereft of technology. I worked very hard to try to understand a lot of it. I think that's what women do when they are the first and only or the only member of a board. You're convinced that if you fall flat on your face they will never ask another woman. I think a lot of that is changing now, but at the time I went on the board I was certainly self conscious about that."[64]

Dana Badgerow, another prominent Honeywell executive, is a vice president and the general manager of Skinner Valve, a Honeywell division purchased in 1979 that boasts sales of $40 million. Among a myriad of industrial applications, Skinner Valves are used to regulate the flow of fuel at gas stations, slowing volume to a trickle when the desired amount is pumped. In addition, a wide range of applications include dispensing condiments in fast food restaurants or regulating the flow of water through dental equipment. Badgerow said she doesn't mind being the only female plant general manager at Honeywell. "It's not a big deal to me. I'm the first and only at the moment, although I know there are all kinds of people coming up the ranks. To be honest with you, it's not a plus or a minus. It just is."[65]

People with disabilities have also contributed to Honeywell's success. George Olson, described in 1950 as "the first and only blind person in Minnesota industries,"[66] worked at Honeywell for some 40 years. Eventually several other disabled people worked in the Coil Winding department with him. Honeywell actively sought the assistance of disabled people outside the company. For example, production subcontracts were regularly awarded to the Society for the Blind in Minneapolis, where vision-impaired workers turned out hundreds of thousands of components for Honeywell thermostats, valves, and other items. The company called its employment of disabled workers an example of successful "human engineering," and in 1950 Honeywell received recognition from the Minnesota Federation of Engineering Societies for its employment of disabled people.

Vietnam Veterans at Honeywell

Honeywell's commitment to the special needs of employees also extended to veterans. After the company's extensive production in World War II, Honeywellers felt a special connection to those who had served. Veterans of the Vietnam War also found the company receptive to their concerns.

In 1981, Honeywell formed a steering committee that studied the special concerns of the 125 Vietnam vets employed in Minneapolis at that time. The company then sponsored awareness seminars, a communications newsletter, family counseling program, career development and stress management courses, along with a referral service for Vietnam veterans and their spouses. [67] Counseling was a particularly successful aspect of the program. One vet, Tim Woodruff from the Residential Division in Golden Valley, Minnesota, said, "I only wish something like this had been available ten years ago. I was a young kid when I went to 'Nam and not much older when I came back, and settling into civilian life would have been a lot easier with support like I've found within the steering committee."[68]

Bob Nelson, a vet in the Avionics Division said, "I view myself with a much more positive attitude. An experience like Vietnam can cause a person to turn inward and bury the anger, fear, etc., but somewhere along the way you have to learn to deal with those feelings."[69]

The Honeywell Foundation

By the 1980s, Honeywell's commitment to corporate responsibility was given full expression in the form of an independent operating unit, the Honeywell Foundation. A non-profit

George Olson worked for Honeywell for over four decades beginning in 1920. For many years, he was believed to be the only blind worker in Minnesota industry.

organization to which Honeywell Inc. gave two percent of its U.S. pre–tax profits, the Foundation awarded money to selected nonprofit agencies and institutions. With its own board of directors, the group establishes its own policy and approves the final disbursement of funds. As part of the Foundation's charter, support is given to all communities where Honeywell facilities are located. Funds are allocated to Honeywell divisions nationwide, so that each can give locally. The Honeywell Foundation also makes annual contributions to the United Way, a long-standing tradition, wherever major company operations are located.[70] Throughout the 1980s, the Foundation's budget ranged from $5 to $10 million annually.

Honeywell's 'Core of Integrity'

Integrity is frequently mentioned when Honeywellers talk about their company. "This company has a core of integrity," said Mannie Jackson, who worked many years in labor relations. He recently retired as senior vice president of marketing and administration to pursue other business interests, including his ownership of the world–famous Harlem Globetrotters. "Honeywell has a sense of purpose like no group or no organization that I know of. And I could always count on the honesty and goodwill of both the senior people and the operating people in this company to deliver on whatever they committed to." [71]

"It's a company that values its integrity first and foremost," said Dana Badgerow, vice president and general manager of Skinner Valve. "Sometimes maybe to its own detriment in terms of financial results, but its clearly a company with integrity. It's a company that's got all the right ingredients right now for a terrific success." [72]

Some observers feel that Honeywell's success is a direct result of the culture fostered first by W.R., and refined by H.W. Sweatt. Herb Bissell called H.W. Sweatt "one of the best businessmen I've ever met."[73] Part of what made Sweatt so exceptional was his ability to see across organizational lines, an ability he encouraged in others. Roger Jensen, who worked in the patent department for more than 40 years, said "H.W. had incredibly good talents in the technical and engineering area. He was probably the perfect executive because he had expertise and aptitude in many different disciplines, not just

Mannie Jackson (center) recently retired to devote more time to other businesses, including his world–famous Harlem Globetrotters. Hired in 1968, he was later named vice president and general manager of the Communication Services division and eventually became senior vice president of marketing and administration for the corporation.

finance and management. He was very strong in marketing and engineering." [74]

In addition to solid management, the success of the company has also relied upon the loyalty of the union, which has represented Honeywell employees in Minneapolis since the 1940s. Warde Wheaton said of Local 1145 of the Teamsters, "Over the years the local union has been a very wisely and competently led organization. One result: we have had almost no strikes. In the last 50 years, there may have been one or two work stoppages. Bill Tyler, [longtime union leader] and his people knew full well if they did good work then they would prosper. If they fought the company, they would not. They were tough. They stood up for their workers, but they were never destructive." [75]

In the early 1980s, Wheaton delivered an address to the union about quality control, safety, and other issues of mutual interest.

"I stood up with my white shirt and my tie and my blue suit, and I started giving a presentation about quality improvement. And when I was partway through, one of the crustier old stewards in the back row raised his hand and said, 'Well, that was nice, but what's in it for us?' What was the incentive for changing their ways and learning new skills? And as I began with a too–technical response, Tyler, who was a man of very few words, but a very wise human being, interrupted me, stood up, and said to his own union steward, 'We do good work, you get to keep your job.' What he said was correct. If you do good work, then your customers will come back to you. If you don't, they'll go someplace else." [76]

Sweatt was a hands–on executive, said former CEO Jim Binger. "I recall a time when we had difficulty with some aluminum. A carload of aluminum came in and it turned out that it was too soft a grade. He went right down into the receiving department. He taught me something. He said, 'Don't believe because you tell somebody to do it, they're going to do it. You have to take a look once in a while to find out if things are being done as you expect them to be.'" [77]

Another time, H.W. visited the shipping dock. "A guy was sitting there in the shade, just sitting there," Randall said. "And H.W. got furious and fired the guy. The guy said, 'You can't fire me. I'm driving the truck that they're loading.' He didn't even work for the company!" [79]

Sweatt's approach included keeping a keen eye on the various lawsuits in which Honeywell was involved. Once, in the 1930s, Minneapolis-Honeywell "had its clock cleaned" by a competitor in Milwaukee, at the hands of a brilliant Chicago attorney named Will Freeman. After the suit, H.W. approached Freeman and said, "Mr. Freeman, you did a good job and I would just like to think that maybe next time Honeywell has some kind of a patent problem we'd like to call on you to represent us." [80] That's precisely what happened. Sweatt and Freeman developed a successful long-term professional relationship. H.W. Sweatt would be a "good role model for even modern day executives," Jensen suggests, "as far as having the ability to communicate with many different functions within his company and really understanding what they're doing." [81] He "had a tremendous curiosity, and he set the shirtsleeve style" which has been such an important part of Honeywell's success over the years. [82]

"From Harold Sweatt's time," longtime Honeywell executive Ed Lund commented, "Honeywellers have always been extremely ethical people. What a remarkable group of human beings Honeywell management was and is. And that's been its success story." [83]

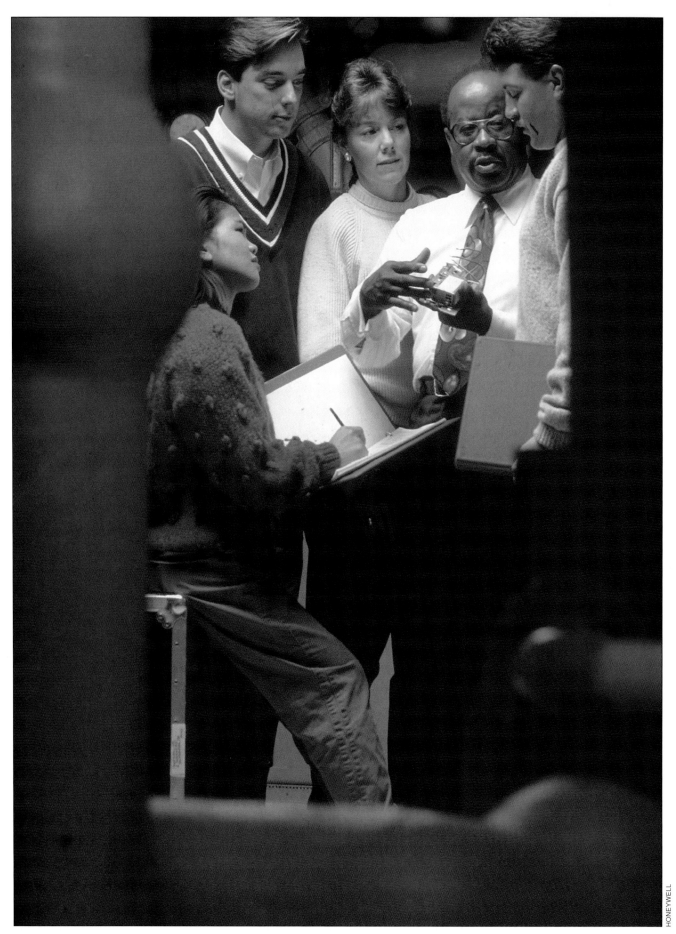

Continuously improving the knowledge skills and abilities of every employee helps Honeywell meet the challenges of rapid change now and in the future.

CHAPTER TEN

1985-1995
A DECADE OF REDEDICATION

"This is a company that has been successful for 110 years. We have a tremendous franchise. We have tremendously loyal customers. When you have been successful for that long, you run the risk of beginning to take the very essence of your success for granted. If I were to put a single hallmark on my time in this office, it would be a rededication to our customers."

— CEO Michael Bonsignore, 1995.

Honeywell marked its 100th anniversary in 1985. CEO Ed Spencer distributed a centennial pin to each employee, and celebrations were held in the United States and abroad. Despite the festivities, it was a year of soul–searching for Honeywell. Between 1982 and 1985, the company sold all or part of nine businesses, worth about $200 million annually, that were not related to controls. The company's top leadership—Ed Spencer and Jim Renier—began forging an aggressive new direction focusing on Honeywell's core business of controls.

By 1995, Honeywell would be streamlined and aggressive, ready to grow as the undisputed leader of control. Through divestitures and staff reductions, employment had dropped from 94,000 in 1985 to 52,000 in 1993. Dramatic changes in Honeywell's portfolio have kept annual sales at around $6 billion. CEO Michael Bonsignore has said it is time to reverse this trend, and he has set the goal of $10 billion in annual sales by the year 2000.

Honeywell's new direction was announced in 1987, when Jim Renier wrote that "a new Honeywell rededicated itself to a century old heritage: helping people control their world. Control technology began with a Honeywell invention. It grew with Honeywell innovations. It remains the core of our business, as we provide control that enables people around the world to live better and work more productively."[1] A new corporate slogan, "Helping You Control Your World," underscored the company's direction.

The rededication was partly a response to Ed Spencer's 1986 decision to get Honeywell out of the computer business, possibly the toughest decision the company ever made. Ed Lund, who was vice president of administration, explained, "It was either devote all the energy of the corporation to trying to make the computer business work, or preserve a truly excellent hallmark set of systems and devices that we owned, like the thermostat. Honeywell had a wonderful long-term future in its charter businesses."[2]

In 1989, Honeywell initiated a program to enhance shareholder value. The program had five parts: divest the Defense and Marine Systems, sell part of its equity in Yamatake-Honeywell, convey the proceeds of these divestitures directly to shareholders, improve operating profit, and deliver these improved profits to shareholders with increased dividends.[3]

Without Information Systems, Honeywell is now divided into three areas—Space and Aviation Control, Home and Building Control, and Industrial Control. All three businesses continue to drive the company's success. By 1993, Honeywell controls could be found in over 100 million residences and five million commercial businesses worldwide. On the industrial side, Honeywell controls can be found in 24 of the world's 25 largest oil refiners and 15 of the world's 20 largest chemical companies. In Space and Aviation Control, Honeywell systems are aboard nearly every commercial airliner and business jet produced around the world, as well as a wide range of spacecraft and military aircraft.[4] Said Bonsignore:

> *"Honeywell controls essentially sense and measure a condition, like temperature or altitude. Then they initiate action to make something happen, they provide feedback and they start the process all over again. You can see this across Honeywell in every single business we have. That, fundamentally, is the control business. It is based on sensing technology that I believe is second to none in the world."[5]*

Divesting From Computers

Under increasing pressure to improve Honeywell's financial performance, Ed Spencer

1988, it reduced its ownership from 42.5 percent to 19.9 percent,[7] and in April 1991, Honeywell divested completely from Honeywell Bull.

Spencer called the divestment "a crucial step for Honeywell, leaving us free to concentrate on businesses where we have solid market share and can achieve higher returns."[8] The move addressed management's concerns about possible vulnerability to corporate raiders, and, in that respect, Honeywell Information Systems had become a serious liability.

"The biggest challenge was the computer business," Spencer said, reflecting on the problems he faced when he became CEO in 1974. "We were not earning the cost of capital." But at that point he was not thinking of divestiture. "It was so competitive that even a whisper of a thought

Edson Spencer became chief executive officer of Honeywell in 1974. He started with the company in 1954 and oversaw the difficult period of the 80s when Honeywell finally withdrew from the computer business.

Dr. James Renier became chief executive officer of Honeywell in 1987, and served until his retirement in 1993. He refocused Honeywell on the controls business.

decided in 1986 to concentrate on the company's traditional and successful product lines and divest from computer production. Honeywell restructured its Information Systems organization in 1986, selling 57.5 percent of its computer business to Compagnie des Machines Bull of France and NEC Corporation of Japan, to create a new company jointly owned by Honeywell, Bull, and NEC.[6] Honeywell then gradually divested from the new company, called Honeywell Bull and based in Billerica, Massachusetts. In

of divestiture could have rippled throughout the organization and caused all kinds of trouble. So divestiture was not talked about in the halls of the company. In hindsight I can look back and say that my own mind was really made up when we spun off part of Bull. The alternative would have been to try and buy out the French partners and run it ourselves."[9]

Looking back, it was easy to say that Honeywell never should have entered the computer business. Steve Keating said the computer business "was maybe the only big mistake that Harold Sweatt ever made. And he would say it if he was here today."[10] Throughout the Sixties and Seventies, the computer business took valuable resources from the rest of the company by altering the balance sheet in ways that some claim affect the company still.[11]

From a practical point of view, it was a real challenge to get out of the computer business. "The longer we stayed in," Keating said, "the more we got wrapped up, the harder it was to disengage from it."[12] Part of the problem was Honeywell's longtime axiom that a market, once entered, would never be abandoned. This philosophy was strengthened by the fact that the company had never failed in any market it had entered.

Michael R. Bonsignore became Honeywell's chairman and chief executive officer in April 1993. When he joined Honeywell right out of the Navy in 1969, it was his "first look at civilian life." His vision for the company calls for delighted customers, worldwide leadership in control, and profitable growth.

After Jim Renier became CEO in 1987, he unapologetically summed up the new corporate strategy: "We were no longer going to be a supplier of computer hardware, but an integrator of computer hardware into advanced automation systems."[13] Board member Geri Joseph said Renier "felt that it's very costly to try to keep up in the computer industry if that is not your central focus. You can get behind in the game very quickly. It became quite evident that it would be a mistake to hang in there, so it was a good thing we sold it.[14]"

Honeywell's new approach was really a reaffirmation of its traditional one. It would continue to incorporate advances in high technology within integrated automatic control systems. But it would no longer be burdened by unnecessarily developing, building, and marketing computers.

By the early 1990s, the divestment was paying off. In 1992, company earnings rebounded to $327 million, returning a profit of $2.36 per share on company-wide sales of $6.22 billion. This recovery was especially impressive because it took place during a generally weakened worldwide economy.

Spinning Off Defense

At the height of the Cold War, the U.S. government devoted substantial resources to developing, manufacturing, and maintaining the world's most advanced defense systems. But during the mid-1980s, Honeywell's ordnance division reflected the slowdown in defense spending after the boom years of the Reagan administration. Honeywell executives decided to phase out the company's commitment to weapons and weapons systems. In 1986, company officials noted that "the U.S. Federal deficit emerged as a critical domestic issue. Allegations of mismanagement and waste in the [defense] industry, coupled with the perception of progress in strategic arms talks, are creating a belief that the rate of defense spending can be reduced without endangering national security."[15]

Honeywell was the only top weapons company never indicted for government contract fraud, said Dana Badgerow, today a Honeywell vice president and general manager, who was formerly the company's vice president of Contract Management. "Honeywell was at times close to the top ten of defense contractors, and was always in the top 25. We were the only company amongst its ranks that was never indicted for a government contract fraud, much less found guilty. Many were indicted, many were found guilty. Honeywell was never even *charged*."[16]

By 1986, Honeywell had become the 12th–largest defense contractor in the country, and nearly half its total revenues came from its aerospace and defense businesses, with 1987 sales of $1.2 billion and an operating profit of $103 million. New products and programs in 1987 included contracts to supply the MK46 torpedo to 23 allied countries, completion of the MK50 program for a next–generation torpedo, and initiation of the Sense and Destroy Armor weapons program (SADARM).Between 1987 and 1988, Honeywell's defense business generated sales of $1.4 billion. On January 16, 1990, the board of directors approved a plan to spin off Honeywell's Defense and Marine Systems business, its Test Instruments Division, and its Signal Analysis Center. On September 28, 1990, the defense spin–off, Alliant Techsystems, began operation as an independent company. On October 9, shareholders received one share of Alliant stock for every four Honeywell shares. About 9.3 million shares of Alliant Techsystems were distributed to Honeywell shareholders, and the new company was listed on the New York Stock Exchange as ATK.[17]

Steve Keating, who had retired by the time Honeywell divested its weapons systems, specu-

General Manager of the Ordnance Division was one of many titles held by Ed Lund during his 31 years at Honeywell. He was hired as a special production assistant in the Aero Division, and was corporate vice president of administration when he retired in 1981. The Lund Award, which recognizes managers who excel at employee development, is named for him.

lated that "it wasn't a very good business in terms of profit or cash-flow, and they found out they couldn't sell it, so they spun it off."[18]

According to the 1990 Annual Report, Honeywell had tried to sell the business, "however, the sale could not be consummated under acceptable terms."[19] In financing the spin–off, Honeywell borrowed $185 million, paid back $20 million, and turned the rest of its debt over to Alliant. The spin–off distribution resulted in a reduction of Honeywell's retained earnings of $129.3 million.[20]

Jim Renier, CEO at the time of the spin–off, said getting out of the defense business was something of a relief. "We were looking into a market that was going away and that had problems associated with it. We were looking at the need to strengthen our core business and spend our resources there as opposed to chasing a diminishing market."[21] Though the defense industry was consistently profitable, he said, it hurt other business. "It was a great business, with a lot of great people, but at the same time it definitely was not in the controls category. It dragged the whole business down in terms of what was expected by shareholders."[22]

Communications executive Dean Randall agreed that the decision was financial. "After the end of the Cold War, I don't think anybody saw very bright prospects in the defense industry."[23] John Dewane, president of Space and Aviation Control, said, "I basically agreed with the reasoning of people at the time. The defense business was obviously facing a long-term decline. Certainly the value of that business was not being recognized [by investors] when it was a part of Honeywell. The company's price/earnings ratio was taken down because of it. I think the subsequent spin–off with Alliant's and Honeywell's value increasing, was certainly the right move."[24]

Warde Wheaton, who retired in 1989 as president of Aerospace and Defense, struck a philosophical note when he said the defense area was always profitable, and the spin–off "did not make a whole lot of economic sense."[25] But Wheaton noted that there were special challenges to the defense industry, even when it was thriving. One constant consideration was the high degree of information control for purposes of confidentiality on sensitive technologies for national security. "Any time you control information you hurt yourself a little."[26] However, many defense systems were so sensitive that they were followed by a massive paper trail documenting their quality assurance, confidentiality, and specifications. Former Ordnance Manager Lund remembered that executives and scientists in the company's defense-related divisions used to joke about the fact that a device you could hold in your hand was often accompanied by a box-car load of paper documentation.[27]

The Sperry Acquisition

In 1986, the company reinforced its shift from ordnance to aerospace by acquiring Sperry Aerospace for $1.029 billion. "This is one of the most important acquisitions Honeywell has made," said Edson Spencer, chairman and CEO at the time. "Both Honeywell's and Sperry's operations have complementary strengths for the avionics instruments markets."[28] The acquisition contributed to sales growth of 24 percent in 1987, with sales of $6.7 billion that year. Honeywell enjoyed a commanding position in flight controls, especially the air transport and business jet segments. Sperry's Aerospace Group, based in Phoenix, Arizona, was a leading supplier of flight instrumentation, advanced avionics, and other electronic systems. The company had entered the automatic flight control market shortly after World War II, and had been a direct competitor of Honeywell's for many years, particularly in the autopilot and computer lines.

"With the opportunity to buy Sperry flight control business we could marry the flight control and navigation system into an integrated instrument system in the cockpit, which is what customers were asking for," Spencer said. "It was customer driven, that merger. It gave us a leading position in navigation systems and a leading position in flight control systems."[29] Honeywell's Aerospace and Defense revenues were "growing from about $400 million in the Seventies to ... over two billion by the middle Eighties," said Warde Wheaton, vice president of the aerospace and defense business until 1989. "And then we acquired Sperry and that took us to three billion in revenues by 1987."[30]

The acquisition solidified Honeywell's position in avionic controls for corporate jet aircraft. The Gulfstream IV, Canadair CL601, Falcon 900, and Cessna Citation were equipped with Honeywell navigational and flight control systems. The Sperry group contributed other sophisticated technologies to Honeywell's lines, like the first FAA-certified wind shear warning system.

With the acquisition of Sperry in 1986, Honeywell became the world's leading integrator of avionics systems. This Cessna Citation X flies with a Honeywell integrated cockpit.

Honeywell developed a wind shear warning system, the first of its kind to be certified by the FAA for comercial use.

Sperry had also been a successful contractor for space vehicles, bringing more extensive experience to Honeywell's aerospace units. When Sperry announced in August 1986 that it was for sale, it attracted interest from more than 30 companies, said Larry Moore, a top executive at Sperry and now president of Honeywell. By the middle of November, Honeywell emerged as the successful bidder. "Sperry had a very good impression of Honeywell, and I think that's something that Honeywell can be very proud of. Honeywell is thought of by customers and even competitors as a company of very high integrity and a very solid company."

In 1987, the division won contracts to upgrade space shuttle controls and to develop space station guidance and control. It is now working closely with Boeing, the world's largest airplane manufacturer. Honeywell designed a smaller, lighter avionics system for the 777, the world's largest twin-engine jet aircraft scheduled to enter service in 1995.

Between 1991 and 1994, Space and Aviation Division has been reduced from 21,000 employees to 10,000. "Space and aviation is a very cyclical business," CEO Bonsignore said.

As can be seen from the interior of the Space Shuttle, many Honeywell controls are used for space flight control. The acquisition of Sperry, Honeywell has positioned itself to benefit from the inevitable recovery in space and aviation. CEO Michael Bonsignore looks for Honeywell to "compete aggressively for virtually every plane they're going to build for the next 25 years."

The cockpit of an F-15 is equipped with an array of Honeywell and Sperry flight management and precision navigation controls.

"It's either growing fast or declining fast. We're on the bottom of a very dramatic three year decline, and our hope is that we will see a recovery start in 1995. If it's a typical cycle, we could see six or seven years of solid growth and profitability."[31]

"When the market recovers in this business, we will be in excellent shape for the future because we have invested throughout this down period to be able to compete aggressively for virtually every plane they're going to build for the next 25 years."[32]

Moore believes that the air transportation industry is turning around. "It's definitely a long term growth industry and we expect it to grow at least five to six percent worldwide over a long period of time. If there are more passengers then, by definition, there are more airplanes. We're very comforted by that fact."[33]

In 1994, Space and Aviation Control won more than $2 billion in new business, or 90 percent of the opportunities it pursued.[34] To ensure profitable growth over the long term, Space and Aviation Control has three focus areas: aggressive cost containment, continued development of new systems and products, and proactive movement of technology from one market to another. This focus has led to the introduction of breakthrough technologies such as liquid-crystal flat-panel displays, introduced in 1994.[35]

Continued Growth for Home and Building Control

Several factors in the domestic and international marketplace encouraged Honeywell executives in their effort to "get back to basics." Increasing environmental concern bodes well for Honeywell's Home and Building Control lines. Honeywell control products have always helped manage energy resources, and Honeywell sensing technologies are ideal for efficiently monitoring and controlling industrial processes that use precious raw materials.

"I think Home and Building Control has the most potential for growth," Bonsignore said. "This is our original franchise, and it has demonstrated above-average growth for the company. It's a $2 billion business today. I don't see why we shouldn't be able to grow it to $4 billion by the end of the decade if we just do a few things right. We see opportunities in energy conservation, human comfort, safety and air quality.[36]

In 1986, Honeywell embarked upon the SmartHouse project with the National Association of Home Builders. The project found ways to link the heating, security, lighting, appli-

Left: D. Larry Moore, president and chief operating officer, came to Honeywell with the acquisition of Sperry. Hired by Sperry in 1962, he started out as an information systems analyst and worked his way up to general manager.

Right: John Dewane, president, Space and Aviation Control, joined Honeywell in 1960 and served in a variety of field and divisional marketing positions during the next decade. After a succession of management promotions, he was named vice president of the Commercial Flight Systems Group in 1989, before taking his present post in 1993.

ances, and telephones of a single-family home through a common network. This project led to Honeywell's TotalHome integrated home control system, introduced in 1992. The system integrates heating and cooling systems, security, lighting and appliance control. The system can be controlled at the touch of a button, or accessed remotely by touch–tone phone.

In 1987, the business introduced several new products, including the 2000e Home Protection system, DeltaNet fire protection system, and a retail line of thermostats, detectors and sensors available in hardware stores. The following year, the division introduced retail home radon detectors, and indoor air quality diagnostic services.

In the 1990s, a growing fear of crime prompted larger markets for, and greater reliance on, security systems. Honeywell provides integrated access control to Munich Airport and many other places. Access control and fire detection systems are becoming centralized and simplified, as marketplace demands converge with emerging digital technologies. Security systems manufactured by Honeywell are increasingly being incorporated into more complete systems of environment control. As a good example, the company's Delta 1000 system for complete environmental control was used at the 1984 Olympics in Los Angeles.[37]

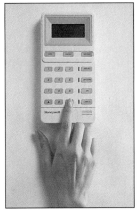

With TotalHome™ consumers can control the heat, security, lighting and appliances in their home with the touch of a button.

In 1992, the company's Residential Controls, Commercial Buildings Systems, and Protection Services businesses were merged into Home and Building Control.

The EXCEL 5000, introduced in January, 1993, is Home and Building Control's key building control system. The EXCEL is a worldwide building control platform that integrates all control functions, including heating, ventilating, air conditioning, fire, security and lighting systems, plus a building's mechanical and electrical systems. The system features an open system architecture, allowing supervision and control not only of Honeywell controls, but other systems as well. Because of technology like EXCEL, Home and Building Control President Brian McGourty believes, "We're postured for continuing growth as we move into 1995. We think we can grow this business 10 percent a year at least."[38]

In 1993, Home and Building Control acquired the Enviracaire air cleaner business, and began its introduction to the worldwide market. Honeywell was one of the first companies to enter the residential air cleaner business in 1960.

In 1994, Home and Building Control sales grew 10 percent to $2.7 billion.[39] About 85 percent of the division's business stems from upgrading existing homes and buildings to improve energy efficiency and reduce costs.

Honeywell's initiatives to broaden its residential offerings are showcased in "Comfortville," a 2,000 square-foot attraction at EPCOT in Walt Disney World in Florida. Comfortville features Honeywell's broad portfolio of products, systems and services for home comfort, convenience, security, communications and entertainment, including the TotalHome automation system.[40]

Industrial Control

"Honeywell control is at work in your world in ways you may not be aware of," reads *A Profile of Honeywell*, published in 1988.

> *"The newspaper you read with your morning coffee is probably produced with our help. Pulp and paper mills everywhere use our systems to automate production. For that matter, Honeywell control may have roasted and packaged your coffee. Our systems are widely used in the food and beverage industry.*
>
> *Chances are, the car you drive has Honeywell controls under the hood to help the engine deliver top performance and fuel efficiency. And when you travel by air, Honeywell travels with you. We're the leading supplier of control systems for commercial aviation."[41]*

Industrial Control is made up of two businesses. The larger one is Honeywell Industrial Automation and Control, and the smaller is Sensing and Control.

In 1993, CEO Bonsignore said Honeywell "must take undisputed worldwide leadership in control—this is what Honeywell is famous for. Leadership in control means offering solutions for transnational and transcultural problems—productivity, energy efficiency, environmental protection, comfort and safety and national security. This is what the world needs. And this is what we can provide."[42]

This rededication to controls means that Honeywell's Industrial Control business is probably more important than ever. The division combined nine sites into one factory in Phoenix.

Ed Hurd, president of Industrial Control until January 1995, said Honeywell's industrial business grew from $264 million in 1972 to $1.835 billion in 1994, a seven–fold increase.[43] And the company is poised for even greater growth. "If we do it right, the chances for growth and profitability exceed what we've done in the past. I think we've really picked out an excellent area to participate in and if we

Ed Hurd, senior vice president, has been with Honeywell 32 years. He served as president of Industrial Control from 1993 to 1995, and before that, he was vice president and general manager of Industrial Automation and Control Group.

Brian M. McGourty was named president of Honeywell's worldwide Home and Building Control in April, 1994. He joined Honeywell Limited, Canada, in 1969, and transferred to Minneapolis in 1991 as vice president, Field Operations, Home and Building Control for the U.S. Region.

Markos I. Tambakeras became president of Industrial Automation and Control in 1995. Prior to this position, he was vice president of marketing for Industrial Automations Division, and he served seven years in Honeywell's South African affiliate, rising to the post of managing director.

With the Expert Window of the TDC 3000 Universal Station, instantaneous, accurate information is available at the touch of a finger.

execute our global strategies we're really going to succeed big time."[44]

Hurd, hired in 1952, won a Sweatt Award in 1967 for a circuitry design. The same year, he was the design architect for an innovative assignment called Project 72. A group of four was given a simulated request from "Intergalactic, Inc." to develop a control system that would take advantage of the latest technologies and "provide significant customer benefits in the process industry." Working for about two years, the group "synthesized what a next-generation control system would look like, taking advantage of the latest and greatest technology and providing significant customer benefits in the process industry." The project eventually led to the TDC 2000, a distributed control system that "took us from $5 million a year to $500 million in five years. It just swept the market."[45]

Since that time, Hurd has continued improving the process industry through constant innovations. Having enjoyed tremendous success with the TDC 3000 system, Industrial Automation and Control has expanded the scope of its offerings to include TotalPlant Open Solutions, a unique combination of technologies, advanced applications and services, which are designed to enhance the manufacturing competitiveness of its customers.

"Customers benefit in several ways. First, through TotalPlant solutions, the automation technologies within and between departments are better integrated. Plants can be managed more comprehensively on the basis of operational information that is widely shared in a timely fashion. Second, customers can achieve global consistency in their operations because of the consistent level of expertise, technology and experience, we are able to deliver at the local level around the world. And third, TotalPlant solutions enable customers to grow their automation solutions incrementally to meet their own needs— from a simple, small system, to a sophisticated, large or complex configuration. Our commitment to the consistent evolution of our offerings also protects customers' investments in both the systems and the applications they have implemented."[46]

The Northwest Shelf Development project in Australia, relies on TDC 3000 systems.

Hurd said new environmental laws will benefit Honeywell. "Probably 60 to 70 percent of our business in Europe and the United States is tied to environmental solutions for our clients," he said. "Our equipment makes plants more efficient. Our software and services, make these plants run with less pollution. In other words, they're cleaner, they're higher quality, there's less waste. It's just the very nature of our business that as our customers have to make more investments in environmental control, we get the benefit of those investments."[47]

The industrial business recently won an $18.9 million contract to modernize a Phillips 66 refinery in Borger, Texas. This contract represents the largest single U.S. order ever received by the division.

In 1995, Bonsignore said, "We see unlimited growth opportunity in our core control businesses. Even last year, with a recession in Europe, Home and Building Control and Industrial Automation Control grew ten and nine percent respectively."[48]

In 1995, Markos Tambakeras, formerly president of Honeywell Asia Pacific, became president of Industrial Automation and Control when Ed Hurd was promoted to senior vice president. "Our customers are focused on improving oper-

ating efficiency," Tambakeras said. "They require manufacturing flexibility to quickly change production based on market demand and the raw materials available."[49]

Honeywell's Sensing and Control business provides industry's most extensive line of sensors, switches and solenoid valves. As communications technology has improved, Honeywell has pushed control capabilities down to a more basic level. "We're working to bring intelligent controls into the smallest sensors on the factory floor," said Ray Alvarez, vice president and group executive for Honeywell Sensing and Control. "We expect this kind of technology—called distributed machine control—to become a $10 billion industry over the next 10 years."[50]

The 'Delighted Customer'

In April 1993, Bonsignore succeeded Renier as CEO. Bonsignore had joined Honeywell in 1969 out of the Navy and worked in the Marine Systems Division. In 1981, Spencer tapped him to be president of Honeywell Europe. He remained for five years, returning in 1987 to run the International division. He was also responsible for the Home and Building Control business before being elected CEO and Chair-

The Asahi Beer Company Brewery in Tokyo, Japan, relies on Honeywell technology to improve productivity. Honeywell enjoys a strong presence in Japan, thanks to a joint venture with Yamatake that dates back to 1953.

man. Bonsignore has crafted a vision for Honeywell that has three elements—delighted customers, undisputed worldwide leadership in control, and profitable growth. The "delighted customer" concept is a key element in Bonsignore's Vision for Honeywell.

> "I had a fundamental anxiety when I took over the chairmanship of the company that we had begun to take our customers for granted. This is a company that has been successful for 110 years. We have a tremendous franchise. We have very loyal customers. And when you have been successful for that long, you run the risk of taking the very essence of your success for granted. If I were going to put a single hallmark on my time in this office, it would be the genuine rededication to our customers. I feel strongly about that for two reasons. First, it's what our customers deserve. And second, my international experience has convinced me that global competitive forces will only increase over the next decade. I don't want Honeywell to be unprepared for that. There's no doubt in my mind that the customer of the 1990s and into the next century will be king and queen. You see this everywhere, in every industry. And for us to miss the point would be a tragedy after 110 years of success."[51]

In a 1994 commentary written for the Minneapolis *Star Tribune*, Bonsignore wrote that merely meeting customer expectations is not enough to survive today's tough business climate.

> "Delighted customers are the gold medal in today's global competition. And each time we astound our customers with our performance, we've just set the bar of expectations for quality one notch higher. Quality is defined by the customer, which makes it a moving target — one that sets new records even as you read this. The bar keeps being raised. In a world of continuous improvement, today's excellence is tomorrow's mediocrity. It's that simple."[52]

Yamatake and the Asian Market

Honeywell continues to expand its presence in Asia, hoping to penetrate a Chinese market that has been implementing capitalist-style economic reforms for the past 10 years. Change in the Asian marketplace has also affected the relationship between Honeywell and its Japanese partner, Yamatake-Honeywell.

In the mid–Eighties, Honeywell was the target of several takeover threats, and "rumors were everywhere," said Renier, CEO at the time. "The stock was gyrating all over the place."[53] The company sold part of its Yamatake holdings in order to generate value for shareholders and stave off these threats. In 1989 and 1990, Honeywell sold half of its 50 percent stake in Yamatake for $407 million The transaction was

completed in 1990 when the company received an additional $35 million.

Honeywell now finds itself competing with its Japanese counterpart with the same product lines in the vast potential markets of the Pacific Rim. The challenge is real, as described in a 1993 article in the Minneapolis *Star Tribune*.

> "[Honeywell's] Japanese ally has turned into a rival that hopes to sell the same products to the same customers, particularly in China. Ironically, the two companies had worked so closely until now that Honeywell, which is based in Minneapolis, has transferred the bulk of its industrial and commercial controls technology to Yamatake. That means Yamatake's products are virtually a mirror image of Honeywell's. Shaking a rival with identical products is a particularly nettlesome problem."[54]

The article quotes former CEO Ed Spencer, who was in charge of Yamatake when he was Far East regional manager.

> "Spencer, the former Honeywell chief, said Yamatake officials think they were double crossed by Honeywell when the company abruptly unloaded its Yamatake stock through a private sale that cost Yamatake tens of millions of dollars to help arrange.
> 'Yamatake management, certainly some of those at the top, are saying, "Well, maybe Honeywell

In 1988, Honeywell funded a Minneapolis YWCA's child care program.

Honeywell's Retiree Volunteers Program puts retirees to work for volunteer organizations in the Twin Cities, a match that benefits both the retired person and the organization. By 1994, 1,100 former employees had become involved.

will sell the rest of its [Yamatake] shares some-day,'" said Spencer, who visited Tokyo last month.

Therefore, Yamatake is preparing for the worst case and backing away from its allegiance to Honeywell before Honeywell does anything more to undercut Yamatake, Spencer said."[55]

Bonsignore described the changing relationship with Yamatake as a challenge for the Nineties:

"The relationship evolved more from expediency and from opportunity than from real strategic purpose. Of course, Yamatake got bigger and more qualified and capable, and Japanese industry was branching out into the rest of Asia. In some cases that created a duplication of effort in a given country, what with the infrastructure Honeywell already had in place. Had our product developments since 1953 been more complementary than duplicative, I think we would have run into fewer problems."[56]

Bonsignore stresses that Honeywell and Yamatake will continue to work together in Asian markets. "I believe that Honeywell and Yamatake are inherently better off with each other than without. Our current relationship with Yamatake is strong and focused in the present, with a careful eye on how we continue to adapt to the future."[57]

"The question is," said former CEO Renier, "can one develop sufficient mutual trust and respect in working relationships to carve out our respective market niches? What I'm saying is the technologies can be similar but we can be expert at different things." [58]

More Global Change

The 1990s are a period of great opportunity on the global scene, as a direct result of the end of the Cold War. In 1993, the company opened affiliates in Abu Dhabi, China, Oman, Romania, South Africa, and the Ukraine. Honeywell now serves customers in 95 countries, through 83 wholly owned non–U.S. subsidiaries and 13 joint ventures.

"The European operation is doing fine," said Giannantonio Ferrari, president of Honeywell Europe. Despite a continuing recession, the organization generated $1.5 billion in revenue and $130 million in profits in 1994, he said. The TotalPlant system will strengthen market penetration, he said. "We are enjoying excellent market share in Europe and of course we have to make sure we keep this trend up."[59]

With the dismantling of the Soviet Union and its related spheres of economic and cultural influence in eastern and central Europe, large but volatile markets are opening up for Honeywell.

As capitalism takes its first uncertain steps in formerly communist countries, Honeywell is ready to profit from experience and a presence dating back to the 1930s.

CEO Bonsignore said: "We are well positioned to capitalize on what the world is going to need in the foreseeable future. Look at the energy conservation implications for Eastern Europe, the environmental and productivity implications. These countries need to upgrade their infrastructures and get competitive. This is wonderful news for Honeywell."[60]

As early as 1974, Jim Binger had established a one-person office in Moscow to develop business during the period of detente between the United States and the Soviet Union.

In 1987, the Soviets opened their country to joint ventures for the first time. The following year, Honeywell became one of the first to seize on this opportunity by forming STERCH, a joint effort with the Soviet government's Ministry of Mineral Fertilizer. The venture was chartered to provide modern process controls to Soviet industry.

After the breakup of the Soviet Union in 1991, Honeywell increased its ownership share in STERCH to 70 percent. By 1994, the company was serving the Commonwealth of Independent States through more than 200 employees, generating about $20 million in revenues. By this time, Honeywell's original presence in Moscow has expanded to comprise six operations, one of them Honeywell Aviation Control Moscow formed in

1992 to supply avionics to Russian aircraft manufacturers. In the building control market, two of Honeywell's most visible customers are the Russian Parliament Building and the State Hermitage Museum, one of the world's premier museums.

In the industrial controls field, Honeywell completed a unique energy–saving demonstration project in Tushino, a Moscow suburb. Four central boiler houses supply hot water for home heating to residents throughout Tushino. As originally designed, the system was inefficient. Honeywell's installation of a TDC 3000 and heat exchange controls cut the system's gas consumption and reduced costs by more than $2 million annually.

Change also affected Honeywell's long-term presence in South Africa in the late Eighties and early Nineties. Honeywell decided to sell its South African subsidiary in 1986, citing worsening conditions and continuing apartheid. After the historic fall of apartheid in the early 1990s, Honeywell was one of the first companies to reinvest in South Africa.

When Michael Bonsignore became CEO in 1993, he assessed Honeywell's position in China. "At first we entered the Chinese market cautiously and carefully, struggling to fully understand the business and political environment. In recent years we've moved more aggressively. Our success so far has been based on recognizing the importance of China and drawing on as much of our Asian experience as possible."[61]

More than 800 Honeywellers volunteered to work for the International Special Olympics, hosted by Minneapolis and St. Paul in 1991.

HONEYWELL

HONEYWELL

Honeywell's Schools Program was started in 1985 to help the nation's public education institutions save money through the efficient management of energy resources. By 1990, the program had saved public schools some $132 million. By the mid Nineties, the program had saved public schools some $819 million.

"Since 1986 we have learned a lot. We've learned there is an excellent supply of good technical manpower in China. For example, we put a three–line classified ad in the Bejing newspaper for an entry–level engineer and got 1,400 resumes. We interviewed 80 people and hired four....From 1986 to 1992 our business in China grew slowly but steadily. Our frustrations were manageable and we didn't lose our resolve. By 1992 Honeywell had achieved a reputation in China for experience in industrial and building controls."[62]

In 1992, Honeywell was approached by Sinopec, the largest petroleum company in China, and a jointly–owned company, Sinopec-Honeywell, was approved in 1993. Honeywell owns 55 percent of the equity, and Sinopec owns 45 percent. "I'm convinced that if we're willing to deal with China pragmatically, take some risks and plan for the long term," Bonsignore said, "there is no reason why American industry can't take its rightful place in the overall development of China."[63]

Recent numbers bear him out. In 1994, Honeywell had 800 employees in China and sales of $150 million. Bonsignore expects to double that sales figure within three years.

Community Involvement

In 1985, Honeywell's program of social responsibility became a highly–defined strategy of special projects, volunteer work, contributions, and partnerships. Special projects included the Futurist Awards, established as a competitive forum in which European college students submit essays on the shape of the future, and five winners receive full one–year scholarships to the American college or university of their choice.

In 1994, Honeywell mourned the death of executive Ron Speed, the moving force behind many important Honeywell charitable programs including the Honeywell Retiree Volunteers Program and the Futurist Awards.

The 1985 plan renewed the company's commitment to making direct contributions to agencies, institutions, and organizations. Direct financial donations, in fact, had been made by Honeywell even before the company had made a profit. In 1891, the year W.R. Sweatt arrived in Minneapolis from Fargo, the directors of Consolidated Temperature Controlling Company organized contributions for the founding of the Minneapolis Institute of Arts.

Partnerships in education are a relatively new approach through which the company joins with other corporations or public agencies to effect positive social change. One successful partnership in 1985 joined Honeywell with the White Earth Chippewa of Minnesota for a series of seminars, with an eye toward hiring more Native Americans.[64]

Another special project was a series of conferences entitled "Prospects for Peacemaking." At the height of the Honeywell Project demonstrations at Honeywell Plaza, Honeywell funded a series of town hall meetings to generate public discussion of defense policy and arms control issues. "Prospects for Peacemaking" was broadcast on television and radio to an estimated audience of 500,000 listeners.

The Honeywell Retiree Volunteer Project, another important innovation developed under the Honeywell Foundation, linked company retirees with non-profit organizations in the Twin Cities. By 1994, 1,100 retirees had become involved in Minneapolis alone. The HRVP served the retired person as well as the non-profit community, and helped to maintain a rewarding relationship between the company and its valued retired employees.

The company's efforts to implement equal opportunity and affirmative action were complemented in the late 1980s by a program to increase employee awareness of the value of diversity in the workplace.

"Honeywell will achieve a highly productive workforce by utilizing the diversity found in our society and fully developing the unique talents found in each individual employee," noted one policy statement.[65]

> *"As we seek new customers and new employees, we must appreciate the increasing diversity of the world in which we operate. This diversity brings to the workplace new ideas, values and relationships. Therefore, we believe that one key to achieving our long-term financial goals is to attract, retain, and develop a diverse workforce, while reducing the barriers to reaching our full human potential. With a workforce reflecting the diversity of our society, our customers, and our communities, Honeywell's continued success in the marketplace will be enhanced."[66]*

Present–day Honeywell employees continue a long tradition of volunteerism. In 1991, 800 Honeywellers volunteered for the International Special Olympics hosted in Minneapolis and St. Paul. In 1990, the company also founded the New Vistas School. In collaboration with Minneapolis public schools, the company opened a progressive high school — within the walls of its corporate headquarters — for teenage girls who are either pregnant or already have children. By 1992, New Vistas had graduated 24 students and 20 had gone on to college. The school features child care, early childhood education, health and social services, parenting classes, and medical services— all on site.

In 1992, echoing a long-standing Honeywell commitment to the nation's youth, Jim Renier said, "Collaboration among business, government, schools, and social service agencies, is the only way to solve urgent social problems – to provide the early development that kids need to grow into educated and productive adults."[67]

The Litton Suit

One of the greatest success stories of Honeywell's aeronautical electronics business has been the ring laser gyroscope system (RLG). RLGs are a critical component of the inertial guidance system used to navigate aircraft and other mobile platforms. Developed by Honeywell since 1958, the RLG became standard equipment aboard many aircraft by 1990. By 1991, Honeywell had manufactured and shipped 45,000 of the devices. So important is this technology that the RLG system became the focus of a landmark patent suit filed by Litton Industries against Honeywell in 1990. It concerned patents relating to special optical coatings applied to the mirrors in the RLG Inertial Guidance system. Litton charged Honeywell with patent violations relating to this coating, and sought damages of nearly $2 billion, and asked the court to increase damages to $6 billion because it said Honeywell's infringement had been willful. Interestingly, Honeywell had earlier sued Litton for its infringement of Honeywell's significant RLG patent portfolio, and the suit was settled prior to trial by Litton paying Honeywell $400,000 for a license to all Honeywell RLG patents.

On January 9, 1995, the U.S. District Court found for Honeywell. The court nullified a $1.2 billion jury verdict returned on August 31, 1993, finding that the patent was unenforceable because it was obtained by inequitable conduct and that it was invalid because it was an invention that would have been obvious from combining existing processes.

"The court's decision is a clear and complete victory for Honeywell," said Edward Grayson, Honeywell vice president and general counsel. Even before the decision, executives were confident. "The basis for the whole thing was absolutely ridiculous," asserted former CEO Jim Renier.[68]

Because the company depends so heavily on new and sophisticated technologies, it aggressively defends its patents from infringement. In 1992, Honeywell success-

Honeywell is well positioned to command the leadership role in integrated avionics for business jet, commercial airline and military applications.

fully sued Minolta for infringing Honeywell's autofocus patents by using Honeywell technology in its cameras. After winning this trial and obtaining a jury verdict of $94 million, Honeywell settled all claims against Minolta pending future royalties for $127 million. Renier, who was CEO at the time, pointed out that "because technology is our franchise, aggressively protecting our technology and patents is critical."[69]

The Future

"Profitable growth. Delighted customers. Worldwide leadership in control. This is our vision for Honeywell," says CEO Bonsignore. "It embodies what we want to be. It underpins how we set our goals. And it defines how we will fulfill the purpose of Honeywell —which is to create value for our shareholders."[70]

With annual sales about level at $6 billion over the past several years, Bonsignore notes that Honeywell is now in a position to grow. "We have addressed very real problems by divesting, cutting and consolidating. Now it is time to reverse that trend and *grow forward* to $10 billion in sales by the year 2000."[71]

Honeywell is aggressively pursuing this goal and is investing capital and people resources in a five–part strategy to grow the company. The strategy calls for increasing business with current customers, since winning a new customer costs five times as much as keeping an existing one. Honeywell also plans to build on its strength in systems integration, allowing customers to rely on it as a long–term partner. A third part of the strategy is that Honeywell will pursue high–growth segments of the market, such as schools, hospitals and industrial buildings. Expanding Honeywell's global presence is also part of the strategy, and the final part calls for pursuing complementary alliances and acquisitions.

As the company that leads the controls industry worldwide, Honeywell is poised for growth. A changing world has made Honeywell resilient to changes in the types of technologies the company develops and markets. Bonsignore states with confidence:

"We are applying our technology to help customers around the globe save energy, protect the environment, improve productivity, and increase comfort and safety. These are growing needs that transcend borders and cultures, and they call for highly precise, highly reliable sensing and control expertise. We want to be able to do that better than anybody else."[72]

In 1994 with input from more than 1,200 employees worldwide, Honeywell developed a statement of eight guiding values that will help the company achieve its vision. They are: integrity and the highest ethical standards; mutual respect and trust; communication that is open, consistent and two-way; diversity of people, cultures and ideas; innovation and encouragement to challenge the status quo; teamwork; and performance with recognition for results. Says Bonsignore:

"Honeywell has a purpose and vision, and a set of values for attaining both. Some may argue that this is 'soft science,' but I believe any great company must have a blueprint and implementation guidelines."[73]

All indications are that Honeywell is well poised to embrace its successful history while positioning itself for an exciting second century.

"We have a good shot at achieving our vision — of reaching our dream, of being what we want to be. Much remains to be done. But we are striving to create an environment for employees that brings out their very best — their creativity and passion for world–class performance, and most of all, a desire to set our own high standards of excellence. This is how we will create value for all the stakeholders— customers, employees, shareholders, suppliers and communities—who depend on our success."[74]

THE LEGEND OF HONEYWELL
NOTES TO SOURCES

Chapter One

1. C.W. Nessell, "From Uncontrolled Fire To Regulated Heat," *Trade Winds,* (Minneapolis–Honeywell Regulator Company: Minneapolis, 1960), 19.
2. *Ibid.*, 20.
3. C.W. Nessell, "Comfort from a Tank of Oil," *Trade Winds,* (Minneapolis–Honeywell Regulator Company: Minneapolis, 1960), 39.
4. Nessell, "Uncontrolled Fire," 18–19.
5. *Ibid.*, 19.
6. *Ibid.*
7. *Ibid.*
8. *Ibid.*
9. *Ibid.*
10. *Ibid.*, 21
11. *Ibid.*
12. *Ibid.*
13. *Ibid.*
14. *Ibid.*, 21–22
15. C.W. Nessell, "What's So Good About The Good Old Days," *Trade Winds,* (Minneapolis–Honeywell Regulator Company: Minneapolis, 1960), 4ff.
16. Nessell, "Uncontrolled Fire," 22.
17. *Ibid.*, 23.
18. *Ibid.*, 22–23.
19. Nessell, "Good Old Days," 5.
20. *Honeywell: The First 100 Years,* (Honeywell Inc.: Minneapolis, 1985), 2.
21. Minneapolis and St. Paul City Directories, 1881 to 1888 inclusive.
22. *Honeywell: The First 100 Years,* (Honeywell Inc.: Minneapolis, 1985), 5.
23. C.W. Nessell, "The Evolution of The Thermostat," *Trade Winds,* (Minneapolis–Honeywell Regulator Company: Minneapolis), 9–11.
24. *Ibid.*
25. *Minneapolis Sales Information Book,* (Minneapolis Heat Regulator Company: Minneapolis, 1917).

Chapter Two

1. *Honeywell World Centennial Issue,* 7 January 1985, (Honeywell Inc.: Minneapolis), 4.
2. *Ibid.*
3. It is possible that no damper–flappers had yet been produced or sold, and Butz proposed to act as a distributor *in the event* they were finally manufactured. This theory would support the view that Butz had no interest in managing the business.
4. The Guion advertisement depicts a device nearly identical to the Butz damper–flapper. Since Consolidated bought Guion, the Butz organization is credited with the original invention. The Consolidated advertisement from 1888 suggests that Guion had manufactured the product based on the Butz patents without arrangement or authorization.
5. *Minneapolis Sales Book,* (Minneapolis Heat Regulator Co.: Minneapolis, 1919), 9. The text asserts that "a satisfactory motive power had not been developed" to perfect the Butz system for heat regulation, and the "Guion motor embodying the patented forked switch feature, was put on the market in Elmira, N.Y. and the Minneapolis company purchased the Guion Company and succeeded to all of its rights and business."
6. *Bulletin of the National Association of Watch and Clock Collectors, Inc.,* vol. XXVII, No.1, February 1985, 4–14.
7. *Centennial,* 4.
8. Pyle would write the definitive biography of Hill in 1917, *The Life of James J. Hill* (Garden City, N.Y.: Doubleday, Page & Co., 1917).
9. C.W. Nessell, *Honeywell The Early Years,* (Minneapolis–Honeywell Regulator Company: Minneapolis, 1960), 4.
10. *Circulator,* 11 June 1948, 1 through 4.
11. *Circulator,* 11 March 1985, 4
12. *Ibid.*
13. *Centennial,* 6.
14. *Ibid.* It is possible that Sweatt was among this group of guarantors, for the first time taking an active part in the affairs of the company.
15. Notes from Michael J. Stapp, taken from minutes of Board of Directors meeting, 15 August 1893.
16. *Ibid.*
17. C.W. Nessell, *Early Years,* 5; *The Restless Spirit,* (Minneapolis–Honeywell Regulator Company: Minneapolis, 1963) 10. This anecdote is typical of Nessell, in that it is nearly impossible to verify, but appears to be an exaggeration. Both works are marred by a sometimes uncritical admiration of the Sweatt family.
18. Nessell, *Early Years,* 6.
19. *Centennial,* 4.
20. Nessell, *Early Years,* 7. The accuracy of this anecdote is also dubious. Part of the mythology to which Nessell contributed concerning the Sweatt family was this quality of "reluctant genius."
21. Stapp minutes of Board of Directors meeting, 15 August 1893.
22. *Circulator,* 11 March 1985, 4.
23. *Centennial,* 4.
24. Nessell, *Restless,* 16.
25. Honeywell historian Michael J. Stapp made this discovery in 1985. For more than 50 years, company artists had perpetuated the inaccuracy.
26. Nessell, *Restless,* 24.
27. *Ibid.*
28. Erik Wistrand, quoted in *Centennial,* 4.
29. Nessell, *Restless,* 24.
30. *The Wilderness World of John Muir,* ed. E.W. Teale, (Houghton Mifflin: Boston, 1954), 51–59.
31. "Diary of a Patent Suit," *Honeywell Factbook: the First 100 Years,* (Honeywell Inc.: Minneapolis, 1985), 5.
32. *Ibid.*
33. C.W. Nessell, "From Uncontrolled Fire to Regulated Heat," *Trade Winds,* (Minneapolis–Honeywell Regulator Company: Minneapolis, 1960), 28.
34. "Looking Back From 1938," *Circulator,* March 1938, 1ff.
35. A thermometer mounted right on the thermostat would ideally show how accurate Honeywell's heat

regulators were, but more often than not they probably showed that how accurate they were not.

36. *Centennial*, 10.
37. *Sheet Metal Worker*, quoted in Nessell, *Restless*, 26.
38. *Centennial*, 11.
39. Nessell, *Restless*, 28.

Chapter Three

1. *M–H News–Circulator*, June 1938, 2.
2. H.W. Sweatt, quoted in *Honeywell World Centennial Issue*, 7 January 1985, (Honeywell Inc.: Minneapolis), 11.
3. C.W. Nessell, *Honeywell the Early Years*, (Minneapolis–Honeywell Heat Regulator Company, Inc. :Minneapolis, 1960), 14.
4. *Honeywell World Centennial*, p. 11.
5. Nessell, *Early Years*, 14.
6. *Ibid.*, 9.
7. *Ibid.*, 10.
8. "Minneapolis–Honeywell," *Fortune*, November, 1937, 126.
9. "The Ten Point Demonstration for All 'Minneapolis' Salesmen," (Minneapolis Heat Regulator: Minneapolis, 1927), 13.
10. Nessell, *The Restless Spirit*, (Minneapolis–Honeywell Heat Regulator Company: Minneapolis, 1960), 15.
11. *Ibid.*, 52–53.
12. *Ibid.*, 88.
13. *Minneapolis Sales Information Book*, (Minneapolis Heat Regulator Company.: Minneapolis, 1919), 12.
14. *Ibid.*, 11.
15. Nessell, *Early Years*, 12.
16. *Ibid.*, 11.
17. *Circulator*, July 1938, 2.
18. *Centennial*, 12.
19. C.W. Nessell, "Comfort

From a Tank of Oil," *Trade Winds*, (Minneapolis–Honeywell Heat Regulator Company, 1960), 40.
20. *Ibid.*
21. *Ibid.*
22. *Ibid.*
23. *Ibid.*
24. Nessell, *Early Years*, 15.
25. Nessell, "Comfort," 41.
26. *Ibid.*, 42.
27. *Ibid.*, 39.
28. *Centennial*, 12. According to tradition, H.W. worked out some of the initial details of the Series 10 while on a train trip to Chicago.
29. Nessell, "Comfort," 41.
30. C.W. Nessell, "How Man Harnessed the Ghost," *Trade Winds*, (Minneapolis–Honeywell Regulator Company: Minneapolis, 1960), 29.
31. *Ibid.*
32. *Ibid.*
33. *Ibid.*, 30.
34. *Ibid.*
35. *Ibid.*
36. *Ibid.*, 29.
37. *Ibid.*
38. *Ibid.*, 30.
39. *Ibid.*, 31.
40. *Ibid.*, 32.
41. *Ibid.*
42. *Ibid.*
43. *Ibid.*, 33.
44. "Minneapolis–Honeywell," 222.
45. *Ibid.*, 220.
46. Nessell, *The Early Years*, 16.
47. "Minneapolis–Honeywell," 125.
48. Anthony Gohl, "A Jewelled Clock – Minneapolis 77," *Bulletin of the National Association of Watch and Clock Collectors, Inc.* vol. XXVII, no. 1, February 1985, 9.
49. "The Tower" at Honeywell World Headquarters in Minneapolis has a facade graced by limestone

reliefs of the 1927 de luxe "Minneapolis" thermostat, the "Model 77."
50. Gohl, "A Jewelled Clock," 14.
51. Nessell, *The Early Years*, 13.
52. Gohl, "A Jewelled Clock," 14.
53. *Ibid.* During research for this book, a "Minneapolis 77," from about 1928 graced the Honeywell offices temporarily housing the company archives. Research assistant Hans Eisenbeis wound the clock and it ran perfectly.
54. *Sales Information Book*, (Minneapolis Heat Regulator: Minneapolis, 1926), 18–19.
55. Andy Jones, quoted in *Centennial*, 12.
56. Carl Smith, quoted in *Centennial*, 7.
57. Wayne Stone, quoted in *Centennial*, 14.
58. Nessell, *The Early Years*, 14.
59. *Ibid.*
60. *Centennial*, 15.
61. "Diary of a Patent Suit," *Honeywell the First 100 Years*, (Honeywell Inc.: Minneapolis, 1985.
62. "Minneapolis–Honeywell," 220.
63. Doug Fetherling, *Shaped by Crisis*, (Honeywell Limited: Toronto, 1980).
64. Nessell, *Restless*, 73. This is a longstanding Honeywell tradition that is not backed up with substantial evidence.
65. *Centennial*, 15.
66. *Ibid.*, 16.
67. W. R. Sweatt, quoted in *Centennial*, 16.
68. *Ibid.*
69. *Ibid.*, 15.
70. *Honeywell Fact Book*, 1985, (Honeywell Inc.: Minneapolis, 1985).

71. "The Brown Instrument Company," *Instrument Maker*, Jan/Feb 1935, 2, claims the earlier date of 1858. The date of 1860 is cited in *Centennial*, 15.
72. "Brown Instrument," 2.
73. Nessell, *Restless*, 94.
74. *Fact Book*.
75. This was not strictly the case, since Honeywell began international operations in Canada when Time–O–Stat had established an office in Toronto which became a Minneapolis–Honeywell property.
76. *Centennial*, 16.
77. Nessell, *Restless*, 94.
78. "Minneapolis–Honeywell," 225.
79. *Ibid.*
80. Lawrence Bird, quoted in *Centennial*, 17.
81. In fact, this tower and facade were rendered in ink to illustrate the cover of a number of annual reports during the Thirties and Forties. The facade in these drawings was always altered to read "Minneapolis–Honeywell." In 1994, the facade still read "Minneapolis Heat Regulator Co."
82. *Minneapolis Tribune*, 2 March 1937, 1; *St. Paul Pioneer Press* 3 March 1937, 1.
83. *Minneapolis Sales Information Book* (Minneapolis Heat Regulator Company: Minneapolis, 1919), 11.
84. Nessell, *Restless*, 92.
85. *M–H News–Circulator*, September, 1939, 1.
86. *Ibid.*
87. Nessell, *Restless*, 92.
88. "Minneapolis–Honeywell," 121.
89. *Ibid.*, 226.
90. Charles Hoyt, quoted in *Centennial*, 6.
91. *M–H News–Circulator*,

June 1938, 2.

92. *M–H News–Circulator,* July 1939, 2.

93. *M–H News–Circulator,* April 1939, 2.

94. Report of Commission, United Electrical Radio & Machine Workers Union Local No. 1145 and Minneapolis Honeywell Regulator Company," *State of Minnesota Divsion of Reconciliation Notice No. 1114,* 21 April 1941, 1.

95. *Ibid.,* 3.

96. *Ibid.,* 9.

97. *Ibid.,* 10.

98. *Ibid.*

99. *Ibid.* 11.

Chapter Four

1. *M–H News–Circulator,* August 1940, 1.

2. *M–H News–Circulator,* September 1940, 1.

3. *M–H News–Circulator,* September 1940, 1.

4. *M–H News–Circulator,* July 1941, 1 ff.

5. *Ibid.*

6. Judy Haaverson, "World War II: Hard Work, Long Hours, Women Enter Factory," *Circulator,* 23 September 1985, 3–4.

7. *M–H News–Circulator,* July 1941, 4.

8. *M–H News–Circulator,* October 1941.

9. *M–H News–Circulator,* July 1941, 4.

10. *M–H News–Circulator,* February 1941, 4.

11. *M–H News–Circulator,* July 1941, 4.

12. *M–H News–Circulator,* December 1942, 1–2.

13. *M–H News–Circulator,* 14 July 1944, 1.

14. C.W. Nessell, *The Restless Spirit.* (Minneapolis–Honeywell Heat Regulator Company: Minneapolis, 1960), 105.

15. *Ibid.,* 107.

16. *Aero,* March 1944, 5.

17. *Honeywell World Centennial Issue,* 7 January 1985, 21–22.

18. Alonzo Mullendore, quoted in *Centennial,* 8. Mullendore was an employee in the Wabash plant from 1926 to 1970. His story has the sound and cadence of an invented joke. Still, it captures the sense of Minneapolis–Honeywell's brash approach to traditional problems of design and production.

19. *M–H News–Circulator,* July 1941, 6.

20. *M–H News–Circulator,* December 1941, 2.

21. *M–H News–Circulator,* August 1942, 1.

22. Army–Navy "E" Award. *Program of Presentation,* (Minneapolis–Honeywell, December 23, 1944). The extension of this award to civilian production facilities underscores the important role of industry in war for the first time in history.

23. Val Sherman, *Speech,* "E" Award Presentation to Minneapolis–Honeywell, (3rd Award), December 23, 1944.

24. *Centennial,* 20.

25. Historical Office, Air Technical Service Command, Wright Field (USAF) "Case History of Norden Bombsight and C–1 Automatic Pilot," *Historical Study No. 77,* January 1945, 1–13.

26. Mike Raphael, "Secret War Secret Device Now a Curio," [sic] *Santa Barbara News–Press,* 13 November 1988, B2.

27. *True* magazine, July 1967.

28. Michael Nisos, "The Bombadier and His Bombsight," *Air Force* magazine,

September 1981.

29. Allen Raymond, "Bombsight Solves Problems," *Popular Science,* December 1943, 119.

30. Ladislas Farago, *The Game of the Foxes.* (New York: D. McKay Co., 1972), 38–49.

31. Letter from Chamberlain to Roosevelt, 25 August 1939.

32. Letter from Roosevelt to Chamberlain, 31 August 1939.

33. Raymond, "Bombsight," 214.

34. Raymond, "Bombsight," 343.

35. Raymond, "Bombsight," 119.

36. Historical Office, "Case History," 2.

37. *Ibid.,* 7.

38. *Ibid.,* 9.

39. *Centennial,* 21.

40. *Ibid.*

41. Letter from Chief of Bureau of Ordnance to Commanding General, Army Air Forces, 5 October 1942.

42. Letter from Col. O.R. Cook, Air Corps Chief, Production Engineering Section, to Commanding General AAF Materiel Command, 12 October 1942.

43. Bill Kossila, quoted in *Centennial,* 31.

44. *Aero,* March 1945, 1.

45. Letter from Robert Lovett, Office of Assistant Secretary for War, to Chief of Air Staff, Washington D.C., 30 June 1944.

46. Report on Auto Gyro Levelling Device, from Gri. Gen. F.O. Carroll, Commanding General Army Air Forces, Development Engineering Branch, Materiel Division, to Col. D.B. Diehl, 14 June 1943.

47. Historical Office, "Case History," 12.

48. *Aero,* April 1944, 3.

49. *Ibid,* 3–5.

50. *Aero,* October 1943, 3.

51. *Centennial,* 21.

52. *M–H News–Circulator,* December 1943, 1.

53. *Aero,* December 1944, 3.

54. *M–H News–Circulator,* 27 October 1944, 1.

55. *M–H News–Circulator,* 11 May 1945, 3.

56. *Aero,* May 1945, 1.

57. *Aero,* date????" Modern Magic"

58. *M–H News–Circulator,* November, 1943, 1.

59. *Aero,* October 1943, 3.

60. Willis Gille and H.T. Sparrow, "Electronic Autopilot Circuits." *Electronics,* October 1944, 110–111.

61. *M–H News–Circulator,* 29 September 1944, 2.

62. Eugene Griffen, "Twist of a Knob is All it Takes to Fly Fortress," *Chicago Daily Tribune,* 10 July 1944, 12.

63. *Aero,* February 1945, 3–5.

64. *M–H News–Circulator,* 27 April 1945, 5.

65. *M–H News–Circulator,* 29 December 1944, 5.

66. *Aero,* May 1945, 6.

67. *M–H News–Circulator,* 29 June 1945, 1–2.

68. *Aero,* March 1944, 5.

69. *M–H News–Circulator,* September 1943, 1.

70. *M–H News–Circulator,* 30 November 1945, 1.

71. *M–H News–Circulator,* January 1943, 1.

72. *M–H News–Circulator,* 12 January 1945, 4.

73. *M–H News–Circulator,* 10 August 1945, 3.

74. Judy Haaverson, *Circulator,* 23 September 1985.

75. *M–H News–Circulator,* July 1943, 3.

76. Kate Massee, "Women in War Work," *Chicago Daily Tribune,* date??? look in McDonald scrapbook.

77. Haaverson, *Circulator*, 23 September 1985.

78. *M–H News–Circulator*, 9 February 1945, p. 3.

79. *M–H News–Circulator*, 30 March 1946, 1.

80. *M–H News–Circulator*, 11 May 1945, 1.

81. *M–H News–Circulator*, 30 March 1946, 1.

82. Campbell to Sweatt and M–H, quoted in *M–H News–Circulator*, 26 January 1946, 1.

83. Col. R.L. Rinkenstaedt, *Speech*, at Army–Navy "E" Award Ceremony of Minneapolis–Honeywell Regulator Co. (Aero Division), Chicago, 23 December 1944.

84. *M–H News–Circulator*, 29 September 1944, 2.

Chapter Five

1. *M-H News-Circulator*, 15 September 44, 2.

2. *M-H News-Circulator*, 29 June 1945, 2.

3. *M-H News-Circulator*, 24 August 1945, 1-3.

4. "A Production Record Unmatched in Aviation History," *Minneapolis Star*, 16 November 1953, reprinted in *Contact Point*, December 1953.

5. *Contact Point*, July 1955, 2.

6. *Contact Point*, August 1950, 2.

7. *Contact Point*, June 1955, 2.

8. *Ibid.*

9. *Ibid.*

10. J. Michael Stapp, "A History of Honeywell's Aerospace and Defense 1940–1982," Management Development Center, Honeywell Archival Materials, Photocopy, 20.

11. Russ Whempner, interviewed by Judy Haaverson, 11 January 1983.

12. *Honeywell World Centennial Issue*, 7 January 1985, (Honeywell Inc.: Minneapolis), 22.

13. Steve Keating, interviewed by the author, 22 August 1994. Transcript, 5.

14. *Centennial*, 22.

15. A.M. Wilson to H.W. Sweatt, "Aeronautical Division Report," 23 March, 1946

16. *Ibid.*

17. *Minneapolis Star*, 16 November 1953, reprinted in Contact Point, December 1953., "A Production Unmatched in Aviation History."

18. *Ibid.*

19. *Ibid.*

20. *Ibid.*

21. *Ibid.*

22. Stapp, "Aerospace and Defense," 7.

23. *Ibid.*, 9

24. Ed Lund, interviewed by the author, 16 November 1994, Minneapolis. Transcript, 8.

25. Stapp, "Aerospace and Defense," 9.

26. *Contact Point*, April 1951, Cover.

27. Keating interview, 6.

28. Stapp, "Aerospace and Defense," 10

29. Raymond Nolan, "How a Manufacturer Banks on Research," *Missiles and Rockets*, 21 July 1958.

30. Stapp, "Aerospace and Defense," 10.

31. *Ibid.*, 15

32. *Ibid.*, 17

33. Philip Klass, "Navy to Test Electrically Suspended Gyro," *Aviation Week*, 6 February 1961.

34. Stapp, "Aerospace and Defense," 17.

35. *Centennial*, 23.

36. Stapp, "Aerospace and Defense," 34.

37. *Ibid.*

38. Russ Whempner, interviewed by Judy Haaverson, April 1984.

39. Philip Klass, "Tests Find New Uses for Laser Gyros," *Aviation Week and Space Technology*, 6 September 1982.

40. Stapp, "Aerospace and Defense," 13.

41. *Ibid.*, 13.

42. *Ibid.*, 20

43. Lund interview, 18.

44. Roger Jensen, interviewed by the author, 22 August 1994, Minneapolis. Transcript, 21–22.

45. *NASA News*, Release No. 74-161, "Down To Earth Space Benefits From Moon Missions," 18 June 1974.

46. John Dewane, interviewed by the author, 12 December 1994, Phoenix. Transcript, 6.

47. *Ibid.*, 12.

48. *Ibid.*, 11–12.

49. Stapp, "Aerospace and Defense," 18.

50. *Honeywell Space Systems Background,* (pamphlet, Honeywell Inc.: Minneapolis, 1967).

51. *Ibid.*

52. Stapp, "Aerospace and Defense," 18.

53. J.W.R. Taylor, ed., *Jane's All the World's Aircraft 1968-1969* (New York: McGraw-Hill, 1968), 517. Quoted in Stapp, "Aerospace and Defense," 27.

54. Stapp, "Aerospace and Defense," 34.

55. *Ibid.*, 32.

56. Keating interview, 28.

57. *Honeywell Centennial Factbook*, (Honeywell Inc.: Minneapolis, 1985).

58. *Centennial*, 29.

59. Rone Tempest, "Defense Industry's Impact is Vast, Powerful." *Minneapolis Star and Tribune*, 31 August 1983, 13A.

Chapter Six

1. H.W. Sweatt, quoted in the *Circulator*, 29 April 1954, 1-2.

2. *M–H News Circulator*, January 1944, 1.

3. *M-H News-Circulator*, 27 April 1945, 2. John Haines, a manager in the Air Conditioning Controls division of the Sales department, was included in Sweatt's post-war committee, a sign that Sweatt saw home air conditioning as an important new market.

4. *Ibid.*

5. Charlie Sweatt, interviewed by author, 1994. Transcript, 4.

6. *M-H News-Circulator*, 25 May 1945, 1

7. *Ibid.*

8. *M-H News-Circulator*, 15 June 1945, 1.

9. *Minneapolis Sunday Tribune*, 5 June 1955.

10. Letter from Herb Bissell to Karen Bachman and Fred Klein, 1 March 1995.

11. *Ibid.*

12. Letter from H.W. Sweatt to Herb Bissell, 6 January 1972.

13. *Contact Point*, September 1955, 3-4.

14. *Honeywell World Centennial Issue*, 7 January 1985, 17.

15. Ray Alvarez, interviewed by the author, 22 December 1994. Transcript, 25.

16. *Ibid.*, 24–25.

17. *Ibid.*, 27.

18. *Ibid*, 27.

19. *Centennial*, 13.

20. *Ibid.*

21. Herb Bissell, letter to Russell Flinchum, guest curator of the Cooper–Hewitt, National Design Museum, Smithsonian Instition, 26 August 1993.

22. Dean Randall, inter-

viewed by the author, 4 October 1994. Transcript, 10.

23. Bissell to Flinchum, 26 August 1993.

24. Clyde Blinn, interviewed by the author, 4 October 1994, Minneapolis, Transcript, 14.

25. Bissell to Flinchum, 26 August 1993.

26. Steve Keating, interview by author, 22 August 1994. Transcript, 29.

27. Blinn interview, 10.

28. *Centennial*, 33.

29. "Brain Industry: Honeywell Uses Skilled Labor." *Minneapolis Sunday Tribune*, 18 October 1953.

30. Jim Binger, interviewed by the author, 16 November 1994, Minneapolis. Transcript, 14.

31. 1984 Presentation of the H.W. Sweatt Awards, 1984, *Program*, 2.

Chapter Seven

1. Pete Sigmund, "His was a Zestful Search," *Sperry–Univac News*, February 1980, 7.

2. K.R. Mauchly, "Mauchly's Early Years," *Annals of the History of Computing*, April 1984, 128.

3. "Through the Past Brightly," Special Section, Honeywell 25th Anniversary in Computers, *Patriot*, May 1980, 2.

4. Herb Bissell, interviewed by the author, 4 October 1994. Transcript, 6.

5. *Honeywell Twenty-Fifth Anniversary in Computers*, (Minneapolis: Honeywell, 1980), 2.

6. *Honeywell World Centennial Issue*, 7 January 1985, 27.

7. A.M. Wilson, quoted in Frank Westbrook, "Editorial Memorandum on Honeywell's Electronic

Data Processing Operations," 1961, 1-4.

8. *Ibid.*

9. "Little Big Honeywell," *Forbes*, 15 November 1964, 22.

10. Dean Randall, interviewed by the author, 4 October 1994. Transcript, 16.

11. *Honeywell Twenty-Fifth Anniversary in Computers*. (Minneapolis: Honeywell, 1980), 2.

12. Westbrook, "Memorandum," 7.

13. *Ibid.*

14. *Twenty-Fifth Anniversary*, 2.

15. William Bond, "EDP Created Ten Years Ago," *EDP Data*, April 1965, 3.

16. "Through the Past," Clearly from the first day of operations at Datamatic, IBM was considered the competitor to beat. They remained so for over 30 years.

17. Bond, "EDP Created," 3

18. "Through the Past," 3.

19. Bissell interview, 10.

20. Randall interview, 33.

21. *Twenty-Fifth Anniversary*, 3.

22. Jim Porterfield, "Honeywell Computers to Tally ABC Network Election Returns," (press release), 26 September 1962, 1-2.

23. Bissell interview, 13.

24. Bond, "EDP Created," 5.

25. "Honeywell Unscrambles its Computer Mix," *Business Week*, 27 April 1974.

26. Robert Levy, "The Heat's on at Honeywell," *Dun's Review*, June 1969, 44.

27. *Ibid.*, 45.

28. *Ibid.*, 103.

29. *Twenty-Fifth*, 3.

30. Finke, quoted in "Editorial Memorandum," 20.

31. *Twenty-Fifth*, 3.

32. "The Formation of Honeywell Information Systems Inc.," (internal report), 1971.

33. "Honeywell Unscrambles."

34. Stan Nelson, interviewed by the author, 4 October 1994. Transcript, 33.

35. Mannie Jackson, interviewed by the author, November 11, 1994. Transcript, 5–6.

36. *Ibid.*

37. Ed Spencer interviewed by the author, 7 November 1994. Transcript, 8.

38. *Ibid.*, 6.

39. *Ibid.*, 7.

40. "Honeywell Unscrambles."

41. "Staying the Course," *Forbes*, 15 December 1975.

42. Spencer interview, 3–4.

43. *Ibid.*

44. Robert Flaherty, "Lost Opportunity," *Forbes*, 1 September 1976.

45. *Twenty-Fifth*, 3.

46. "Honeywell Doing Well In Minis," *Datamation*, 1 May 1979.

47. *Ibid.*

48. "Honeywell Unscrambles."

49. Jim Binger, interview by the author, 16 November 1994, Minneapolis. Transcript, 10.

50. Nelson interview, 29.

51. Spencer interview, 9.

52. "Honeywell Doing Well."

53. Gene Bylinsky, "The Second Computer Revolution," *Fortune*, 11 February, 1980, 230-231.

54. Westbrook, "Memorandum," 5.

55. "Little Big Honeywell," 25.

56. *Ibid.*, 23.

57. *Centennial*, 28-29.

58. Westbrook, "Memorandum," 5.

59. *Twenty-Fifth*, 7.

60. *Centennial*, 28–29.

61. Ray Alvarez, interview by the author, 22 December 1994. Transcript, 11.

62. Claudia Waterloo, "Honeywell is Pushing Its

Computer Business Despite Past Problems," *Wall Street Journal*, 25 June 1984.

63. Jim Renier, interview by author, 23 November 1994. Transcript, 15.

64. Spencer interview, 13.

65. Waterloo, "Past Problems."

Chapter Eight

1. J. Michael Stapp, "The Multi-National Company Centennial Project," notes for *Honeywell World Centennial*.

2. Tom McDonald, speech to Northwestern National Bank and Trust Company, 7.

3. *Nederlandsche Honeywell N.V. 50th Year Anniversary* booklet, 1984.

4. Herman Wex may have become a Nazi while working in the Amsterdam office. Several sources speak of Amand's and other employees' experiences of dealing with a Nazi manager who may or may not have been the *Verwalter* (administrator) assigned to the company by German authorities after Pearl Harbor. The evidence of Nazism is purely circumstantial, and inferred from the comments of A.S. Taselaar and P.C. Sharp. When asked about Wex in a 1984 interview, Taselaar said, "Too much, too much. I don't think you should talk about it." (A.S. Taselaar and Theo. Hollema, Interview by Jerry Norbury, Amsterdam, 2 September 1984.) Cran Sharp, interviewed by Dennis Johnson at his residence, August 1984, said, "Ed Cushing... went to Holland to establish a training program. He dealt with a guy who became a Nazi. Cushing also

dealt with A. [S.] Taselaar, Theo Hollema, and Jan Amand. Can't recall who the Nazi guy was."
5.   A.S. Taselaar and Theo. Hollema, interview by Jerry Norbury, Amsterdam, 2 September 1984.
6.   *Nederlandsche 50th Anniversary.*
7.   *M-H News-Circulator,* 14 December 1946, 1.
8.   *M-H News-Circulator,* December 1943, 1-3.
9.   McDonald speech, 4.
10. Sherwood Berryann, letter to P.C. Sharp, 9 November 1973.
11. Taselaar and Hellema interview.
12. *Ibid.*
13. *Netherlandsche 50th Anniversary.*
14. *M-H News-Circulator,* 26 October 1945.
15. *Honeywell World Centennial,* 7 January 1985, 24.
16. Berrywood letter to Sharp.
17. Toshihiko Yamaguchi, letter to P.C. Sharp, 14 November 1973.
18. *M-H News-Circulator,* 16 November 1945, 5.
19. *M-H Circulator,* 14 December 1946, 1.
20. *M-H News-Circulator,* 13 April, 1945.
21. *Centennial,* 25.
22. *Honeywell Europe Presidential Newsletter,* Special Issue, October 1980.
23. *Netherlandsche 50th Anniversary.*
24. *Ibid.*
25. P.C. Sharp, "Report on Cuba and Establishment of Controles Honeywell S.A.", 1951.
26. "The Incomes Board: No Teeth, Little Bite," *The (London) Financial Times,* 9 April 1965.
27. "Honeywell Bets on Automation," *Business Week,* 5 February 1966.

28. James Binger, interviewed by the author, 16 November 1994, Minneapolis, Minnesota. Transcript, 4.
29. Steve Keating, interviewed by the author, 22 August 1994, Minneapolis, Minnesota. Transcript, 35.
30. *Ibid.,* 7.
31. *Ibid.,* 3.
32. "Incomes Board."
33. "New Jobs for Newhouse: Honeywell to take on 100 Extra," *The Scotsman,* 10 April, 1965.
34. "Honeywell Bets."
35. *Honeywell World,* 18 September 1979, 4.
36. *Centennial,* 26.
37. Michael Bonsignore, interviewed by the author, 18 August 1994, Minneapolis, Minnesota. Transcript, 2.
38. Charlie Sweatt, interviewed by the author. Transcript, 10.
39. Keating interview, 19.
40. "Industrial Capabilities," filmstrip, 1978 script-photocopied.
41. Bonsignore interview, 23.
42. Giannantonio Ferrari, interviewed by the author, 25 January 1995.
43. *Ibid.*
44. *Ibid.*
45. Michael Bonsignore, presentation to European Editors, 11 March 1987.
46. Edson Spencer, speech, 1980, 1.
47. Geri Joseph, interviewed by author, 15 November 1994. Transcript, 6.
48. Tom Donahue, letter to Judy Haaverson, 1984.
49. William George, "Contrast in Management Styles — Europe and the United States," lecture to Institution of Electrical Engineers, London, England, 25 January 1983.
50. *Honeywell World,* 18

September 1979, 5.
51. *Honeywell World,* 16 July 1984, 4.
52. R.E. Maroukian, *Notes On South African Affiliate,* to Judy Haaverson, 1982.
53. Ferrari interview.
54. *Honeywell World,* 16 July 1984, 4.
55. Donahue letter to Haaverson.
56. Yoshiro Kurose, telex to Jerry Norbury, 12 December 1984.
57. *Honeywell World,* 25 June 1984, 1ff.
58. *Honeywell World,* 18 September 1979, 5.
59. Ed Spencer, letter to P.C. Sharp, 27 November 1973.
60. Sharp interview by Johnson, 1984.
61. *Honeywell World,* 12 July 1976, 2.
62. John Wadsworth, interviewed by the author, 7 March 1995.
63. *Ibid.*
64. *Ibid.*
65. *Honeywell World,* 5 October 1970, 1.
66. *1985 Honeywell Factbook.*
67. Jim Renier, letter to P.C. Sharp, 10 December 1973.
68. Jim Binger, interviewed by the author, 16 November 1994, Minneapolis. Transcript, 15–16.
69. *Honeywell World,* 5 October 1970, 1.
70. Chuck Ungemach, quote provided by Honeywell.
71. Dean Randall, interviewed by the author, 4 October 1994. Transcript, 18.
72. Keating interview, 16.
73. *Honeywell World,* 5 October 1970, 1.
74. *Ibid.*
75. *Ibid.*
76. Bonsignore interview, 4.
77. Edson Spencer, address to the House Ways and Means Committee's

Subcommittee on Trade, April 1984.
78. *Ibid.*

Chapter Nine

1.   Bill Harrison, interviewed in "Reminiscences of Honeywell Oldtimers," *A Minneapolis-Honeywell Miscellany,* (Minneapolis-Honeywell Regulator Co.:Minneapolis, 1960).
2.   Charlie Nelson, interviewed in "Reminiscences."
3.   Chet Lyford, interviewed in "Reminiscences."
4.   "Mrs. Honeywell Receives Special Eisenhower Award," *Wabash Plain Dealer,* 31 March 1971.
5.   Minneapolis Heat Regulator Company, *Minutes,* Director's Meeting 11 January 1932, 3.
6.   Herb Bissell, interviewed by the author, 4 October 1994. Transcript, 4.
7.   *M-H News Circulator,* March 1941, 2.
8.   *M-H News Circulator,* July 1941, 2.
9.   *Honeywell Circulator,* 12 May 1950, 2.
10. *Minneapolis-Honeywell Circulator,* 29 October 1948, 1.
11. *M-H News-Circulator,* 26 October 1946, 3.
12. *Honeywell Circulator,* 11 August 1950, 1.
13. Gerry Morse, "The Challenge Is Ahead," Speech to Equal Employment Opportunity Seminar at the University of Pennsylvania, 13 November, 1964.
14. *Ibid.*
15. *Ibid.*
16. Fred Laing, *Circulator,* 15 September 1968.
17. *Ibid.*
18. *Ibid.*
19. Bob Ehler, "Fifteen Years of Protest," *Minneapolis Star and Tribune*

Sunday Magazine, 16 December 1984.

20. Warde Wheaton, interviewed by the author, 16 October, 1994, Minneapolis. Transcript, 10.

21. Jim Binger, interviewed by the author, 16 November 1994, Minneapolis. Transcript, 7–8.

22. Jim Renier, interviewed by the author, 23 November 1994, Minneapolis. Transcript, 10.

23. Steve Keating, interviewed by the author, 22 August 1994, Minneapolis. Transcript, 25.

24. Karen Bachman, interviewed by the author, 15 November 1994, Minneapolis. Transcript, 13.

25. *Ibid.*

26. *Ibid.,* 10.

27. Ehler, "Fifteen Years."

28. Ed Spencer, Memo to all Honeywell Employees, 23 April 1983.

29. *Ibid.*

30. Ehler, "Fifteen Years."

31. Warde Wheaton, interviewed by the author, 16 October 1994, Minneapolis. Transcript, 11.

32. Ehler, "Fifteen Years."

33. *Ibid.*

34. Dean Randall, interviewed by the author, 4 October 1994, Minneapolis. Transcript, 21.

35. R.J. Boyle, "The Role of the Corporation in Defense: What's a Nice Company Doing in A Business Like That?" Address to League of Women Voters' *National Security: Not For Experts Only* Conference, 4 February 1984.

36. *Ibid.*

37. Mike Kaszuba, Jim Dawson, Delia Flores, "256 Arrested in Protest at Honeywell," *Minneapolis Star and Tribune,* 28 April 1984.

38. Catherine Watson, "City Businesses Give $14,000 to Study Coalition on Race, Poverty," *Minneapolis Tribune,* 13 September, 1967.

39. Maurice Hobbs, "Honeywell President Names Chairman of Urban Coalition," *Minneapolis Star,* 18 January, 1968.

40. "Coalition Head says Racism Killed Dr. King," *Minneapolis Tribune,* 5 April, 1968.

41. Glenn Hovemann, "New Breed of Business Man has Social Concern. Honeywell President Keating Heads Urban Coalition," *Minnesota Daily,* 8 May 1968.

42. *Ibid.*

43. "Keating Tells it as it Is: Honeywell Cites 1968 Progress in Minority Hiring Activities," *Minneapolis Spokesman,* 27 February 1969.

43. Tom Langenfeld, "Mission: Search and Employ. Honeywell's Human Problem Solver," *Minneapolis Tribune,* 29 September 1968.

44. Catherine Watson, "General Mills, Honeywell, to Aid Learning Centers," *Minneapolis Tribune,* 27 August 1968.

45. Hovemann, "New Breed of Businessman."

46. Hallock Seymour, "Businessmen Can Solve Urban Ills – Keating," *Minneapolis Star,* 9 May 1968.

47. *Minnesota Daily,* 9 May 1968.

48. "Keating Steps Down," *Minneapolis Star,* editorial, 11 December, 1968.

49. Ed Spencer, "The Bottom-Line Value of Hiring Minority Engineers," *Graduating Engineer,* January 1982, 96-98.

50. *Ibid.*

51. *Ibid.*

52. *Honeywell Factbook,* (Honeywell Inc.: Minneapolis, 1985).

53. *Honeywell World Centennial Issue,* 7 January 1985, 7. The author of this article asserts that the payment may have been "possibly severance pay for several years of work." It is a speculation drawn from the relatively large amount (for the 1890s) and the notation, "with the Company's thanks."

54. *Centennial,* 8.

55. Helen Haertzen, quoted in *Centennial,* 14.

56. *Minneapolis Star,* 24 October 1969.

57. *Aero,* August 1943.

58. *Aero,* February 1944.

59. *Honeywell Women's Council Communique,* Spring 1986.

60. *Honeywell Circulator,* 21 July 1950, 1.

61. *Agenda,* October 1983.

62. Bachman interview, 5–6.

63. *Ibid.*

64. *Ibid,* 2ff.

65. *Ibid.*

66. Geri Joseph, interviewed by the author, 15 November 1994. Transcript, 4.

67. Dana Badgerow, interviewed by the author, 12 December 1994, New Britain, Ct. Transcript, 16.

68. *Honeywell Circulator,* 2 February 1950, 2.

69. *Report of Honeywell Vietnam Veterans Steering Committee,* 1981.

70. *Honeywell Community Responsibility Report 1985,* Honeywell Inc.: Minneapolis, 1985).

71. Mannie Jackson, interviewed by the author, 11 November 1994. Transcript, 15.

72. Badgerow interview, 21.

73. Bissell interview, 3

74. Roger Jensen, interviewed by the author, 22 August 1994. Transcript, 6.

75. Wheaton interview, 36.

76. *Ibid.,* 3.

77. Binger interview, 34.

78. Randall interview, 7.

79. Jensen, 7.

80. *Ibid.,* 8.

81. *Ibid.*

82. Ed Lund, interviewed by the author, 16 November 1994, Minneapolis. Transcript, 38-39.

Chapter Ten

1. James Renier, *1987 Honeywell Annual Report,* 1.

2. Ed Lund, interviewed by the author, 16 November 1994. Transcript, 29.

3. *1989 Honeywell Annual Report.*

4. *Honeywell at a Glance,* (Honeywell, Inc.: Minneapolis, 1994).

5. Michael Bonsignore, interviewed by the author, 17 August 1994. Transcript, 21.

6. "Honeywell Completes Restructuring; Financial Impact Announced." (news release, Kathy Tunheim, Honeywell Inc.), 17 December 1986.

7. "Honeywell Reduces Ownership in Computer Firm." (news release, Kathy Tunheim, Honeywell Inc.), 29 December 1988.

8. *1986 Honeywell Annual Report 1986.*

9. Edson Spencer, interviewed by the author, 7 November 1994. Transcript, 12.

10. Steve Keating, interviewed by the author, 22 August 1994. Transcript, 8.

11. *Ibid.,* 9. Keating said, "With all due respect to my successors... we are still struggling from [the computer business] today."

12. *Ibid.*, 11

13. James Renier, *Presentation to European Editors,* 3 November 1987. Transcript.

14. Geri Joseph, interviewed by the author, 15 November 1994. Transcript, 2.

15. *1985 Honeywell Annual Report,* 12.

16. Dana Badgerow, interviewed by the author, 12 December 1994, New Britain, Connecticut. Transcript, 2.

17. "Honeywell to Pursue Spin–Off of Defense and Marine Business." (news release, Susan M. Eich, Honeywell Inc.), 17 April 1990.

18. Keating interview, 27.

19. *1990 Honeywell Annual Report.*

20. *Ibid.*

21. James Renier, interviewed by the author, 23 November 1994. Transcript, 11.

22. *Ibid.*, 9.

23. Dean Randall, interviewed by the author, 4 October 1994. Transcript, 25.

24. John Dewane, interviewed by the author, 12 December 1994. Transcript, 5.

25. Warde Wheaton, interviewed by the author, 16 October 1994, Minneapolis. Transcript, 13.

26. *Ibid.*, 18.

27. Lund interview, 18.

28. "Honeywell to Acquire Sperry Aerospace Business." (news release, Susan M. Eich, Honeywell Inc.), 14 November 1986.

29. Spencer interview, 18.

30. Wheaton interview, 38.

31. Bonsignore interview, 15.

32. *Ibid.*, 20

33. Larry Moore, interviewed by the author, 30 November 1994. Transcript, 9.

34. *1994 Honeywell Annual Report.*

35. *Ibid,* 19.

36. Bonsignore interview, 15-17.

37. *1984 Honeywell Annual Report,* 10.

38. Brian McGourty, interviewed by the author, 1 December 1994. Transcript, 4.

39. *1994 Honeywell Annual Report.*

40. *Honeywell at a Glance,* 19.

41. *A Profile of Honeywell,* (Honeywell Inc.: Minneapolis, December 1988), 2.

42. Michael R. Bonsignore, "Vision for Honeywell," Honeywell Internal Communications, 20 April 1993, 65.

43. Ed Hurd, interviewed by the author, 23 January 1995.

44. *Ibid.*

45. *Ibid.*

46. *Ibid.*

47. *Ibid.*

48. Bonsignore, "Vision for Honeywell," 57.

49. *1994 Honeywell Annual Report,* 16.

50. *Ibid.*

51. Bonsignore interview, 9.

52. Michael Bonsignore, "Quality Defined by Customer in Today's World Competition, *Minneapolis Star Tribune,* April 25, 1994.

53. Renier interview, 13.

54. Mike Meyers, "Honeywell Engaged in High Stakes 'Bridge Building.'" *Minneapolis Star Tribune,* 13 December 1993.

55. *Ibid.*

56. Bonsignore interview, 4.

57. *Ibid.*, 5.

58. Hurd interview.

59. Renier interview, 14.

60. Giannantonio Ferrari, interviewed by the author, 25 January 1995.

61. Bonsignore interview, 19.

62. "Honeywell in the Commonwealth of Independent States," (editorial backgrounder, Meta Gaertnier, Honeywell Inc.), January 1995.

63. Michael Bonsignore, "The China Market: Strategies for the 90s." (Honeywell internal communications), 19 October 1993, 2.

64. *Ibid,* 4.

65. *1984 Honeywell Annual Report.*

66. Diane Beezer, memo to Corporate-Wide Diverse Workforce Goaling Committee, 18 May, 1987.

67. *Ibid.*, 22

69. Renier interview, 21.

70. Bonsignore quote, provided by Honeywell.

71. *1991 Honeywell Annual Report,* 19.

72. Bonsignore quote, provided by Honeywell.

73. *Ibid.*

74. *Ibid.*